Internet and E-mail for Seniors
with Windows Vista

Studio Visual Steps

Internet and E-mail for Seniors with Windows Vista

For everyone who wants to learn to use the Internet at a later age

www.visualsteps.com

This book has been written using the Visual Steps™ method.
Translated by Chris Holingsworth and Grayson Morris
Edited by Ria Beentjes, Yvette Huijsman and Marleen Vermeij
© 2007 Visual Steps B.V.
Cover design by Studio Willemien Haagsma bNO

First printing: April 2007
ISBN 978 90 5905 284 0

Resources used: Some of the computer terms and definitions seen here in this book have been taken from descriptions found online at the Windows Help and Support website. (http://windowshelp.microsoft.com/Windows/en-US/default.mspx)
Additional technical resources include:
The Microsoft TechNet forums (http://forums.microsoft.com/technet/default.aspx?forumgroupid=204&siteid=17),
The Windows Vista Community website (http://www.microsoft.com/windowsvista/community/default.mspx),
The Windows Vista Developer Center website (http://msdn2.microsoft.com/en-us/windowsvista/aa904962.aspx) and
Tips&Tricks (http://www.windowsvistatnt.com/).

Would you like more information?
www.visualsteps.com

Do you have questions or suggestions?
E-mail: info@visualsteps.com

Website for this book:
www.visualsteps.com/internetvista
Here you can register your book.

Register your book
We will keep you aware of any important changes that are necessary to you as a user of the book. You can also take advantage of our periodic newsletter informing you of our product releases, company news, tips & tricks, special offers, etc.
www.visualsteps.com/internetvista

Table of Contents

Foreword

The Internet has ushered in a whole new era. Until a few years ago, most computers were isolated from one another. Since the emergence of the Internet, people are able to communicate with other connected computer users on a worldwide basis. The Internet has gradually become so vast that you can browse in even the most obscure libraries and communicate with people and organizations no matter where in the world they are.

More and more applications are being created that have advantages for computer non-experts as well. For example, e-mail is increasingly replacing the telephone, regular mail and the fax.

The purpose of this book is to acquaint you with the Internet. Then we will teach you the essential skills needed to take full advantage of what the Internet can offer. We have also given a lot of attention to Internet safety and privacy. We will we alert you to potential dangers when using the internet. Finally, we will show you what kind of measures you can take to protect your computer.

We have created a special website to accompany this book, where you can safely practice what you have learned before you set out on your own on the Internet.

This book makes use of the Visual Steps™ method specifically developed for adult learners by Addo Stuur.
We hope you enjoy this book and wish you a pleasant journey on the Internet.

The Studio Visual Steps Authors

P.S. Your comments and suggestions are most welcome. Our e-mail address is: mail@visualsteps.com

Introduction to Visual Steps™

The Visual Steps manuals and handbooks offer the best instruction available for anyone new to computers. Nowhere else in the world will you find better support while getting to know the computer, the Internet, *Windows* and other computer programs.

Visual Steps manuals are special because of their:

- **Content**
  The adult learners needs, desires, know-how and skills have been taken into account.
- **Structure**
  Get started right away. No lengthy explanations. The chapters are organized in such a way that you can skip a chapter or redo a chapter without worry. Easy step by step instructions and practice exercises to reinforce what you have learned.
- **Illustrations**
  Every single step is accompanied by a screenshot. These illustrations will guide you in finding the right buttons or menus, and will quickly show you if you are still on the right track.
- **Format**
  A sizable format and pleasantly large letters enhance readability.

In short, I believe these manuals will be excellent guides.

Dr. H. van der Meij

Faculty of Applied Education, Department of Instruction Technology, University of Twente, the Netherlands

What You Will Need

In order to work through this book, you will need a number of things on your computer.

The primary requirement for working with this book is having the US version of *Windows Vista Home Basic* or *Windows Vista Home Premium* or *Windows Vista Ultimate* on your computer.
You can check this yourself by turning on your computer and looking at the *Welcome Screen*.

 Network and Internet
View network status and tasks
Set up file sharing

You need a functioning **Internet connection**. Contact your *Internet Service Provider* or your local computer store if you need help.
If you need help setting up your dial up connection, you can read *Appendix A Setting up a Dial-up Connection* at the end of this book.
If you need help setting up your broadband Internet connection (cable, DSL or ISDN), please contact your *Internet Service Provider* or consult the manual you have received. Each provider has a different protocol for setting up a connection. Detailed documentation containing this type of technical information goes beyond the scope of this book.

 **Internet**
Internet Explorer

 **E-mail**
Windows Mail

The following programs for working with the Internet should be installed on your computer:
- *Windows Internet Explorer 7*
- *Windows Mail*

These programs are included in *Windows Vista*.

You also need:

A computer mouse. If you are working on a laptop with touchpad, you may want to purchase an external mouse in order to more easily follow the steps in this book.
If you want to learn more about using the touchpad to operate your laptop, surf to the website www.visualsteps.com/internetvista/news and read the Tip *Working with a Touchpad*.

Prior Computer Experience

This book assumes a minimum of prior computer experience. Nonetheless, there are a few basic techniques you should know in order to use this book. You do not need to have any prior experience with the Internet. But you do need to be able to:

- click with the mouse
- start and stop programs
- type and edit text
- start up and shut down *Windows*

If you do not know how to do these things yet, you can read the book
Windows Vista for Seniors first:

ISBN 978 90 5905 274 1

Paperback

US $19.95
Canada $26.95

Windows Vista for Seniors has been specifically written for people who are taking their first computer steps at a later age. It is a real "how to" book. By working through this book, you will learn all the techniques needed to operate your computer. You will gradually become more confident and comfortable using the computer. The step-by-step method makes instruction easy to process so you quickly gain basic computer skills.

What You Will Learn
When you finish this book, you will have the skills to:
• work independently with your computer
• write a letter using your computer
• adjust your computer settings so you can work with it most comfortably

For more information, visit
www.visualsteps.com/vista

How This Book Is Organized

This book is set up in such a way that you do not necessarily have to work through it from the beginning to the end. It is a good idea, however, to work through the chapters containing basic techniques first.

The Basics
- connecting to the Internet — Chapter 1
- surfing the Internet — Chapters 1 and 2
- sending e-mail — Chapter 5

After you have mastered these basic techniques, you can choose among the following chapters. Each one can be worked through separately. These cover the following subjects:

Optional Subjects
- searching the Internet — Chapter 3
- saving text and pictures — Chapter 4
- your *Contacts* folder and e-mail attachments — Chapter 6
- formatting e-mail — Chapter 7
- using *Windows Calendar* — Chapter 7
- downloading files — Chapter 8

The last chapter of this book is specifically devoted to security and privacy. Here you can read about specific settings and programs that enhance your safety when you use the Internet.

- security and privacy — Chapter 9

How to Use This Book

This book has been written using the Visual Steps™ method. It is important that you work through each chapter **step by step**. If you follow all the steps, you will not encounter any surprises. In this way, you will quickly learn how to use the Internet without any problems.

In this Visual Steps™ book, you will see various icons. This is what they mean:

Techniques
These icons indicate an action to be carried out:

 The mouse icon means you should do something with the mouse.

 The keyboard icon means you should type something on the keyboard.

 The hand icon means you should do something else, for example turn on the computer.

Sometimes we give you a little extra help in order to work through the book successfully.

Help
You can get extra help from these icons:

 The arrow icon warns you about something.

 The bandage icon can help you if something has gone wrong.

 The check mark icon appears in the exercises. These exercises help you independently practice the techniques you have learned.

 Have you forgotten how to do something? The number next to the footsteps icon tells you where you can find it in the appendix *How Do I Do That Again?*

This book also contains a great deal of general information and tips about the Internet, computers and *Windows*. This information is given in separate boxes.

Extra Information
Information boxes are denoted by these icons:

 The book icon gives you extra background information that you can read at your convenience. This extra information is not necessary for working through the book.

 The light bulb icon indicates an extra tip for using *Windows* and the Internet.

The Screen Shots

The screen shots in this book were made on a computer running *Windows Vista Home Premium.* To enhance the readability of the book we have adjusted certain settings on the computers we used for creating the book. For example, the mouse pointer will appear larger in the book than it will look on your computer screen. This makes no difference however in performing the requested actions or doing the exercises.

Test Your Knowledge

Have you finished reading this book? Test your knowledge then with the online tests *Internet Explorer 7* and *Windows Mail.* Visit the website: **www.ccforseniors.com**

These multiple-choice tests will show you how good your knowledge of Internet and e-mail is. If you pass the test, you will receive your free computer certificate by e-mail.

For Teachers

This book is designed as a self-study guide. It is also well suited for use in a group or a classroom setting. For this purpose, we offer a free teacher's manual containing information about how to prepare for the course (including didactic teaching methods) and testing materials. You can download this teacher's manual (PDF file) from the website which accompanies this book: **www.visualsteps.com/internetvista**

Visual Steps Newsletter

The free Visual Steps Newsletter will inform you of our product releases, free tips & tricks, special offers, free guides, etc.
It is sent to you periodically by e-mail. Please rest assured that we will not use your e-mail address for any purpose other than sending you the information you have requested and we will not share this address with any third-party. Each newsletter contains a clickable link to unsubscribe from our newsletter.

Register Your Book

You can register your book. We will keep you aware of any important changes that are necessary to you as a user of the book. You can also take advantage of:
Our periodic newsletter informing you of our product releases, company news, tips & tricks, special offers, etc.

1. Starting Out on the World Wide Web

The Internet consists of thousands of computers that are connected to one another by cables, the telephone network and satellite links. The *World Wide Web* is one of the most enjoyable and widely-used parts of the Internet. The World Wide Web is just that: a "spider web" of computers containing information on many diverse subjects.

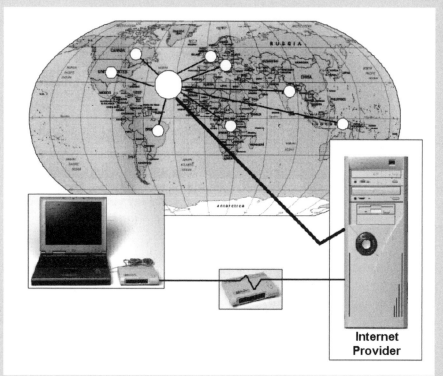

A computer connected to an Internet Service Provider

You can use your computer to open and read these specially formatted documents on the Internet no matter where you are in the world. These documents are called webpages. A website consists of one or more webpages. You can move from one webpage to another with a click of the mouse. You can move from one website to another just as easily. This is called *surfing the Web*.

In order to access the Internet, you will need to connect to a computer that is already connected to the Internet. An *Internet Service Provider*, also called an ISP, offers this type of service.

If you want to use the Internet, you will need a subscription with an *Internet Service Provider*. You will be given a user name and a password, and the ISP will provide software to set up your computer. This gives you access to the Internet.
If you have a regular dial-up (telephone) connection to your ISP, you will have to manually connect in order to surf the Internet. If you have a DSL or cable connection, you do not have to do anything; your computer automatically connects to the Internet. Once you are connected to the Internet, you are online. In this chapter, you will go online and learn how to *surf* the Internet.

In this chapter, you will learn how to:

- start *Internet Explorer*
- connect to your *Internet Service Provider*
- use a web address
- browse forward and back
- use tabbed browsing
- use the scroll bar
- move from one window to another
- zoom in and out
- disconnect from the Internet

⇨ **Please note:**

You must have a working Internet connection in order to use this book.
Contact your *Internet Service Provider* or your computer supplier if you need help.

- You can read the tips on *Connecting by Telephone Line* at the end of this chapter if you need more information about dial-up connections.

⇨ **Please note:**

This book assumes that you are working with a computer mouse. If you are working on a laptop with touchpad, you may want to purchase an external mouse to be able to follow the steps in this book more easily.

- If you want to learn about using the touchpad to operate your laptop, surf to the website **www.visualsteps.com/internetvista/news** and read the Tip *Working with a Touchpad*.

1.1 Starting Windows

Windows starts automatically when you turn on your computer.

☞ **Turn on your computer**

If you have set up user accounts on your computer, you will see the screen below first, where you can choose your own account.
If you did not set up any user accounts on your computer, you will immediately see the *desktop* of *Windows Vista*. In that case, continue reading on the next page.

If you see this screen:

⊕ **Click the icon of your user account**

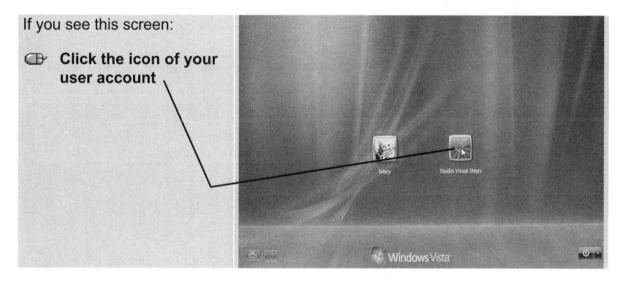

If you have set up a password for the user account, you will have to type it right now:

⌨ **Type the password**

⊕ **Click**

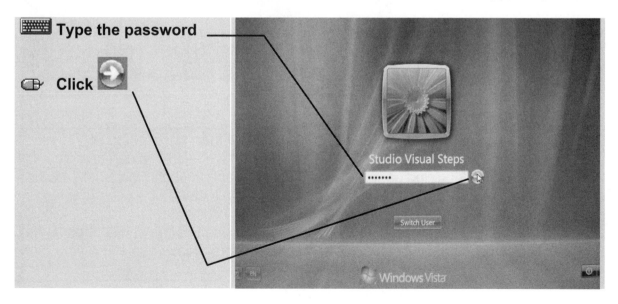

Possibly, you will see the
Welcome Center of *Windows
Vista*:
You can close this window:

 **Click**

The *Welcome Center* will now
disappear.

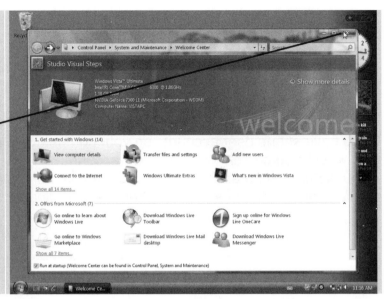

You now see the desktop of
Windows Vista containing
several icons:

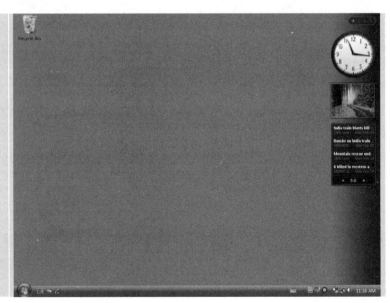

⇨ **Please note:**

The desktop you see on your screen may look different than the desktop you see in
the image above. The settings for the appearance of *Windows Vista* can be adjusted
in many ways. In order to increase the clarity of the images used in this book, a solid
color has been chosen as a background for the desktop instead of a photograph.

The Internet changes on a daily basis. For this reason, the images in this book taken
from the Internet at the time of this writing may differ from those you see on your own
computer.

1.2 Is Your Modem Ready?

Many people use a *modem* and a telephone line to connect to the Internet.
A modem is a device that connects your computer to your telephone line or cable
network. Sometimes it is in a separate box, called an *external modem*. In many
modern computers, however, the modem is already built in – an internal modem.
Before you connect to the Internet, it is important to check that your modem is *ready*.

☞ Make sure your modem is connected to the telephone line or cable network
You can read the tips on *Connecting by Telephone Line* at the end of this
chapter if you need more information about dial-up connections.

Do you have an external modem?
☞ Turn the modem on

Do you have an internal modem?
☞ You do not have to do anything

1.3 Starting Internet Explorer

The program you will use to contact the World Wide Web is called *Internet Explorer*.
Here is how you start this program:

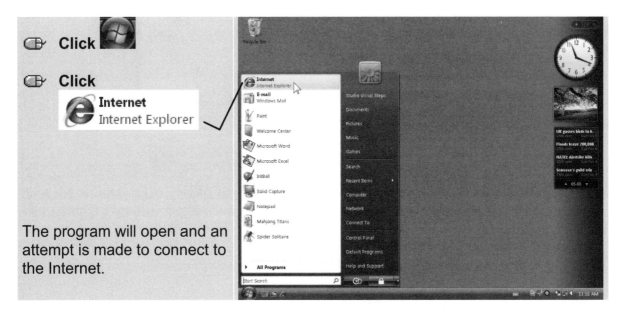

⌨ **Click**

⌨ **Click**
Internet
Internet Explorer

The program will open and an
attempt is made to connect to
the Internet.

If you are using *Internet Explorer* for the first time and you have a *broadband* connection to the Internet (DSL or cable), you will probably see a window like this floating on top of the *Internet Explorer* window:

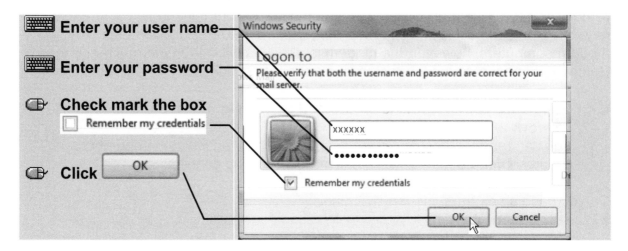

If you are using *dial-up networking* to connect to the Internet, you will see a *Dial-up Connection* window.

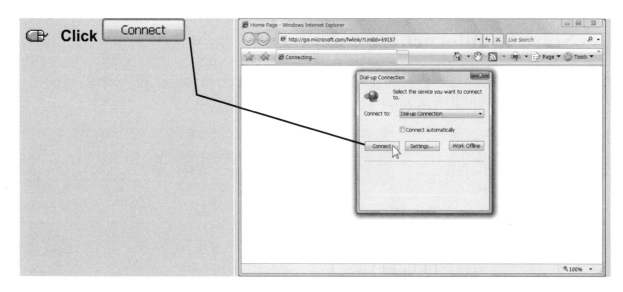

If you have an Internet access subscription, your ISP has given you a *user name* and a *password*. If everything is set up properly, both of these will already be displayed in the next window.

If your user name and password are **not** displayed:

 Type your user name and password in the appropriate boxes

⊕ **Check mark the box**

☐ Save this user name and password f(

⊕ **Click** ○ Me only

⊕ **Click** [Dial]

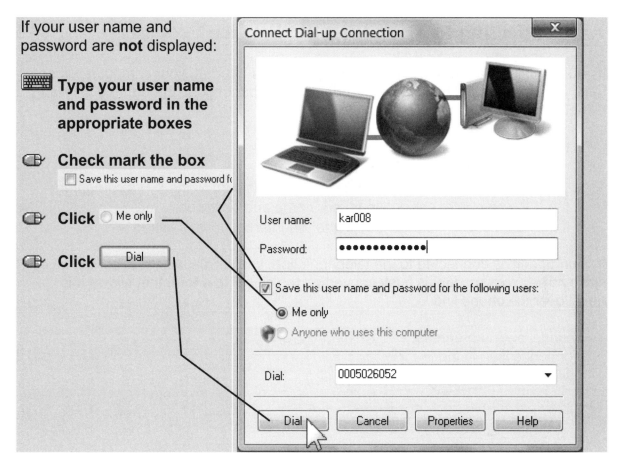

A connection is made to your ISP (*Internet Service Provider*).

🔌 HELP! I do not see windows like these.

Are these windows not shown on your screen? If you are connected to the internet by cable or DSL, then this *Dial-up Connection* window will not appear. You will have a different set up on your computer. *Internet Explorer* automatically connects with the Internet when you open it.

☞ **Just continue reading**

1.4 Connecting to Your Internet Service Provider

If you are using dial-up networking to connect to the Internet, your computer will now try to contact your ISP by using the modem. The modem goes through the following steps:

- the modem dials your ISP's telephone number
- then it connects to your ISP's computer
- your computer sends your user name and password to the ISP's computer
- the ISP's computer checks your user name and password
- if they are correct, your connection to the Internet is established

If your modem is connected to the telephone line, you will usually hear quite a bit of static noise. Your modem is busy converting the signal to a form that allows it to travel over the phone line.

You can follow the progress of your connection in the window:

Connecting to Dial-up Connection...

Dialing 1-456-456-4556

Cancel

If you have a cable, ISDN or DSL connection, *Internet Explorer* automatically connects to the Internet and you will not hear any noise.

Once you are connected to the Internet, the home page will be displayed in the *Internet Explorer* window.

If you have not made any changes to your settings, this is probably a page from *Microsoft*, the company that makes *Internet Explorer*.

Down in the right corner of the *taskbar*, you will see an icon with two computers indicating that you are *online*:

Please note:

The home page on your computer may not be the same as the one in the illustration. You might, for example, see the website of your *Internet Service Provider*.

 HELP! Invalid user name or password?

If you connect but receive the following message "Invalid User name or Password", re-enter your user name and password in the *Dial-up Connection* window and try to connect to the Internet again.

 HELP! There is no connection.

Were you unable to connect to the Internet?
This could be because your ISP's number is "busy":

Dial-up Connection	X
Select the service you want to connect to.	

Connect to: Dial-up Connection ▼

☐ Connect automatically

[Connect] [Settings...] [Work Offline]

Dialing...0005026052
Dialing attempt 1.
Unable to establish a connection.

When that happens, try again a little later.

 HELP! Still no connection?

If you have tried to connect to the Internet a number of times and you still are unable to establish a connection, most likely the settings on your computer are not correct. You will need to contact your ISP for assistance.

1.5 Typing an Address

Every website has its own web address on the World Wide Web. These are the addresses that start with www that you see everywhere.
You can use these addresses to find a website on any computer that is connected to the Internet. The web address of the Visual Steps publishing company is:

www.visualsteps.com

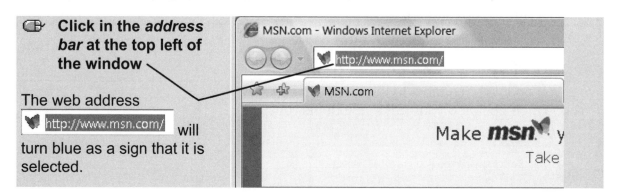

Click in the address bar at the top left of the window

The web address http://www.msn.com/ will turn blue as a sign that it is selected.

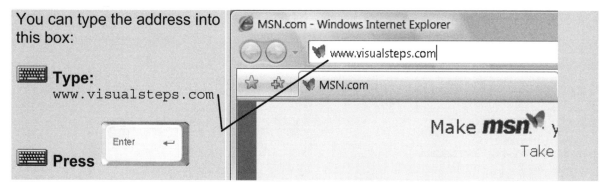

You can type the address into this box:

Type:
www.visualsteps.com

Press Enter ↵

HELP! Where is the Enter key?

The Enter key is located on the right-hand side of your keyboard:

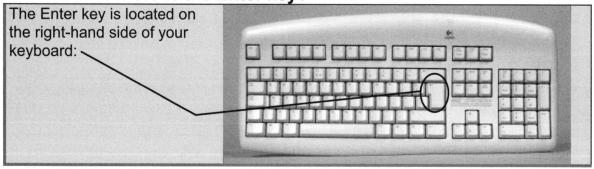

After a few moments, you see the opening page for this website:

This webpage is updated frequently. The picture you see on your computer may be different than the one in this illustration.

1.6 Maximizing the Window

You can maximize the *Internet Explorer* window at any time, so that it fills the entire screen. This makes it easier to view a webpage. Here is how you do this:

Click

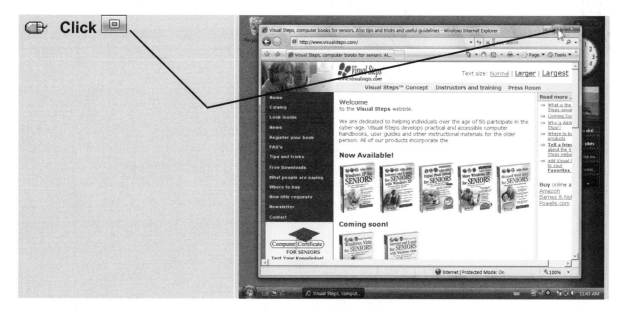

The window now fills your entire screen:

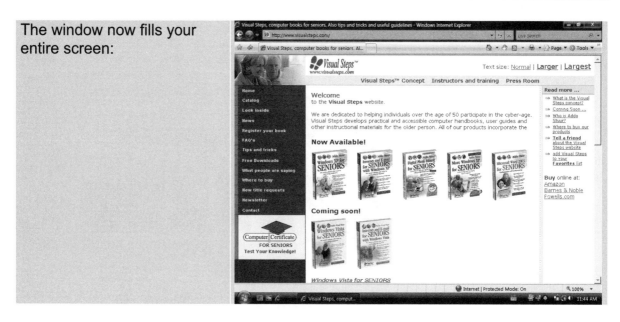

💡 Tip

Unfortunately, *Internet Explorer* does not automatically start with a maximized window. Go ahead and click right after it opens.

You can restore the window to its original size with just one click:

Click

1.7 A Wrong Address

Once in a while a typing error is made when typing a web address. Or a particular web address may no longer exist. This is especially true because the Internet is highly dynamic, changing every day. Private individuals and companies may need to change their web addresses for a variety of reasons.

When typing a web address, pay close attention to the following:

Sometimes you will see an address that starts with **http://**. That is additional information indiating that the address is for a website.
With *Internet Explorer,* you do not need to type **http://**. The program automatically understands that you are looking for a website and will add it to the address.
Make sure that any dots (.) or forward slashes (/) are typed in the correct places. If they are not, you will receive an error message.
Never type spaces in a web address.

If even one dot is missing, an error message will appear. Try it:

Click in the address bar

Type: `www.pbsorg`

Press

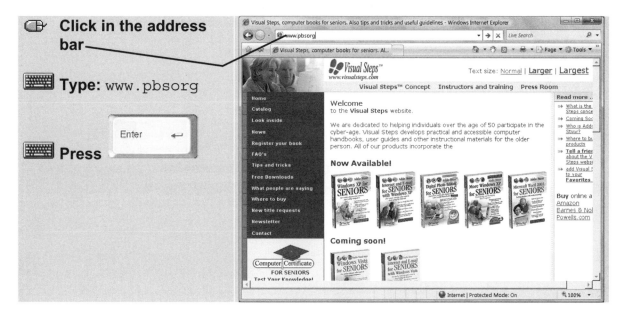

After some time, the following webpage is displayed:

But this is not the webpage you were looking for.
Search provider *Live Search* is trying to help you.

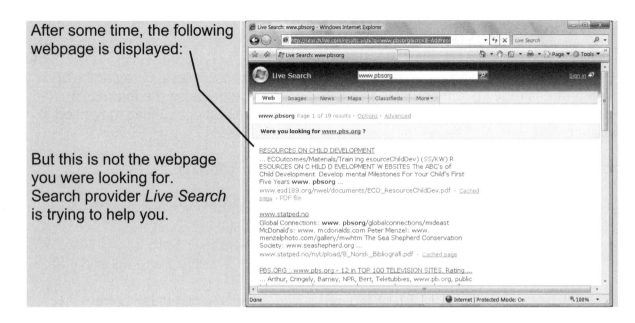

Live Search asks: **Were you looking for www.pbs.org ?** *Live Search* has made this assumption because the address you typed - **www.pbsorg** - was incorrect, but was very similar to an address they have in their database. The dot before **org** is missing. The correct address for the Public Broadcasting Service website is:

www.pbs.org

Try the correct address:

Click in the address bar

Type: www.pbs.org

Press Enter ⏎

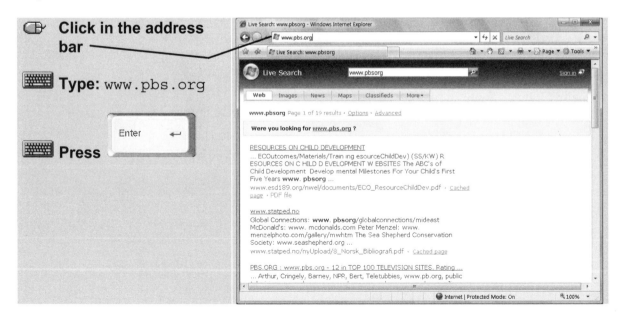

After a short while, you see the home page for the Public Broadcasting Service.

At the time of this writing, this is how the page looked:

Remember, if you forget just one dot the program may not be able to find the website you want.

 Please note:

The website shown above may look different now. The Internet changes all the time.

1.8 Refreshing a Page

Sometimes a page is not displayed on your screen as it should be. When that happens, you can tell *Internet Explorer* to reload the page again: to *refresh* it. Just watch what happens:

Click

You will see that the window will be refreshed and the information is collected once again.

Everything that is shown on your screen must be sent in through the telephone line or the cable. This may take a while. Sometimes it will seem like nothing is happening. But there is a way to check if *Internet Explorer* is still busy loading a page that you have requested:

At the bottom of the screen, the green bar indicates that information is being received:

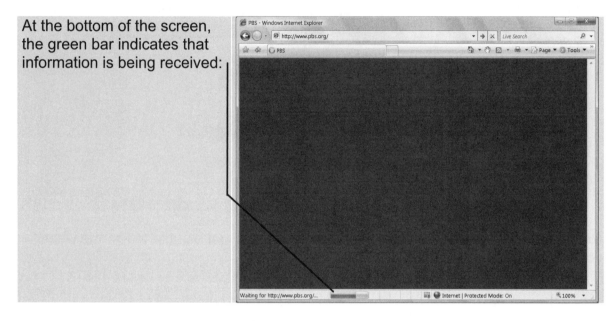

Not all information appears immediately on your screen; it may take time to load the entire page, especially if you are using dial-up networking to connect to the Internet.

1.9 Forward and Back

You do not need to retype the web address of a website if you want to revisit it. *Internet Explorer* has a number of buttons that help you *navigate* the Internet.

At the top left of the window, click ⬅

The previous webpage you viewed will be opened.

What you see now is the website where search provider *Live Search* was helping you:

Perhaps you noticed how quickly this is done. *Internet Explorer* retains the websites you recently visited in its memory so that you can quickly look at them again without the need of requesting the information through your telephone line or cable.

Click two more times

Now you will go back to the website you first visited.

Once again, the start page is displayed:

Now you can no longer browse back. That is because this was the first website you opened.

The button is gray and can no longer be used:

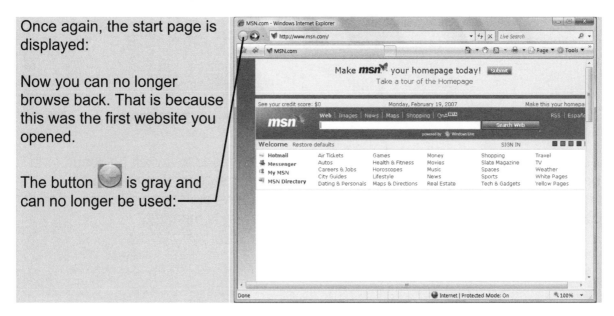

You can, however, browse the other way. There is a special button for this as well.

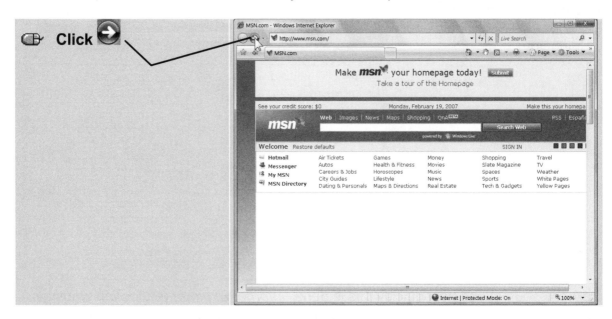

Now you see the same Visual Steps website on the screen as you did before:

As you have seen, the buttons ⬅ ➡ can easily be used to switch back and forth between the websites you have viewed. This is called "surfing" the Internet. However, these websites will not remain in memory forever. When you close *Internet Explorer,* the websites will be removed from the browser's memory.

1.10 Tabbed Browsing

Internet Explorer has an interesting feature that allows you to open multiple websites in a single browser window. This is called *tabbed browsing*. You can start by opening a new, blank tab:

In the new tab you will see a webpage with information about tabs.

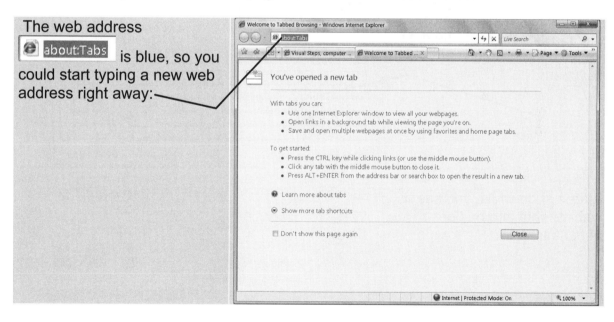

In the next paragraph, you will use the new tab to open a webpage in the *subdirectory* of the Visual Steps publishing company website.

1.11 Subdirectories

Some websites have an additional website added onto the main web address. This extra website is in a subdirectory. The subdirectory is separated from the main address by a / (*slash*). Take, for example, the website for this book:

www.visualsteps.com/internetvista

Type:
www.visualsteps.com
/internetvista

Press Enter

HELP! Where is the / (slash) key?

The / is on the same key as the question mark, in the right bottom corner of the keyboard:

After a short while, you see a website with information about this book:

1.12 Browsing by Clicking

Nearly every website will have a navigation list, a sort of *table of contents* summarizing the subjects you can find on the site. This website has one too. You can see the subjects in a column on the left-hand side. By clicking on one of the subjects, you can go to another page:

Place the mouse pointer on

> Practice website

You see the mouse pointer change into a little hand 🖑 :

Click

> Practice website

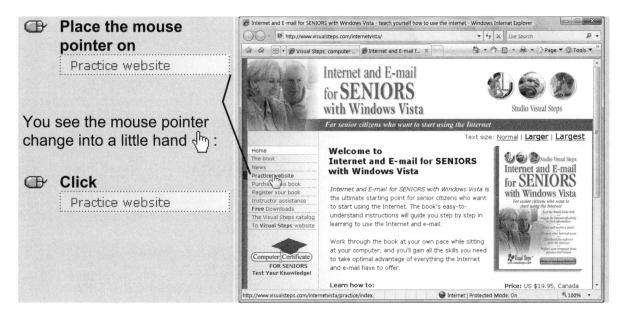

You can click anywhere on a webpage where you see the little hand appear. Not only buttons, but also bits of text or images may be "clickable". A word, a button or an image that you can click is called a *link*. Sometimes the word *hyperlink* is used.

The practice website for this book is opened in the second tab, replacing the website for this book:

On the page you see various buttons that link to other pages:

Click Exercise Page

The exercise page is opened.

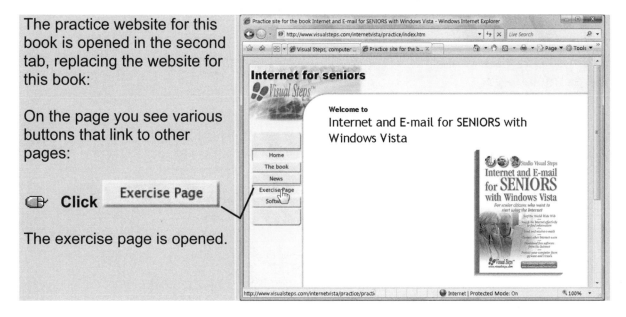

1.13 Opening a Link in a New Tab

When you click a link, the new webpage will replace the old webpage in the tab you are working in. *Internet Explorer* has a trick to open a link directly in a new tab. Try that with one of the links on the exercise page:

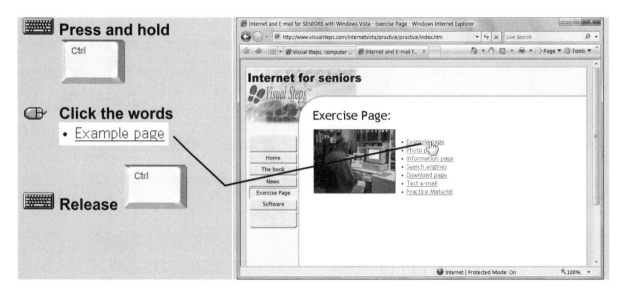

The example page opens in a new tab. That tab is still hidden behind the second tab with the exercise page. You can switch to the third tab by simply clicking it:

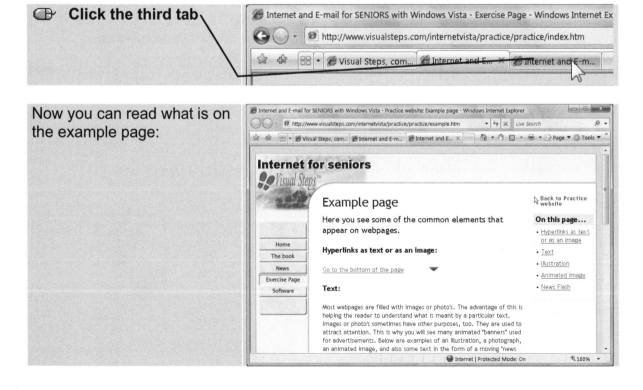

1.14 Using the Scroll Bars

When you view pages on the Internet, you may need to use the *scroll bar*. Even if you maximize the browser window, it might not be large enough to hold all of the information. In order to see the rest of the page, you must use the vertical scroll bar.

Click the scroll arrow
▾ **at the bottom of the scroll bar**

You see the page slide upwards:

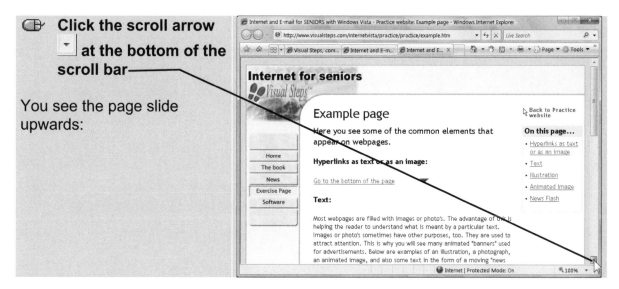

You can move the page back down so you can see the top again.

Click ▴ **at the top of the scroll bar**

You see the page slide back down:

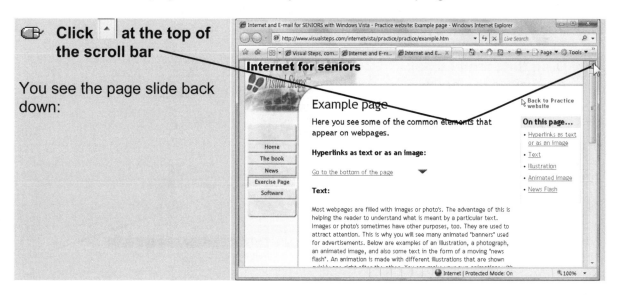

You can move the page very precisely by **dragging** with the mouse. Here is how you drag:

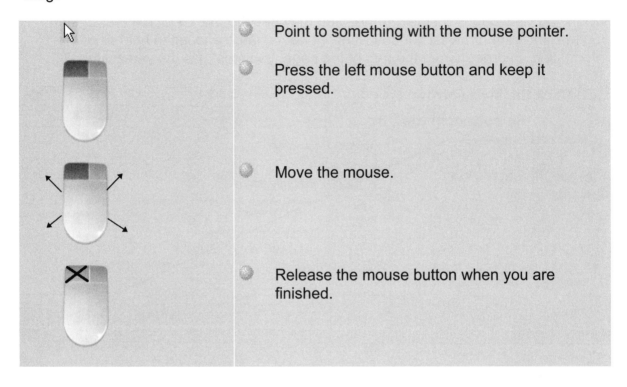

	Point to something with the mouse pointer.
	Press the left mouse button and keep it pressed.
	Move the mouse.
	Release the mouse button when you are finished.

By dragging with the mouse, you can move the slidable part of the scroll bar, called the *scroll box*. Give it a try:

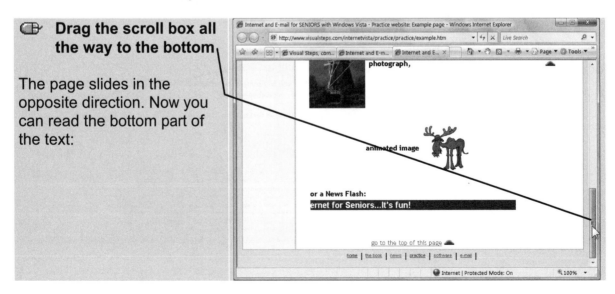

☞ Drag the scroll box all the way to the bottom

The page slides in the opposite direction. Now you can read the bottom part of the text:

This window sliding is called *scrolling* in computer language.

Tip

The scroll wheel
The rapidly growing popularity of the Internet has resulted in various new additions to the mouse, including one called the scroll wheel.
By turning the wheel with your finger, the contents of the window will scroll. This is the same thing that happens when you use the scroll bar, but it is much easier and quicker.

Once you have gotten used to a mouse wheel, you will never want to do without!
To scroll down, roll the wheel backward (toward you).
To scroll up, roll the wheel forward (away from you).

 Tip

Clicking with the scroll wheel
The mouse wheel can also be used to click a link:

⊂🖰 **Place your mouse pointer on a link**
⊂🖰 **Press the scroll wheel down**

Now the link automatically opens in a new tab!

 Tip

Other types of mice

In addition to the classic mouse shape, there are also *ergonomically*-shaped mice with extra buttons for your thumb, for example. You can give these different buttons specific functions.

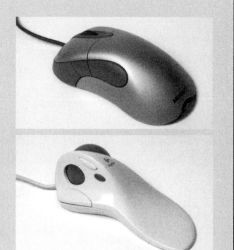

A *trackball* is a kind of "reverse" mouse. The device does not move on your desk, instead you roll the ball with your fingers to move the mouse pointer. The trackball also has a scroll wheel for the Internet and multiple buttons.

1.15 Back to the Home Page

A good website is made in such a way that you can easily move from one page to the next without getting lost. Most websites, for example, have a button marked *Home* or *Start* that when clicked will return you to the website's *home page*.

Click home

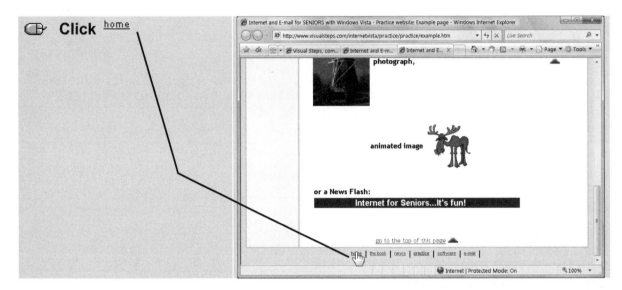

You see the opening page for the practice website for this book:

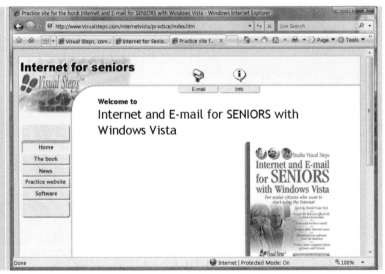

1.16 A Second Window

Up to this point, you have viewed all the webpages in tabs in a single *Internet Explorer* window. However, a website can be designed so that a new browser window is opened when you click a hyperlink. You do not have any control over this, because it has been programmed into the website and happens automatically. There is a hyperlink like this on the exercise page. Give it a try:

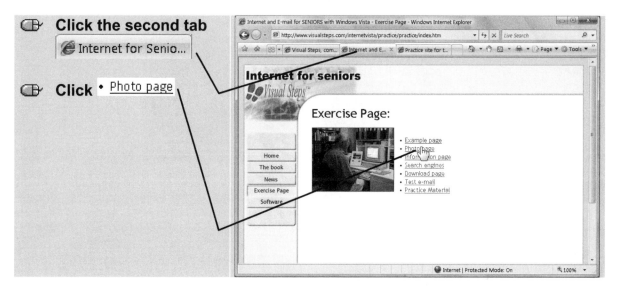

Click the second tab

Click **• Photo page**

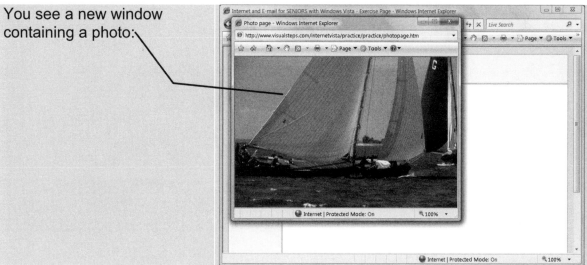

You see a new window containing a photo:

If you do not want to close this page, and would like to keep this window available, you can minimize it.

1.17 Minimizing a Window

Making a window small is called *minimizing*.

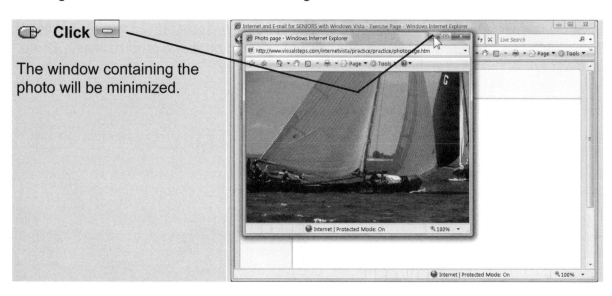

☞ **Click** ⬜

The window containing the photo will be minimized.

Now you see the window with the practice website and the other tabs again:

You can also minimize this window:

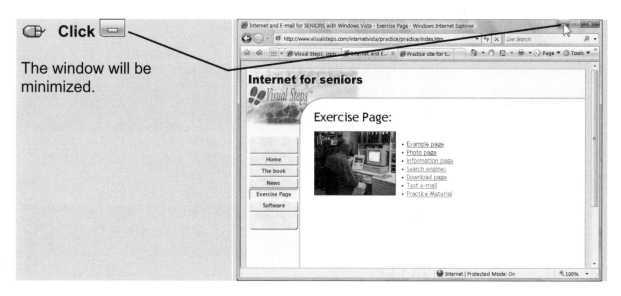

⬚ **Click** ⬚

The window will be minimized.

Now you have minimized two windows: the window with the photo and the windows with the practice site and the other tabs.

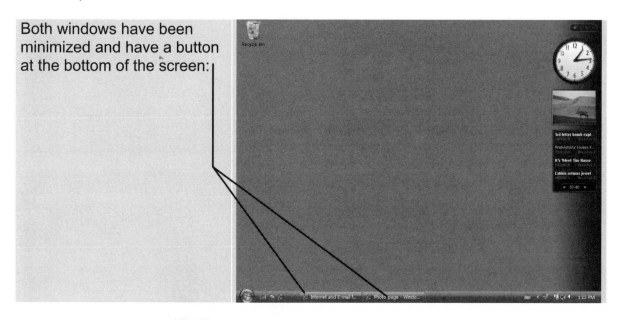

Both windows have been minimized and have a button at the bottom of the screen:

The gray bar next to ⬚ is called the *taskbar*. The taskbar always contains the buttons for the windows you are currently using.

1.18 Opening a Window

You can quickly re-open a window by using the taskbar buttons:

☞ **Click**

    Internet and E-mail f...

on the taskbar

You see the window for the practice site again. Now you can open the window with the photo the same way:

☞ **Point to**

    Photo page - Wi...

on the taskbar

A miniature version of the window is displayed above the taskbar button:

☞ **Click**

    Photo page - Wi...

on the taskbar

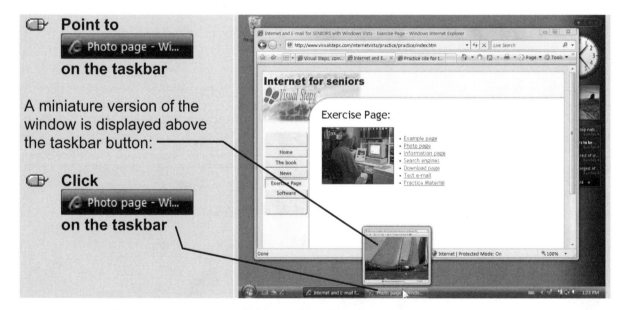

The window with the photo now appears on top of the other window:

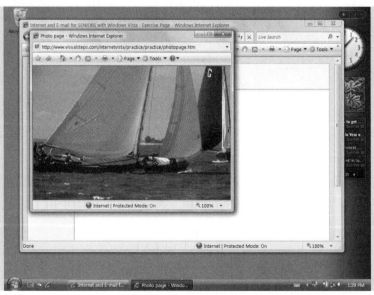

1.19 Switching between Windows

You can use the taskbar to quickly back and forth between windows:

Click

Internet and E-mail f...

on the taskbar

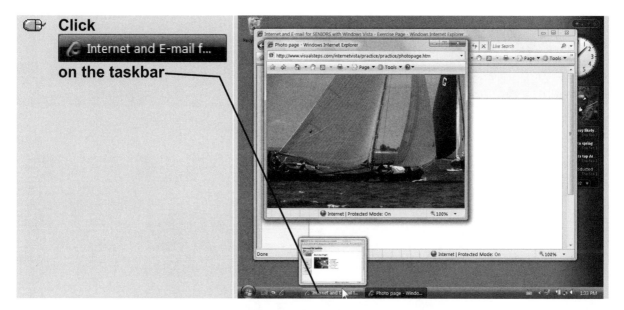

The window with the photo now disappears behind the window for the practice site.

Click

Photo page - Wi...

on the taskbar

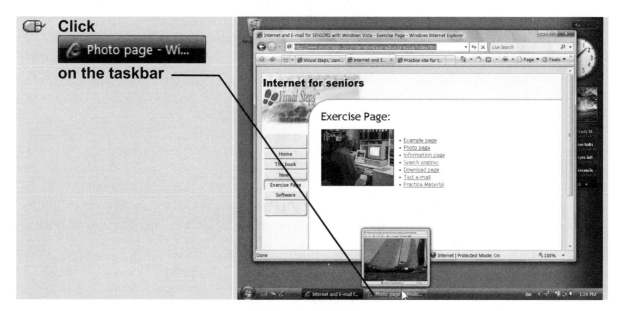

Now the window with the photo pops in front again. You can see how easy it is to switch back and forth between different windows.

1.20 Closing Windows

When you have several windows opened, you can always close the ones you no longer need.

 Please note:

Always keep at least one *Internet Explorer* window open, or the connection to the Internet may be broken.

In this case, you can close the window with the photo.

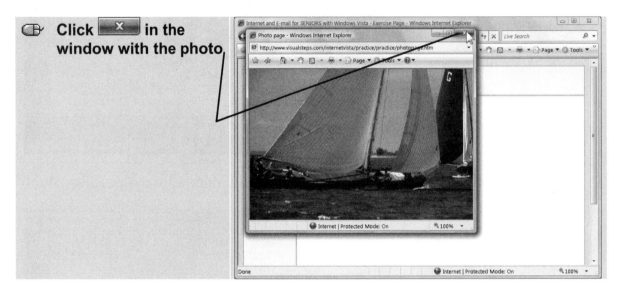

 Click [X] **in the window with the photo**

The window closes and its button on the taskbar disappears.

💡 Tip

Opening a link in a new window
Even when it has not been programmed into the website, you can always open a link in a new browser window, instead of in the same window or a new tab. Here is how to do this:

⌨️ **Press and hold** [⇧ Shift]
👆 **Click the link**

⌨️ **Release** [⇧ Shift]

A new browser window opens and you see the website for to the link you just clicked.

1.21 Closing Tabs

A tab you no longer need can also be closed. Try that with the first tab:

☞ Click the first tab

You see the webpage of the Visual Steps publishing company again.

On the active tab, you see a small button **X** to close that tab.

☞ Click X

The first tab has disappeared. Now you have two tabs left:

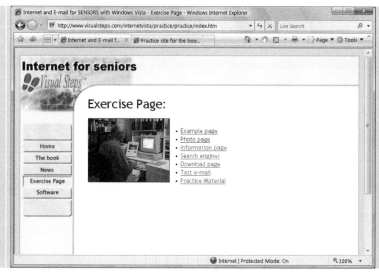

Tip

Quick Tabs
When you have multiple webpages open on separate tabs, *Quick Tabs* provides a miniature view of all your open tabs. This makes it easier to find the webpage that you want to view.

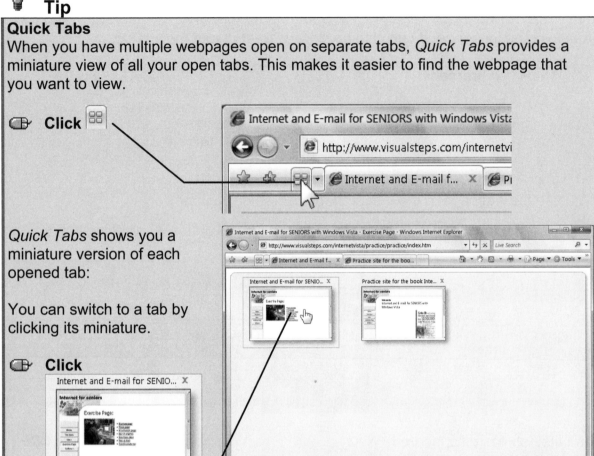

Quick Tabs shows you a miniature version of each opened tab:

You can switch to a tab by clicking its miniature.

1.22 Zooming In and Out

Images and text on webpages can be very small. By zooming in on part of the website, you can see more detail or read the text more easily. You can give that a try on the example page:

You see the *Internet for Seniors* exercise page:

☞ **Click** • Example page

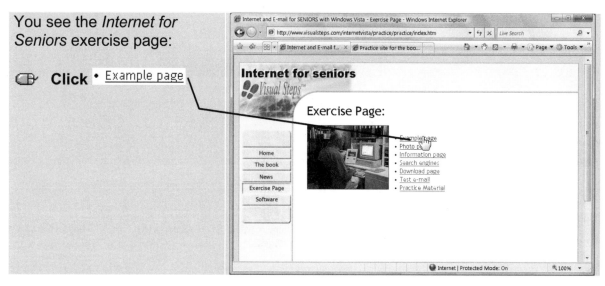

You see this page:

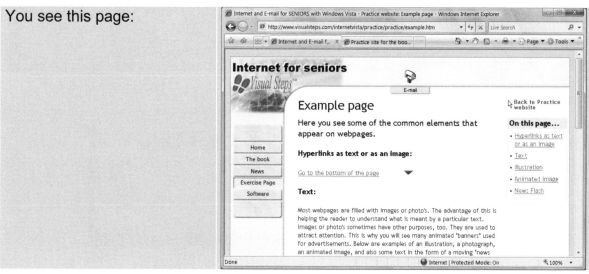

Zooming in will enlarge the text and the objects on your screen.

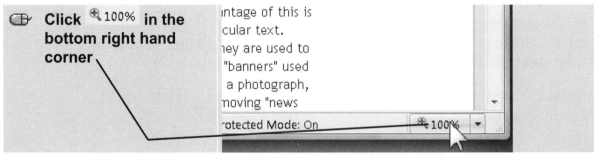

Click 🔍100% **in the bottom right hand corner**

The text and images look quite a bit larger. You will need to use the scroll bars to see everything:

Here you can see that the zoom level has been changed to 🔍125% :

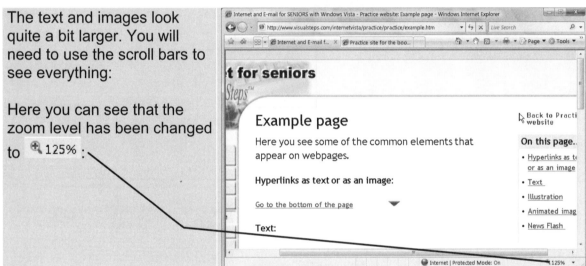

You can zoom in even more:

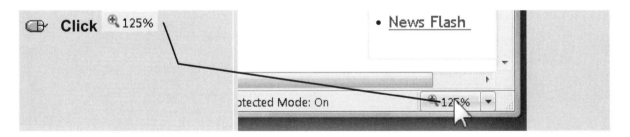

Click 🔍125%

Now the zoom level has increased to ⊕150%. Clicking this button again will not increase the zoom level anymore. Instead, you will go back to the original level of ⊕100%. Try that:

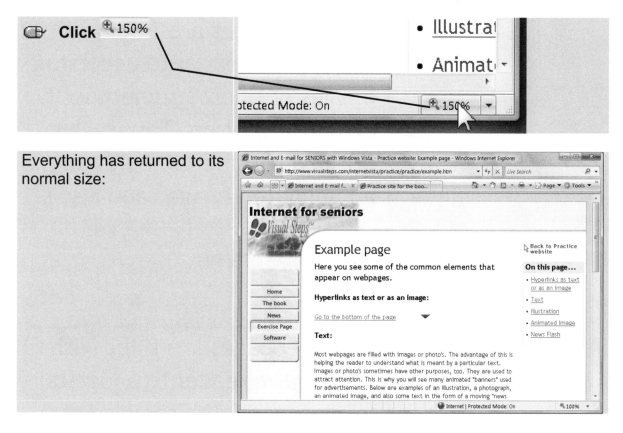

☞ **Click** ⊕150%

Everything has returned to its normal size:

It is possible to zoom in beyond 150%, even up to 400%! This is how you do that:

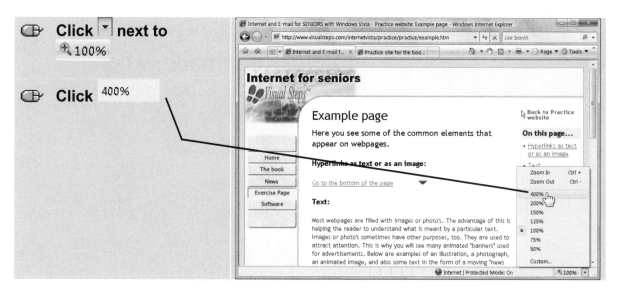

☞ **Click** ▾ **next to** ⊕100%

☞ **Click** 400%

You have zoomed in so far that you can only see a small part of the webpage.

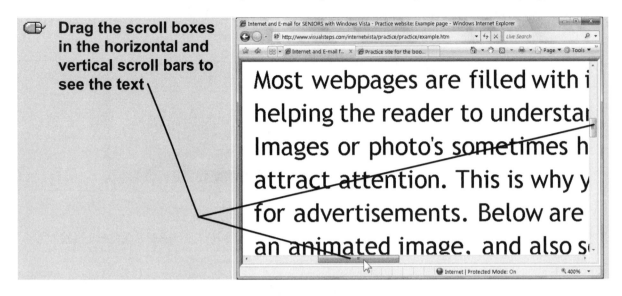

With a zoom level of 50% you can see most of the webpage.

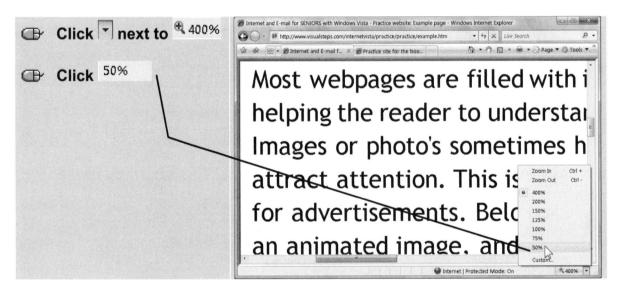

However, most of the text is now very small and difficult to read. Just one click will bring you back to a zoom level of 100%:

☞ **Click**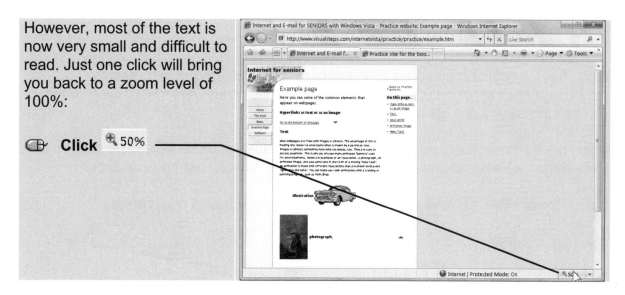

The website is now shown in its normal size.

1.23 Using Large Icons

Zooming in and out does not change the size of the buttons and icons in the *Internet Explorer* window.

By default, the buttons have this size:

You can easily enlarge these as well:

☞ **Right-click between** [ ] **and** 🏠

☞ **Click** Use Large Icons

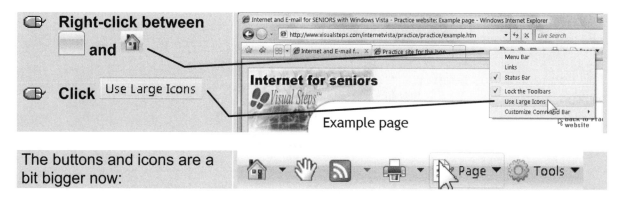

The buttons and icons are a bit bigger now:

To increase readability, *Internet Explorer* will be shown with large buttons in the rest of this book.

1.24 Disconnecting from the Internet

If you have a common analog dial-up connection to the Internet, you have to disconnect each time you stop using the Internet. No other calls can come through to you as long as you are connected to the Internet.

If you have a broadband connection like DSL or cable, you are always connected to the Internet, whether you are using the web or not. You do not have to disconnect.

Follow these steps to close the *Internet Explorer* window and disconnect.

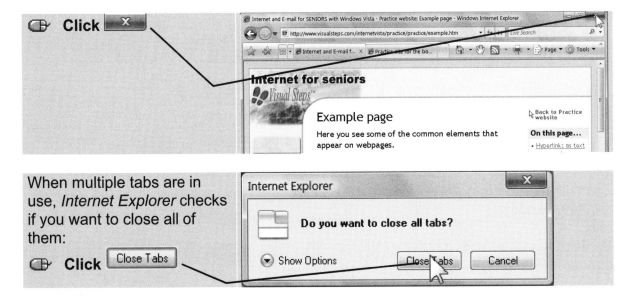

When multiple tabs are in use, *Internet Explorer* checks if you want to close all of them:

☞ **Click** Close Tabs

If you have a dial-up connection, you see the window *Auto Disconnect*:

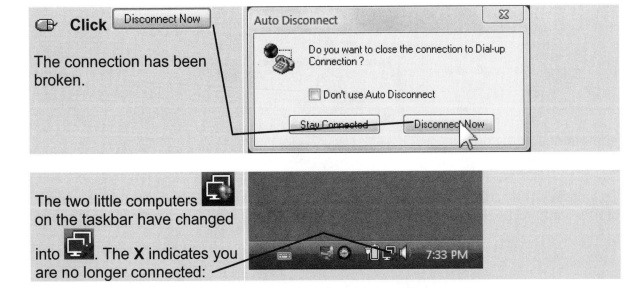

☞ **Click** Disconnect Now

The connection has been broken.

The two little computers on the taskbar have changed into . The **X** indicates you are no longer connected:

If you have a broadband connection such as DSL or cable, you will not see the *Auto Disconnect* window. You will still see in the notification area on the far right side of the taskbar because you are continuously online.

HELP! The connection is not broken.

Do you have a dial-up connection to the internet and you do not see the *Auto Disconnect* window?

Do you still see the computers on the taskbar without the **X**? This means that the connection has not been broken. There is another way to disconnect:

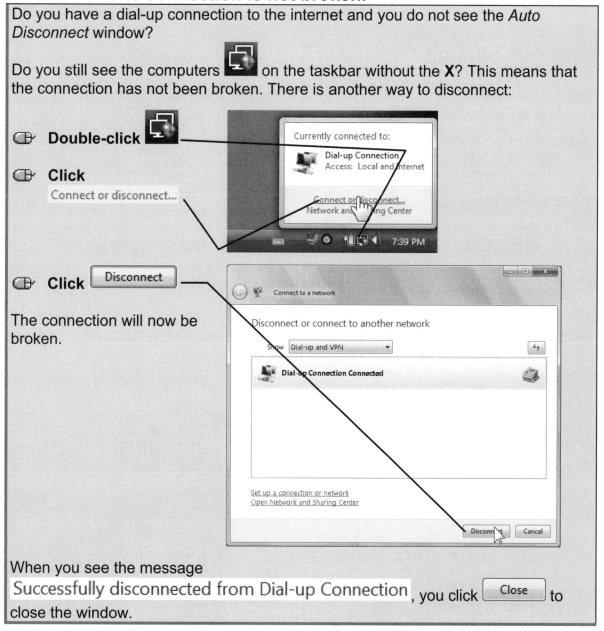

The connection will now be broken.

When you see the message
Successfully disconnected from Dial-up Connection, you click Close to close the window.

In this chapter you learned how to surf the internet. With the following exercises you can practice what you have learned.

1.25 Exercises

The following exercises will help you master what you have just learned. Have you forgotten how to do something? Use the number beside the footsteps to look it up in the appendix *How Do I Do That Again?*

Exercise: Surfing

Going from one website to another is called surfing. In this exercise, you will surf to websites you visited previously.

✔ Start *Internet Explorer*. 🐾1

✔ Connect to the Internet if necessary. 🐾3

✔ Type in the address of the Public Broadcasting Service: www.pbs.org 🐾4

✔ Type in the address: www.visualsteps.com/internetvista 🐾4

✔ Go back to www.pbs.org 🐾6

✔ Refresh the page. 🐾8

✔ Go forward to www.visualsteps.com/internetvista 🐾7

✔ Click Practice website .

✔ Click Exercise Page and then • Example page .

✔ Scroll to the bottom of the example page. 🐾9

✔ Go back to the Public Broadcasting Service website. 🐾6

✔ Close *Internet Explorer*. 🐾2

✔ Close the connection to the Internet if necessary. 🐾5

Exercise: Tabs and Windows

In this exercise, you will practice working with tabs and windows.

✔   Start *Internet Explorer*. $\ell\ell^1$

✔   Connect to the Internet if necessary. $\ell\ell^3$

✔   Type in the address: www.visualsteps.com $\ell\ell^4$

✔   Open a new tab. $\ell\ell^{62}$

✔   Type in the address: www.visualsteps.com/internetvista $\ell\ell^4$

✔   Click Practice website and then Exercise Page .

✔   Open the link • Example page in a new tab. $\ell\ell^{63}$

✔   Click • Photo page .

✔   Minimize the photo page window. $\ell\ell^{11}$

✔   Switch to the first tab. $\ell\ell^{64}$

✔   Minimize the *Internet Explorer* window. $\ell\ell^{11}$

✔   Open the window with the photo by using the taskbar. $\ell\ell^{12}$

✔   Close the window with the photo. $\ell\ell^{13}$

✔   Open the *Internet Explorer* window by using the taskbar. $\ell\ell^{12}$

✔   Close the second tab. $\ell\ell^{65}$

✔   Close *Internet Explorer*. $\ell\ell^2$

✔   Close the connection to the Internet if necessary. $\ell\ell^5$

1.26 Background Information

Glossary

Address bar	The address bar is located near the top of the *Internet Explorer* window. It displays the web address of the webpage you are currently viewing. By typing a new web address and pressing the Enter key you can open another webpage.
Back button	Use the *Back* button to return to the previous webpage.
Broadband connection	A high speed Internet connection. Broadband connections are typically 256 kilobytes per second (KBps) or faster. Broadband includes DSL and cable modem service.
Browser, Web browser	A program used to display webpages and to navigate the Internet. *Internet Explorer* is a web browser.
Cable Internet	Cable Internet access is a broadband connection that uses the same wiring as cable TV. To use cable, you need an account with a cable *Internet Service Provider* in your area. The ISP usually provides any necessary equipment, and often sends a technician to set it up for you.
Desktop	The desktop is the main screen area that you see after you turn on your computer and log on to *Windows Vista*. When you open programs or folders, they appear on the desktop.
Dial-up connection	Connecting to the Internet by using a modem and a telephone line. Usually a low speed analog connection.
Dragging	Moving an item on the screen by selecting the item and then pressing and holding down the left mouse button while sliding or moving the mouse.
DSL	Digital Subscriber Line - a type of high speed Internet connection using standard telephone wires. This is a broadband connection. The ISP is usually a phone company.
Forward button	Use the *Forward* button to go to the website you visited after the one you are now viewing.

- Continue reading on the next page -

Home page	The first page or opening page of a website. Also the page that is displayed when you first start *Internet Explorer.*
Hyperlink, Link	A hyperlink is a navigation element in a webpage that automatically displays the referred information when the user clicks on the hyperlink. A hyperlink can be text or images like buttons, icons or pictures. You can recognize a hyperlink when the mouse pointer turns into a hand 🖑.
Icon	A small picture that represents a folder, program, or object.
Internet	A network of computer networks which operates worldwide using a common set of communications protocols. The part of the Internet that most people are familiar with is the World Wide Web (WWW).
Internet Explorer	A program used to display webpages and to navigate the Internet.
ISP	An *Internet Service Provider* (ISP) is a company that provides you with access to the Internet, usually for a fee. The most common ways to connect to an ISP are by using a phone line (dial-up) or broadband connection (cable or DSL). Many ISPs provide additional services such as e-mail accounts, virtual hosting, and space for you to create a website.
Maximize	Increase the size of a window to full-screen size.
Minimize	Reduce a window to a button on the taskbar.
Modem	A modem is a device that connects your computer to your telephone line or cable network.
Password	A string of characters that a user must enter to gain access to a resource that is password protected. Passwords help ensure that unauthorized users do not access your internet connection or your computer.
Program	A set of instructions that a computer uses to perform a specific task, such as word processing or calculating.
Quick Tabs	*Quick Tabs* gives a miniature view of all your open tabs.
Refreshing	Reloading a webpage.
Restore	Return a window to its former size.

- Continue reading on the next page -

Scroll bars	When a webpage picture exceeds the size of its window, scroll bars appear to allow you to see the information that is currently out of view. You can drag the horizontal or vertical scroll bar to display the desired part of the webpage.
Surfing	Going from one website to another.
Tab	Part of the *Internet Explorer* window on which a separate website can be opened.
Tabbed browsing	Tabbed browsing allows you to open multiple websites in a single browser window. You can open webpages on new tabs, and switch between them by clicking the tab.
Taskbar	The taskbar is the long horizontal bar at the bottom of your screen. The taskbar is usually visible.
User name	Login name.
Web address	The web address of a website uniquely identifies a location on the Internet. An example of a web address is: www.visualsteps.com. A web address is also called an URL (Uniform Resource Locator). People use URLs to find websites, but computers use IP addresses to find websites. An IP address usually consists of four groups of numbers separated by periods, such as 192.200.44.69. Special computers on the Internet translate URLs into IP addresses (and vice versa).
Webpage	A webpage is a resource of information that is suitable for the World Wide Web and can be accessed through a browser.
Website	A website is a collection of interconnected webpages, typically common to a particular domain name on the World Wide Web on the Internet.
Window	A rectangular box or frame on a computer screen in which programs and content appear.
Windows Vista	Operating system: the computer program that manages all other computer programs on your computer. The operating system stores files, allows you to use programs, and coordinates the use of computer hardware (mouse, keyboard).
WWW	World Wide Web - web of computers, connected to each other - containing an infinite amount of webpages.
Zooming in or out	Enlarge or reduce the view of a webpage. Zoom enlarges or reduces everything on the page, including text and images.

Source: Windows Help and Support

The history of the Internet
Soon after the introduction of the first computers, people in offices began connecting them using cables so that every employee could exchange information with others. Computers that are connected to one another are called a *network*.

The first of these networks began in the USA at the end of the 1960s. The Department of Defense had a network called ARPANET. ARPANET was an experiment. The DoD wanted to develop a technology that would allow all the defense computers to communicate with one another, even if part of the connection fell away because of a nuclear attack, for example. The problem was solved by a method that works just like the highway network. If a road is blocked, you can usually still get to your destination by taking a different route. This technique worked. Similar networks appeared in other countries.

At the end of the 1980s, all these networks were connected to one another. The Internet was born. At first, mainly universities and research institutions were connected to the Internet, but in 1990 individuals and commercial companies also gained access to it. From that moment on, the number of users has grown phenomenally, a growth that continues up to this day.

Domain names
A web address associated with a particular name is called a domain name. Every web address has a suffix such as *.com*.

For example: www.visualsteps.**com**

There are several variations on this suffix. In Europe, a country code is often used:

For example: www.visualsteps.**nl**

Other country codes include **.be** for Belgium and **.de** for Germany.
Outside Europe and in the United States, a different system is used. The suffix indicates the type of organization:
.com .... commercial company
.edu .... educational institution
.org .... non-profit organization

Internet Service Providers

Connecting to the Internet is often done over a telephone line. Computers can communicate with one another over the telephone network. Connecting your computer to others usually happens with the help of an *Internet Service Provider* (ISP). This ISP gives access to the Internet by means of a large number of computers, all of which are connected to the Internet. When you make contact with one of the ISP's computers, you gain access to the Internet.

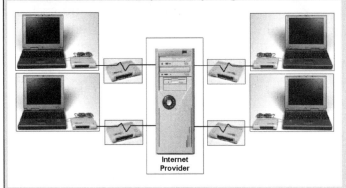

The Internet Service Provider offers access to many users

Most large ISPs have so many *access numbers* (the telephone number for the ISP that your own computer will call) that you can always call locally. If there is no local number in your area, the ISP usually offers a toll-free number you can call. That means accessing the Internet will not cost you a lot of money on your telephone bill.

There are two kinds of subscriptions: free and premium. In practice they offer the same options, though some providers distinguish between them. With a premium subscription, the paying customer will get faster access and more disk space for his own website. You do not have to feel sorry for the free providers, though – they make their money on advertisements placed directly on your screen.
If you have a DSL or cable connection, you pay a fixed amount every month.

What services do ISPs provide?
• access to the World Wide Web (viewing information on the Internet)
• e-mail (electronic mail);
• FTP (download files from other computers)
• newsgroups (discuss topics with a group of other users)
• chatboxes (chat in real time with other users)

During the time you are connected to the Internet, you, the *client*, are in contact with your ISP's computers. These computers are called *servers*. The computers work together according to the *client-server* model.

The modem

It is easy to understand why the telephone network is used to connect computers that may be thousands of miles apart. After all, nearly everyone has a telephone line. Cable TV providers have also entered the Internet market, using the cable network for Internet connections.

You need a special device to connect to the Internet via a telephone line or a cable connection: the *modem*. A modem makes it possible for your computer to communicate with your ISP's computer. There are two kinds of modems:

The first is a separate box that is connected to your computer with a cable. This is called an *external modem*.

Another cable connects the modem to the outlet for the telephone line or the cable TV connection.

External modem

Almost all new computers have a built-in modem. This is called an *internal modem*.

The only part of this you see is a plug for a telephone cable or for a cable connection. These may be found in the back of your desktop computer or on the side of your laptop.

Internal modem

The modem to make a dial-up connection is connected to the telephone jack in your home by a regular telephone cable. You can also use a splitter if you want to keep your telephone connected to this same jack.

Telephone splitter

How to connect the modem

If you have an internal modem, a cable runs from the modem in your computer to the telephone jack. If you use a splitter, you can plug both your telephone and the modem into the same jack.

Computer with internal modem and splitter

If you have an external modem, the modem box is located somewhere between your computer and the telephone jack:

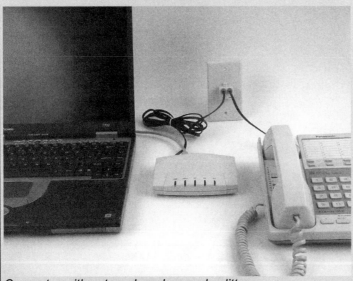

Computer with external modem and splitter

The modem is connected to the computer with a separate cable.

Connecting over a telephone line

The internal or external modem always has an outlet for a *UTP* cable. This is an ordinary telephone cable. There are telephone plugs (also known as *RJ-11* plugs) on both ends. You plug one end of the telephone cable into the modem:

A UTP cable with telephone plugs   *The UTP outlet on the modem*

Plug the other end of the cable into the telephone jack on your wall:

The telephone plug   *The telephone jack*

If you want to connect your telephone to this same telephone jack, you can use a splitter. Some splitters fit directly into the phone jack. Others allow you to place it wherever you like, and connect it to the wall jack with another regular telephone cable:

A telephone splitter you can place anywhere   *A splitter that connects directly to the phone jack*

If you need a longer cable because your computer is too far from the phone jack, you can buy one in a variety of lengths at most appliance stores. Remember, all you need is a regular telephone cable.

1.27 Tips

 Tip

Displaying the menu bar permanently
Like other *Windows* programs, *Internet Explorer* has a *menu bar* that can be used to access various functions: File Edit View Favorites Tools Help . The menu bar is not visible when you use the standard settings of *Internet Explorer*.
This is how you display the menu bar:

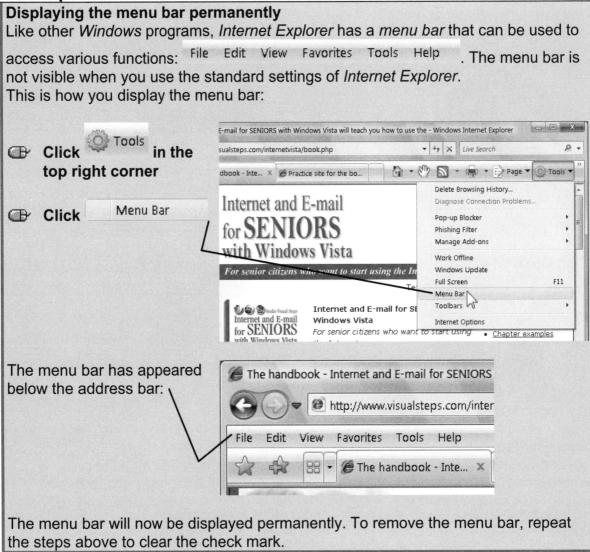

☞ **Click** Tools **in the top right corner**

☞ **Click** Menu Bar

The menu bar has appeared below the address bar:

The menu bar will now be displayed permanently. To remove the menu bar, repeat the steps above to clear the check mark.

 Tip

Displaying the menu bar temporarily
If you want to use the menu bar once without permanently displaying it:

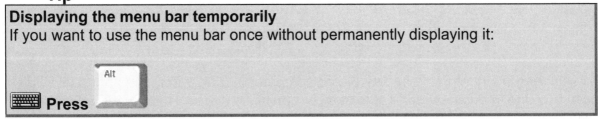

⌨ **Press** Alt

Tip

Increase text size
In this chapter you have learned how to adjust the zoom level on a webpage. There is also another method for making the letters of the text on webpages larger or smaller. This does not enlarge images, or text on buttons. Here is how to choose the largest text size:

☞ **Display the menu bar if necessary** ℰ**66**

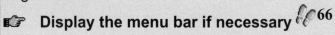 **Click** View

Click Text Size

Click Largest

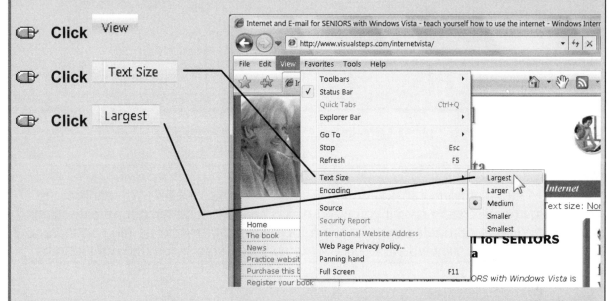

As you can see, the size of the text in the middle of the window has increased:

The images have not changed.

Internet Explorer saves this setting. Next time you start *Internet Explorer*, the text size you chose previously will be used.

Tip

Sometimes you can do things very quickly without having to use the mouse. Do you see that one button has a darker color?

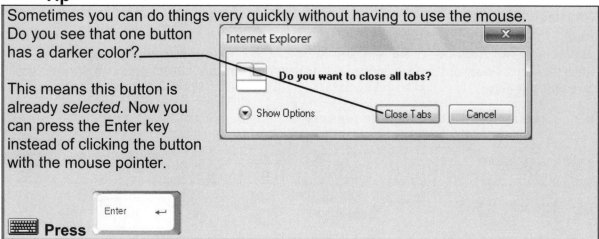

This means this button is already *selected*. Now you can press the Enter key instead of clicking the button with the mouse pointer.

 Press Enter ⏎

 Tip

An extension reel
Make sure the telephone cable is neatly stored against the wall so you can not trip over it. Buy an extension cord if you need one. There are also telephone extension reels, with one or more telephone jacks on the reel and a telephone plug on the end of the cable. These allow you to keep your telephone cable at just the right length.

Tip

A busy signal
Is your Internet connection made through your telephone line?
If you are connected to the Internet and someone tries to call you, they will get a busy signal. If you are expecting a call, you should wait to connect to the Internet.

Is your Internet connection made through an ISDN line?
Then you can connect to the Internet and call or be called at the same time.

Is your Internet connection made through a DSL line?
Then you can connect to the Internet and call or be called at the same time.

Is your Internet connection made through the cable TV line?
Then, of course, you can always call or be called.

Tip

Zooming in up to 1000%
Zooming in is not limited to 400%. You can zoom in as much as 1000%!

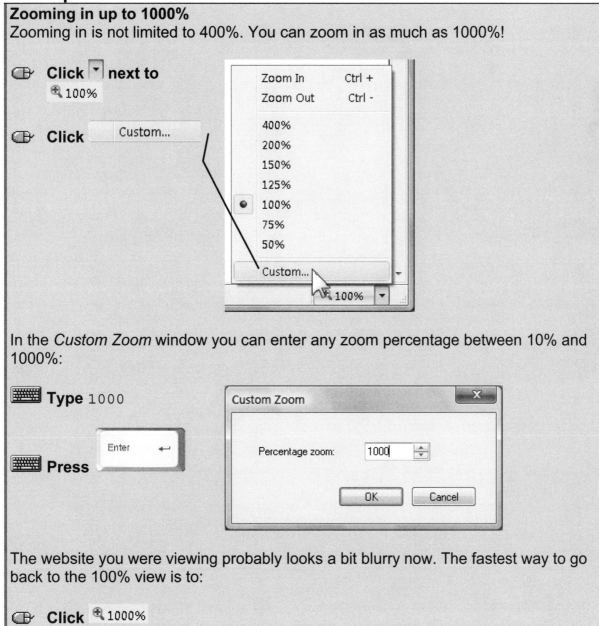

☞ **Click** [▾] **next to**
🔍 100%

☞ **Click** [Custom...]

In the *Custom Zoom* window you can enter any zoom percentage between 10% and 1000%:

⌨ **Type** 1000

⌨ **Press** [Enter ↵]

The website you were viewing probably looks a bit blurry now. The fastest way to go back to the 100% view is to:

☞ **Click** 🔍 1000%

Notes

2. Navigating the Internet

Surfing the Internet is a fun and enjoyable activity. By clicking on various hyperlinks, you can visit many interesting websites and personal home pages. By *website* we mean an extensive system of webpages for a company or organization. A personal *home page* may consist of only a few webpages. It usually belongs to an individual, or contains only a little commercial information about a company.

The World Wide Web is infinitely large and increases by thousands of websites daily. After surfing for a while, you will no doubt want to revisit an interesting website from time to time. All those hyperlinks make it easy to lose your way, however.

Fortunately, *Internet Explorer* has several built-in options to help you get to where you want to go. In this chapter, you will learn how to use these convenient features, allowing you to "navigate" straight to your target: back to the webpages you visited earlier.

In this chapter, you will learn how to:

- open a website from the list of addresses previously typed
- save a web address
- open a *Favorite*
- organize your *Favorites*
- use RSS feeds
- temporarily disconnect
- change the *Internet Explorer* home page
- use the *History*
- give a website its own shortcut

2.1 Starting Internet Explorer

☞ **Turn on the computer**

Do you have an external modem?
☞ **Turn on the modem**

Now you can start *Internet Explorer*:

☞ **Start** *Internet Explorer* 👣¹

Internet Explorer starts, and you can connect to the Internet:

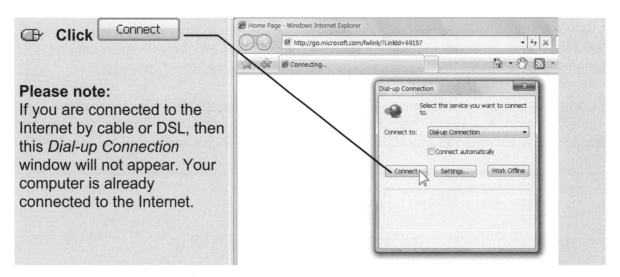

🖰 **Click** [Connect]

Please note:
If you are connected to the
Internet by cable or DSL, then
this *Dial-up Connection*
window will not appear. Your
computer is already
connected to the Internet.

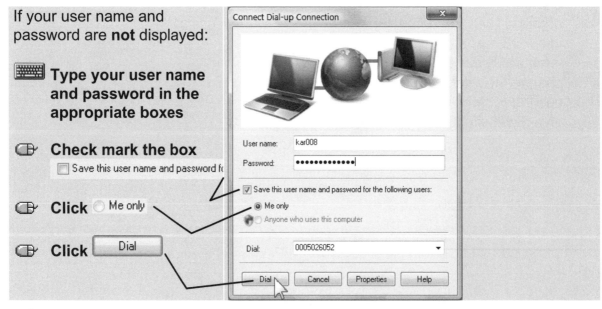

If your user name and
password are **not** displayed:

⌨ **Type your user name
and password in the
appropriate boxes**

🖰 **Check mark the box**
☐ Save this user name and password fo

🖰 **Click** ○ Me only

🖰 **Click** [Dial]

A connection is made to your ISP (*Internet Service Provider*).

You see the home page as it is set up on your computer:

This page might be different on your computer.

You will learn later how to change the page that appears when you start *Internet Explorer*.

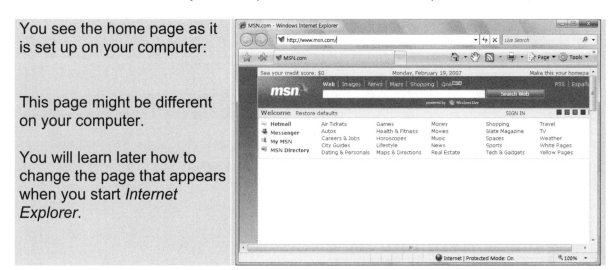

2.2 The Address Bar

Internet Explorer has a useful feature on the address bar. By clicking a button on the address bar, you will see a list of website addresses that you have previously typed. You can use this list to reopen a website without having to retype the web address.

☞ **Click ▾ at the end of the address bar**

You see a list of web addresses you have visited before:

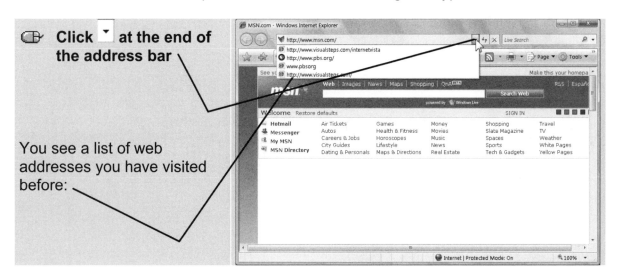

You can click one of these addresses to reopen the associated website:

The website for the Visual Steps publishing company will be opened. This method only works for a website that you recently visited. If you would like to keep a web address for a longer time, it is a better idea to save it.

2.3 Saving a Web Address

Once you have found an interesting website, you can save its address. From then on, you can quickly reopen this website anytime without having to remember the web address or retyping it. Saved websites are called *Favorites* in *Internet Explorer*.

 Please note:

You can only save a web address when the associated website is displayed in the *Internet Explorer* window.

In this case, you see the Visual Steps website:

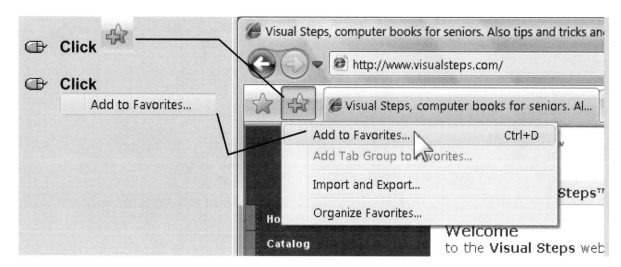

Now you see a small window on top of the webpage in which the name of the website has already been inserted:

👆 **Click** Add

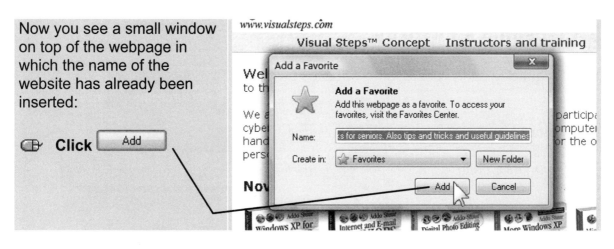

Later, you will see how to quickly reopen this favorite website. To see how a *Favorite* works, you will first need to go to a different website. You can go, for example, to the special website for seniors, *SeniorNet*:

👆 **Click in the address bar**

⌨ **Type:**
www.seniornet.org

⌨ **Press** Enter ↵

You see the *SeniorNet* home page:

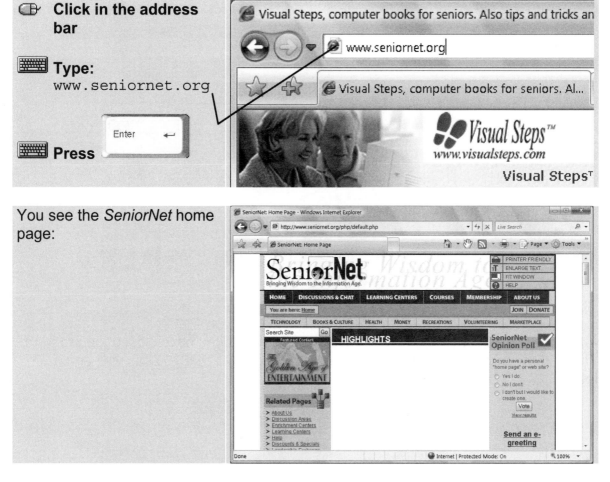

Now you can open the *Favorite* you just saved.

2.4 Opening a Favorite

You can quickly open your favorite websites using the *Favorites Center*:

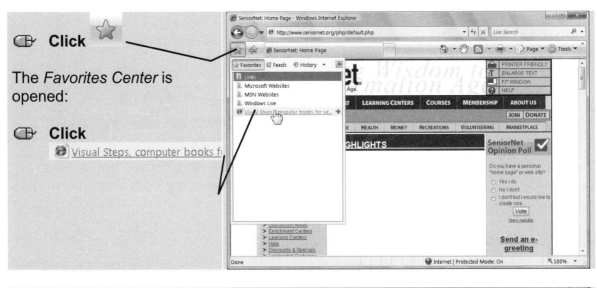

🖱️ **Click** ⭐

The *Favorites Center* is opened:

🖱️ **Click**
🔘 Visual Steps, computer books f

Internet Explorer immediately jumps to the Visual Steps website:

Internet Explorer remembers your *Favorites* even after you have closed the program. This allows you to create an entire collection of websites that you can visit again later.

2.5 Organizing Your Favorites

You can save all your favorite websites in one long list in the *Favorites Center*, but in the long term this is not very practical. It is better to organize your *Favorites* in separate folders. You can save websites according to subject, for example.
You can also use folders to separate your own *Favorites* from those of other users on the same computer.

For practice, you are going to create a folder for websites related to this book.

☞ **Click** ✩

☞ **Click**
Organize Favorites...

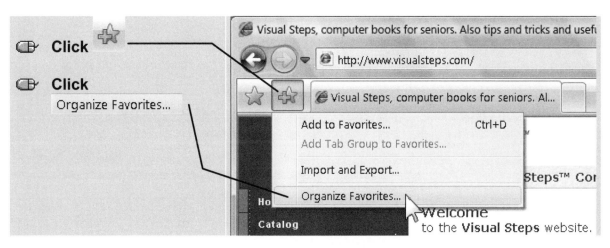

Now you see this window. Usually there are already a few ⬜ folders:

Below these folders is the *Favorite* you saved earlier:

☞ **Click** New Folder

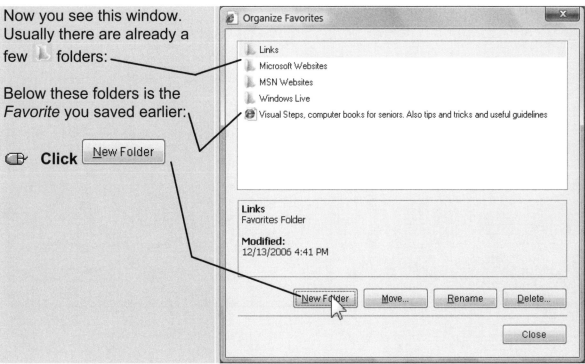

A new 📁 folder appears at the bottom of the list, and you can immediately type a name for it:

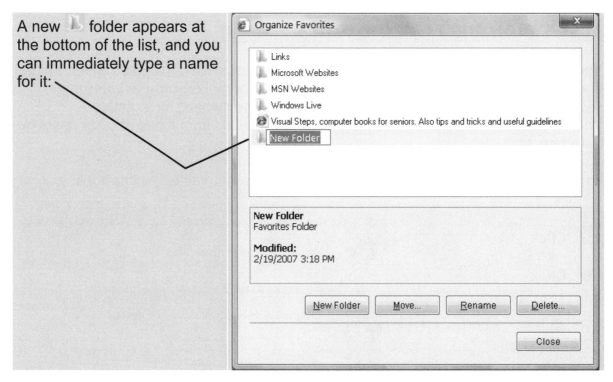

⌨ **Type:** Internet Book

🖱 **Click** [Close]

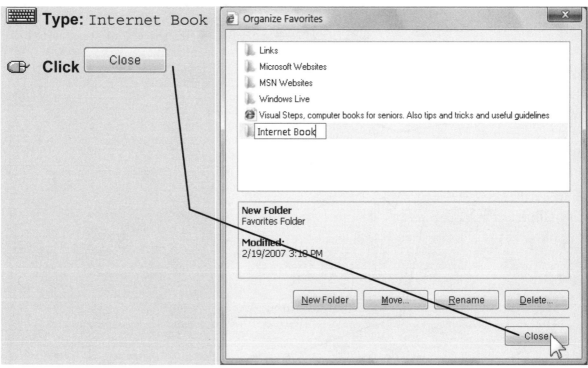

The folder has now been created. You can check this right away in the *Favorites Center.*

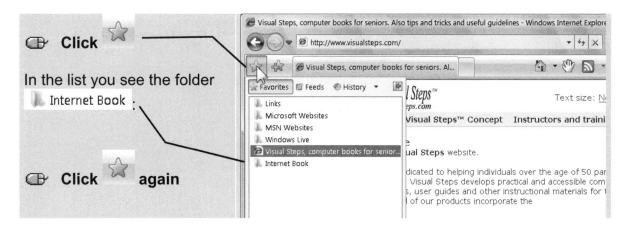

You have seen that the folder has been created. A little later on, you will read how you can save all the websites related to this book in this new folder.

2.6 Typing Part of a Web Address

At the beginning of this chapter you read about the list of web addresses previously visited. This list can get very long, making it hard to find the address you need. Take a look now at what happens when you start typing just part of a web address:

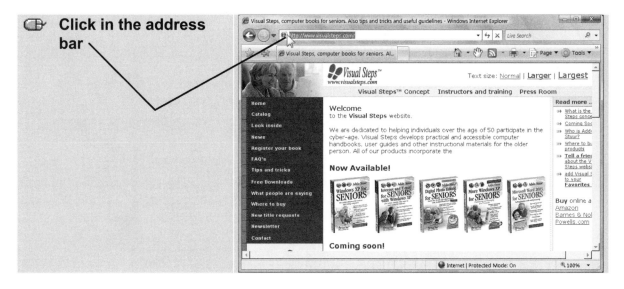

Type: www.visu

Under the address bar, a list of web addresses appears that begins with www.visu:

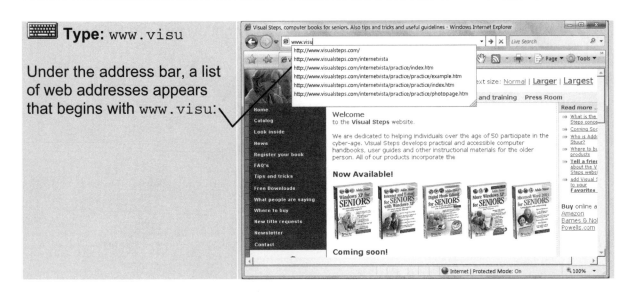

Now you just need to click the desired web address in the list:

Click
http://www.visualsteps.com/intern

The website for this book opens:

 Please note:

Pay attention to which address you click – *Internet Explorer* also remembers incorrectly typed web addresses.

2.7 Saving a Web Address in a Folder

It is pretty easy to save a website in the new folder in the *Favorites Center*.

 Please note:

You can only save a web address when the associated website is displayed in the *Internet Explorer* window.

In this case, you now see the website for this book in the window. You can save this website in the new "Internet Book" folder.

Click ☆

Click

Add to Favorites...

You see this little window again:

The name of the website has already been filled in:

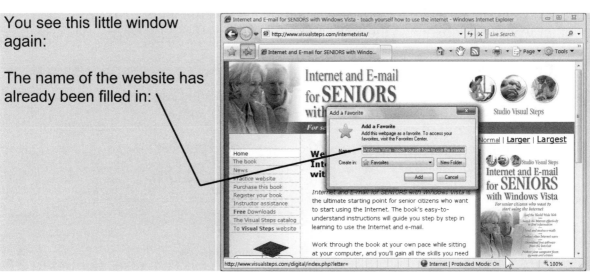

Now you open the folder where you want to save this *Favorite*:

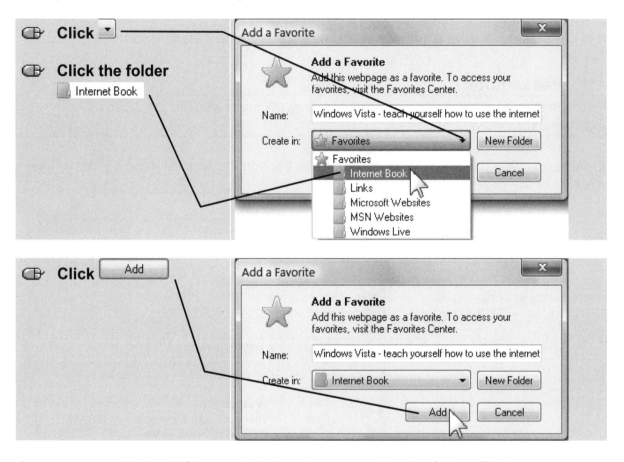

Later on you will check if the website has been saved in the folder. First you open another website, for example the CNN website:

You see the home page for CNN:

On top of the website you may see a small window with a message about the *information bar:*

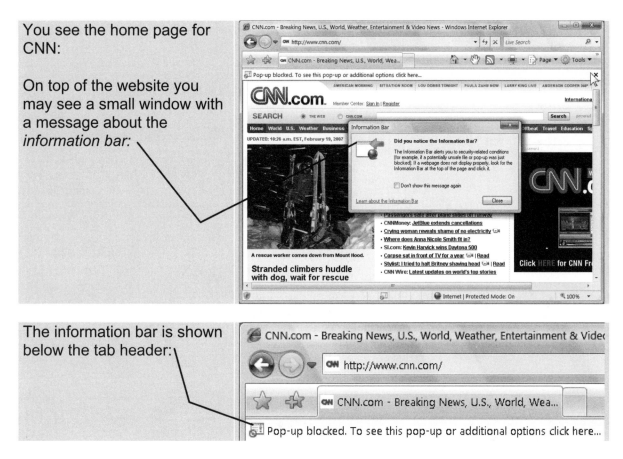

The information bar is shown below the tab header:

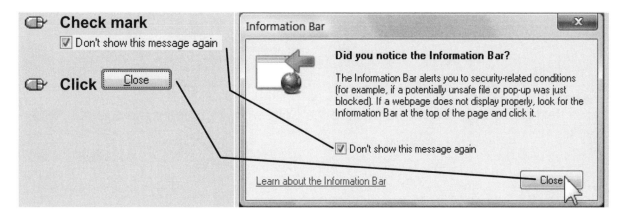

According to the information bar a *pop-up* has been blocked. A pop-up is a small web browser window that appears on top of the website you are viewing. A pop-up window may open as soon as you visit a website. They are often used for advertising purposes.

In Chapter 9: *Security and Privacy* you will learn more about these pop-ups and the *Pop-up Blocker* in *Internet Explorer.* For now, you can close this small window:

Check mark
☑ Don't show this message again

Click ⬚ Close ⬚

Information Bar

Did you notice the Information Bar?

The Information Bar alerts you to security-related conditions (for example, if a potentially unsafe file or pop-up was just blocked). If a webpage does not display properly, look for the Information Bar at the top of the page and click it.

☑ Don't show this message again

Learn about the Information Bar   Close

Next time a pop-up is blocked, you will no longer see this message.

Now you can open the *Favorites Center* to see if the *Favorite* has been stored in the right folder:

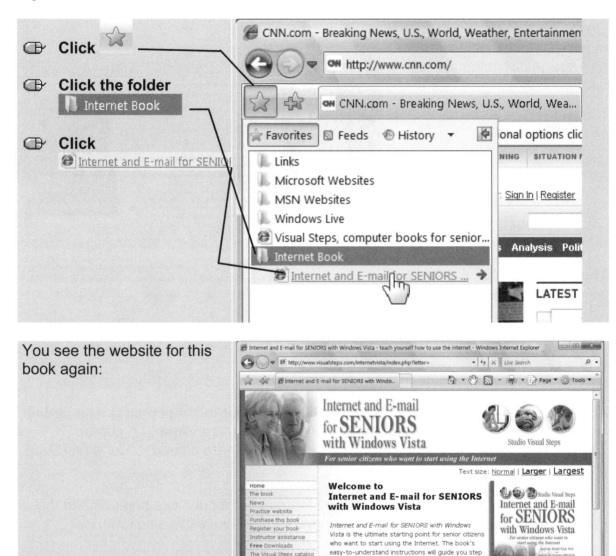

You see the website for this book again:

In the next paragraph you will go back to the CNN website to learn more about *RSS feeds*.

2.8 RSS Feeds

News agencies like CNN and other dynamic websites offer a service called *RSS feeds*. The acronym RSS stands for *Really Simple Syndication*, a format used to publish frequently updated digital content, such as news headlines or sports scores. *Internet Explorer* has a built-in feed reader that can display these feeds. When you subscribe to a news agency feed for example, the latest headlines are automatically sent to your computer when you connect to the Internet.

Internet Explorer looks for RSS feeds on every webpage you visit. When available feeds are found, the *RSS Feed* button will change from gray to orange. You can use the CNN website to practice with RSS feeds:

☞ **Go back to www.cnn.com** 6

The *RSS Feed* button is orange:

☞ **Click**

This will open the webpage where you can view the feeds and subscribe to them. Subscribing to a feed is usually free.

The RSS feeds from *CNN.com* consist of the latest news headlines:

☞ **Click**
⭐ Subscribe to this feed

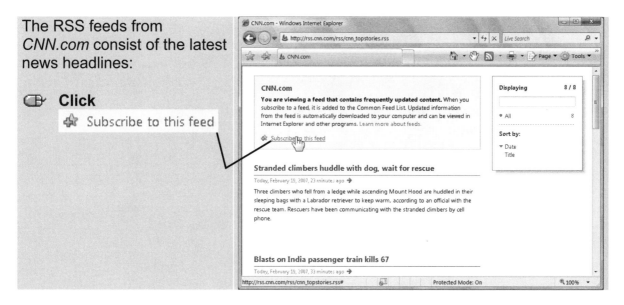

The name of the feed has already been entered:

☞ **Click** Subscribe

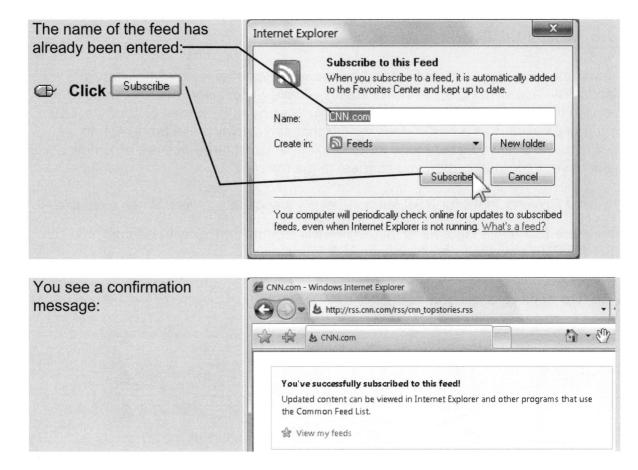

You see a confirmation message:

Now that you have subscribed to this feed, it has been added to the *Common Feed List* in the *Favorites Center*. You can verify this:

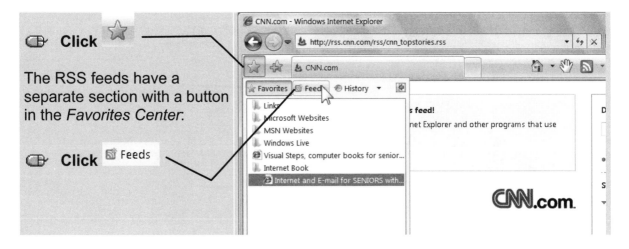

☞ **Click** ⭐

The RSS feeds have a separate section with a button in the *Favorites Center*.

☞ **Click** 📶 Feeds

When you have subscribed to a feed, they will be listed here. In this case, there is only the CNN feed:

Click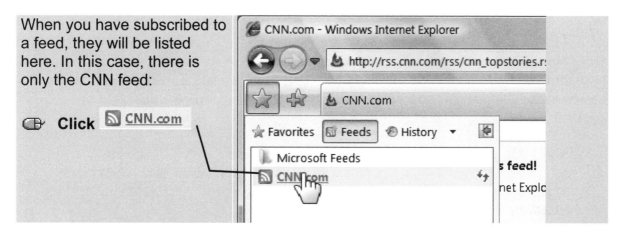

The CNN feed is displayed:

Updated information from the feed is automatically downloaded to your computer, even when you are not using *Internet Explorer*.

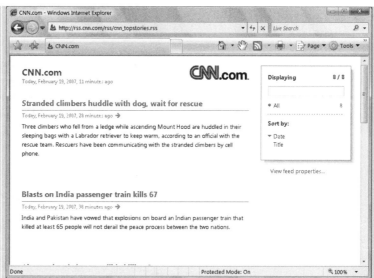

 Tip

Feed facts

- Clicking a headline will open the full news story on the CNN website.

- By default, the feed will be updated once a day. To change this default setting, click View feed properties... on the feeds page.

- After you visit the feeds page, all feeds on the page will be marked as read. Next time you visit the feeds page, these old headlines will be gray instead of blue. This makes it easier to recognize the feeds you have not read yet.

- Many websites offer RSS feeds. Make sure to check the website for your local newspaper, or you favorite sports or news channel.

Tip

Feed Headlines in the Windows Sidebar
Now that you have subscribed to the CNN RSS feed, these headlines are also shown in the *gadget* named *Feed Headlines* in the *Windows Sidebar* on your desktop.

If you want this gadget to display just the CNN headlines, do the following:

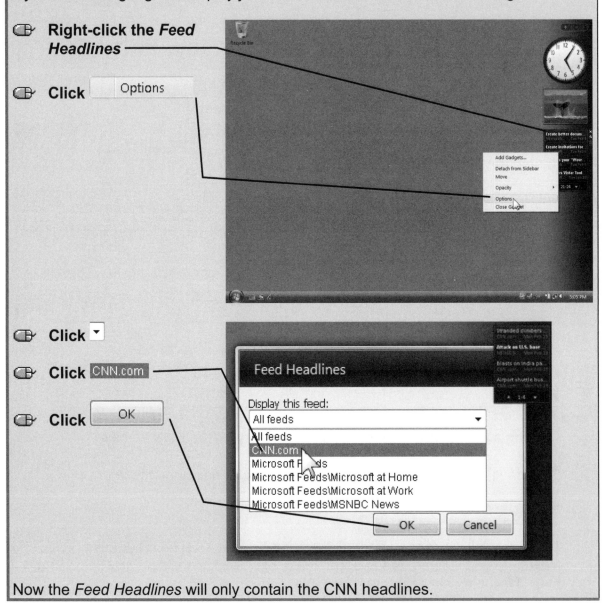

- **Right-click the *Feed Headlines***

- **Click** Options

- **Click** ▼

- **Click** CNN.com

- **Click** OK

Now the *Feed Headlines* will only contain the CNN headlines.

2.9 Temporarily Disconnecting

 Please note:

This section only applies when you use a dial-up connection!
If you have a DSL or cable connection, you do not have to worry about your
telephone line being busy. You can just read through this section.

If you have a dial-up connection where you have to manually connect to the Internet,
you may sometimes want to temporarily break the connection to the Internet to save
on telephone charges. For example if you want to do something else, or when a web
page takes a long time to read. This way you also free up your telephone line in case
someone wants to call you. You do not have to close *Internet Explorer* to do so:

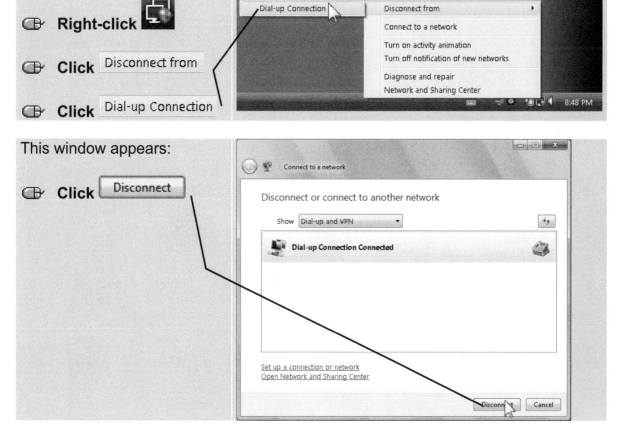

When you see the message

Successfully disconnected from Dial-up Connection , the connection is broken.

With the button [Close] you can close this window.

The two little computers have changed into , the **X** indicates you are no longer connected.

To reconnect, do the following:

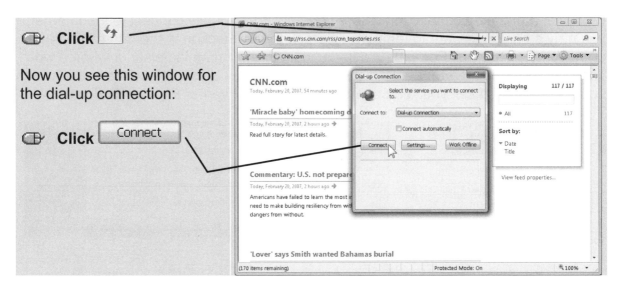

☞ **Click** [↖↗]

Now you see this window for the dial-up connection:

☞ **Click** [Connect]

If necessary:

⌨ **Type your user name and password in the appropriate boxes**

☞ **Check mark the box**
  ☐ Save this user name and password f(

☞ **Click** ○ Me only

☞ **Click** [Dial]

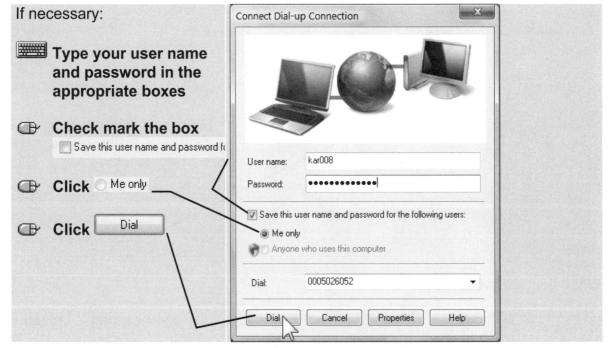

The connection to the Internet is re-established.

2.10 Changing the Home Page

When opened *Internet Explorer* displays a particular webpage, called the *home page*. You can change this setting and make this your favorite page, for example the practice website for this book.

 Please note:

You can make a page your home page when it is displayed in the *Internet Explorer* window.

First you open the website for this book using the *Favorites Center*:

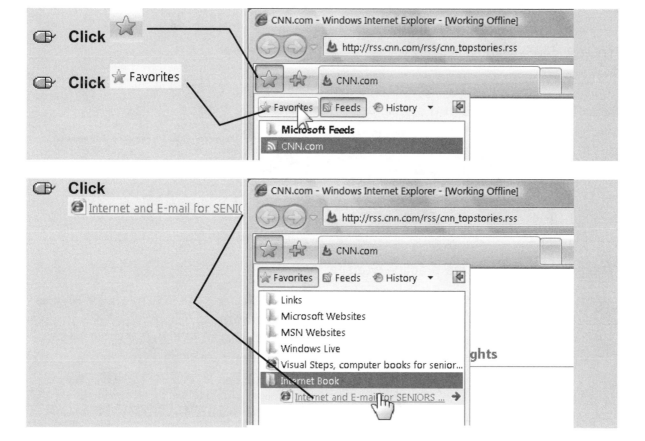

The webpage for this book opens.

Tip

Take a moment to register your book!
You can register your book. Visual Steps will keep you aware of any important changes that are necessary to you as a user of the book. You will also receive our periodic newsletter (e-mail) informing you of our product releases, company news, tips & tricks, free guides, special offers, etc.

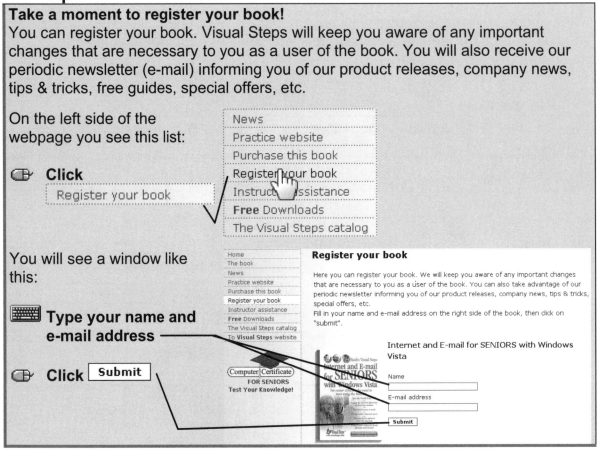

On the left side of the webpage you see this list:

☞ **Click** Register your book

You will see a window like this:

⌨ **Type your name and e-mail address**

☞ **Click** **Submit**

There is also a link to the practice website:

☞ **Click** Practice website

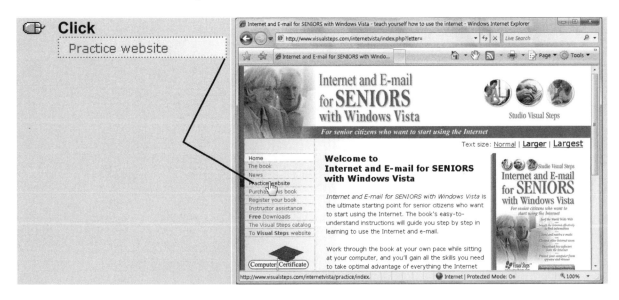

Click next to 🏠

Click

Add or Change Home Page...

Now you see this window:

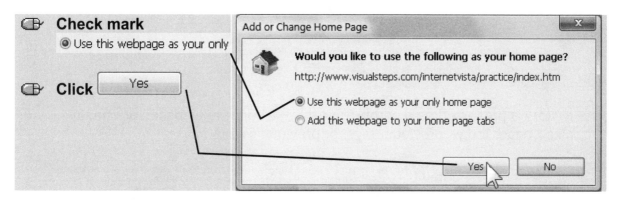

Check mark

Use this webpage as your only

Click Yes

The practice website has now been stored as the home page.

💡 **Tip**

Keeping you Favorites on display
If you want to keep the *Favorites Center* in your viewing window:

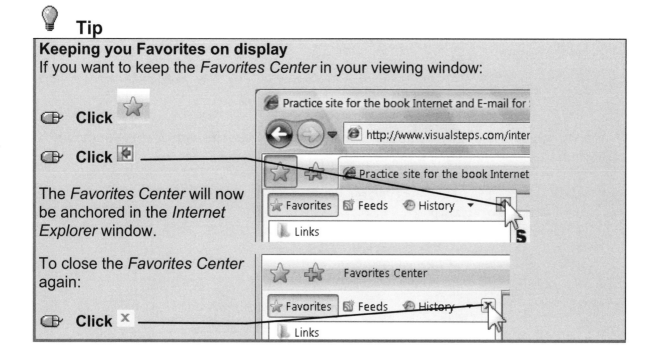

Click ⭐

Click 🔙

The *Favorites Center* will now be anchored in the *Internet Explorer* window.

To close the *Favorites Center* again:

Click ✕

2.11 History

Besides the *Favorites* and RSS feeds, the *Favorites Center* also has a section with a button called *History*. This is where *Internet Explorer* stores links to the websites you have recently visited.

The *History* is presented as a chronological list, where the websites are neatly organized under today, previous days, or previous weeks.

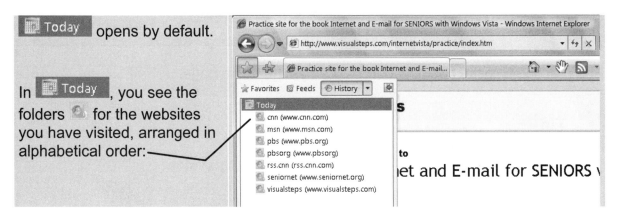

When you open one of these folders, you can see the specific webpages you have visited on that website. Take a look:

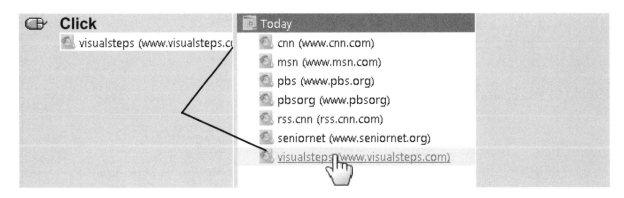

You can click any one of
these links to return to the
corresponding webpage:

Returning to a website in this way is only useful if you remember when you last
visited it. If you are on the Internet daily, however, and you surf to many websites,
this method is not as useful. In that case, it is a lot easier to store these web
addresses as *Favorites*, like you have practiced before.

A website that you look at frequently can also be saved as a shortcut on your
desktop. Continue to the next paragraph to read more about that.

2.12 Shortcuts

You can also put an icon called a *shortcut* for your favorite website on your desktop.
Once you have started *Windows*, you just have to double-click this icon to view the
website. For practice, you can make a shortcut for the *Internet for Seniors* website.
You can make a shortcut when the webpage is displayed in the *Internet Explorer*
window. Here is how to make a shortcut:

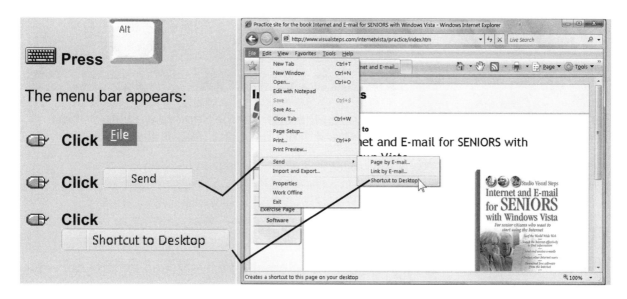

Internet Explorer asks you to confirm this action:

☞ **Minimize the *Internet Explorer* window** 🦶11

When the *Internet Explorer* window is minimized, you see the desktop:

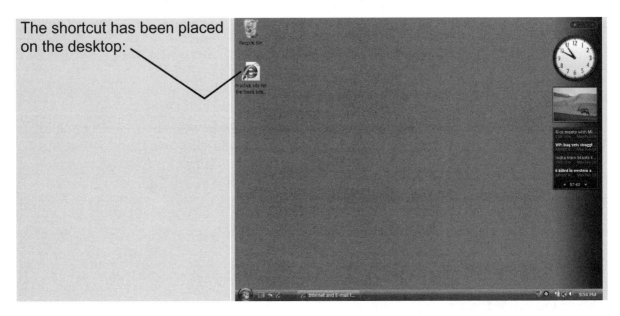

The shortcut has been placed on the desktop:

By double-clicking this icon, you can open the *Internet for Seniors* website without even having to open *Internet Explorer* itself. That happens automatically.

☞ **Close *Internet Explorer*** 🦶2

☞ **If necessary, disconnect from the Internet** 🦶5

Now you know several ways to navigate the Internet effectively, and to find your way back and forth between websites.

You can practice these techniques in the following exercises.

2.13 Exercises

The following exercises will help you master what you have just learned. Have you forgotten how to perform a particular action? Use the number beside the footsteps to look it up in the appendix *How Do I Do That Again?*

Exercise: The SeniorNet Favorite

In this exercise, you will open the websites for SeniorNet and CNN and add them to your favorites.

☑ Open *Internet Explorer*. ℓℓ¹

☑ If necessary: connect to the Internet. ℓℓ³

☑ Use the hidden list under the address bar to open: www.seniornet.org ℓℓ⁶⁷

☑ Make the address for SeniorNet a *Favorite*. ℓℓ¹⁵

☑ Use *History* to open: www.cnn.com ℓℓ¹⁴

☑ Make the address for CNN a *Favorite*. ℓℓ¹⁵

☑ If needed, temporarily disconnect from the Internet. ℓℓ¹⁶

☑ Reconnect to the Internet. ℓℓ⁷⁰

☑ Open the *Favorite* SeniorNet. ℓℓ¹⁷

☑ Open the *Favorite* CNN. ℓℓ¹⁷

☑ Close *Internet Explorer*. ℓℓ²

☑ If necessary: disconnect from the Internet. ℓℓ⁵

Exercise: A New Favorite

In this exercise, you will open the National Geographic website and add it to your favorites in the folder related to this book.

✓ Open *Internet Explorer*. 𝄞¹

✓ If necessary: connect to the Internet. 𝄞³

✓ Type the address: www.nationalgeographic.com 𝄞⁴

✓ Now you see this website:

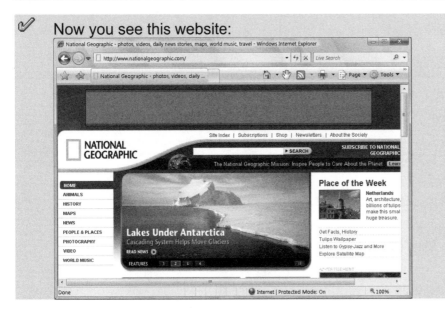

✓ Save the address for the National Geographic website as a *Favorite* in the folder ☐ Internet Book. 𝄞¹⁸

✓ Open the *Favorite* CNN. 𝄞¹⁷

✓ Open the *Favorite* SeniorNet. 𝄞¹⁷

✓ Open the *Favorite* National Geographic. 𝄞¹⁹

✓ Close *Internet Explorer*. 𝄞²

✓ If necessary: disconnect from the Internet. 𝄞⁵

2.14 Background Information

Glossary

Favorites	*Internet Explorer Favorites* are links (bookmarks) to websites that you visit frequently. By adding a website to your *Favorites* list, you can go to that site by simply clicking its name, instead of having to type its address in the address bar.
Favorites Center	The *Internet Explorer* area where you can view and organize your *Favorites*.
Feed Headlines	*Feed Headlines* is one of the default gadgets in *Windows Vista* that is displayed in the *Windows Sidebar*. You can see continuously updated headlines from a website that supplies RSS feeds.
History	The section of the *Favorites Center* that displays the websites you recently visited. By default, the *History* listing is sorted by date.
Home page	The webpage that is displayed each time you open *Internet Explorer* or click the button 🏠.
Information bar	In *Internet Explorer*, the information bar appears below the address bar and displays information about downloads, blocked pop-up windows, and other activities.
Pop-up	A pop-up is a small web browser window that appears on top of the website you are viewing. A pop-up window, often used for advertising purposes, may open as soon as you visit a website.
RSS feeds	RSS feeds contain frequently updated content published by a website, such as news headlines or sports scores. The acronym RSS stands for *Really Simple Syndication*, the format used to publish these feeds.
Shortcut	A shortcut is a link to a website, file or program, represented by an icon. Double-clicking a shortcut will open the file or program.
Windows Sidebar	A long, vertical bar that is displayed on the side of your desktop. Contains mini-programs called *gadgets*.

Source: Windows Help and Support

Why do I have to wait so long sometimes?
Sometimes it takes quite a long time before a page you want loads into your browser. This depends on a number of things:

- Modems can have various speeds. The faster the speed of the modem, the faster text and pictures are transmitted. The speed of the connection type also plays an important part.
  To date, a modem connected with the normal analog telephone line is the slowest type. Other types of connections, such as ISDN, cable and DSL, are significantly faster.
  New developments will present a range of fast transmission possibilities through the regular analog telephone line.

- Some websites have more pictures and illustrations than others. Some pages have numerous pictures or various graphic effects. All those dancing figures, revolving text, pop-up assistants and other graphic effects require information to be sent to your computer, and it all has to be sent via the telephone line if that is how you are connected.
  Receiving pictures takes a particularly long time. The more efficient the web page is designed, the faster it will appear on your screen.

- Sometimes it is very busy on the Internet. So many people are surfing at the same time that traffic jams occur. When that happens, you will have to wait longer than usual.

What can be done about this?

- You do not always have to wait until all the pictures have been received. Sometimes you immediately see the topic you are looking for.

  ☞ **If this is the case, click** ☒ **next to the address bar**
  No more information is sent and you can click to go to a different page.

- Sometimes a website's opening page will have a button that says: *Text only*. If you click that button, only the text will be sent, not the illustrations. That takes much less time.

How does the WWW work?

The World Wide Web (WWW) is one of the more recent and most popular Internet applications. The idea for the web was developed in 1989 by Tim Berners Lee and Robert Cailliau at CERN (the European Organization for Nuclear Research) in Geneva, Switzerland.

The information on the WWW comes to us in the form of *hypermedia*. The word hypermedia is derived from *hypertext*.
A hypertext is a text containing *jump text* (or *hyperlinks*). The words in a hyperlink refer to the address of a different webpage. By clicking on the jump text, you tell *Internet Explorer* to open that other webpage. This page might be located on any Internet-connected computer in the world, even one on the other side of the world.

Words are not the only things that can be used as a hyperlink. Drawings and photos can also be used. Webpages usually contain not only text, but also images, sound and moving images (*multimedia*). That is why you sometimes hear the term *hypermedia* these days; it is a contraction of the words *hyper*text and multi*media*.

How does the Internet system always find the right page? The WWW contains millions of pages. Each page has its own unique address, called an *URL* (Uniform Resource Allocator).

An example of an URL is: **http://www.internetforseniors.com**.
You can read this as follows:

http	HyperText Transfer Protocol
www	World Wide Web
internetforseniors	The domain name or "brand name" of the organization
com	A commercial website (as opposed to e.g. educational)

Based upon the URL, your ISP's computer knows on which computer the website is stored. In order to make communication between computers possible, every computer receives a unique address, the *Internet Protocol Number* (IP number or IP address). You will not use this number in daily practice. Instead, people use the URL, for example www.internetforseniors.com. When computers communicate with one another, this name is automatically converted to the numeric IP address. Sometimes you will see these numbers displayed at the bottom of the *Internet Explorer* window.

HTML
Webpages are written in a special language. This makes it possible for the pages to look the same on completely different computers. *Internet Explorer* translates this language into a readable page for you. This language is called *HTML* or *HyperText Markup Language*.
Every HTML page looks the same in its simplest form.

```
<HTML>
     <HEAD>
            <TITLE>Internet for Seniors</TITLE>
     </head>

     <BODY>
            <p>This will be the text.</p>
     </body>
</HTML>
```

This language is fairly complicated, and therefore not very practical to use. Fortunately, we do not have to wrestle with all these unintelligible codes any more. Software companies like *Microsoft* have created special programs that make it possible to write webpages without the need to know a single word of HTML.
We call this kind of program a *web editor*. One example of a web editor is *FrontPage*. A web editor works just like a text editing program such as *MS Word*. You type in text, add images, and make sure that everything looks nice. The web editor translates all your work into HTML. It could not be easier.

Bandwidth

In the early days of telecommunications, telephone lines were only used for speech. Now that the arrival of the Internet has appropriated these lines for other purposes in recent years – such as sending text, images, audio and video – it has become apparent that the bandwidth of these lines is too limited.

What do we mean by bandwidth?

The term can best be compared to a hallway between two rooms. Imagine that a hundred people are standing in one room. The time it will take for all these people to move to the other room depends primarily on how wide the hallway is. The wider the hallway, the better the flow. People have been searching for years for techniques to increase bandwidth for the Internet.

ISDN

One of these techniques is ISDN (Integrated Services Digital Network). ISDN allows much more information to be sent on the same copper wire in a given amount of time (up to 64 Kilobits per second). It is also possible to send different signals at the same time. That is how ISDN makes it possible to call someone on the phone and use the Internet at the same time. ISDN does have special requirements, however, such as a special modem and a different telephone subscription.

DSL

DSL (Digital Subscriber Line) is another technique for making broadband Internet possible. Here, the connection is split in two: an *upstream* channel (for sending information) and a *downstream* channel (for receiving information). Just as with ISDN, it is possible to call on the phone and use the Internet at the same time. Like ISDN, DSL has special equipment requirements. It also has a unique feature. With DSL, the user has a private line between two modems: one at home and the other at the exchange. This makes the channel secure. Your data goes over your own private line, in contrast to other techniques in which the line is shared with other users. Because you have your own line to the exchange, its speed is not affected by other users.

Cable

High-speed connections are also available through the television cable infrastructure. This connection, however, becomes faster or slower depending on how many other people are using the same cable.

2.15 Tips

 Tip

Clearing the History
You might not like the fact that all the websites you visit are stored in a list. Another user on your computer could easily view your surfing behavior.
Fortunately, you can also clear your surfing history. Chapter 9 will show you how.

 Tip

The Home button

If you click the *Home* 🏠 button, your default home page will be displayed.

 Tip

Organizing Favorites
You might want to remove, rename or move some of your *Favorites* from time to time. Here is how to do this:

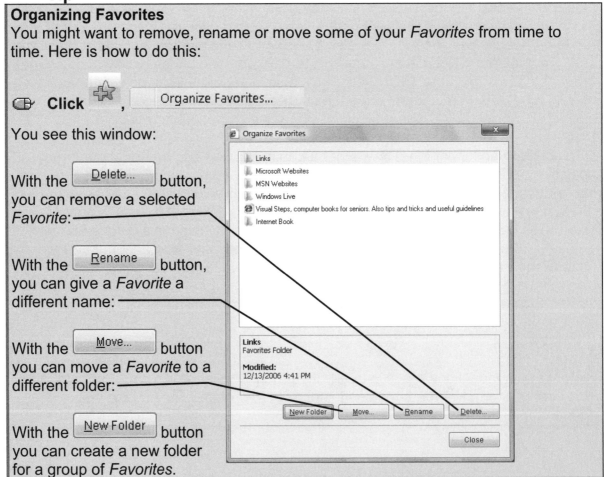

☞ **Click** ⭐ , Organize Favorites...

You see this window:

With the Delete... button, you can remove a selected *Favorite*:

With the Rename button, you can give a *Favorite* a different name:

With the Move... button you can move a *Favorite* to a different folder:

With the New Folder button you can create a new folder for a group of *Favorites*.

3. Searching and Finding on the Internet

The Internet is sometimes compared to a large library full of information on all kinds of subjects. Unfortunately, this library has no librarian. The books in this library are all jumbled up together. This comparison is a pretty good one. There is indeed no supervisory organization that organizes the information on the Internet. Everyone can place his own information on the Internet, which is immediately available to everyone else. This does not make searching on the Internet any easier.

There are a large number of companies and organizations that try to assist Internet users by organizing this enormous mountain of information. This occurs in several ways. The first way is via a *search engine*. This is a computer that is constantly busy indexing webpages. You can use the search engine's webpage to search for all the webpages that contain certain words, your *search terms* which you have typed in to the search term box.

A second method for organizing information on the Internet is a *directory*. In this case, a company has already selected a large number of webpages and categorized them according to subject.

Despite these various resources, searching on the Internet can still be frustrating at times: You know, for example, that information on a particular subject must be out there somewhere, yet you can not find the webpage in question. This chapter will help you perform better searches. It covers various techniques for searching for information. The more you practice these techniques the better you will become at finding the information you want.

In this chapter, you will learn how to:

- use the *Instant Search Box*
- search for information, images and news with *Live Search*
- change your default search engine to *Google*
- do an advanced search in *Google*
- use directories
- search within a webpage

3.1 Starting Internet Explorer

☞ **Turn on the computer**

Do you have an external modem?
☞ **Turn on the modem**

Now you can start *Internet Explorer*:

☞ **Start *Internet Explorer***[1]

After *Internet Explorer* starts, you can connect to the Internet:

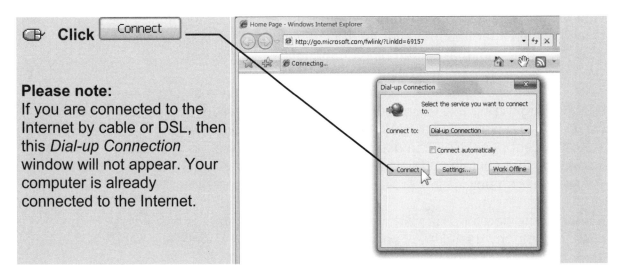

⊞ **Click** [Connect]

Please note:
If you are connected to the Internet by cable or DSL, then this *Dial-up Connection* window will not appear. Your computer is already connected to the Internet.

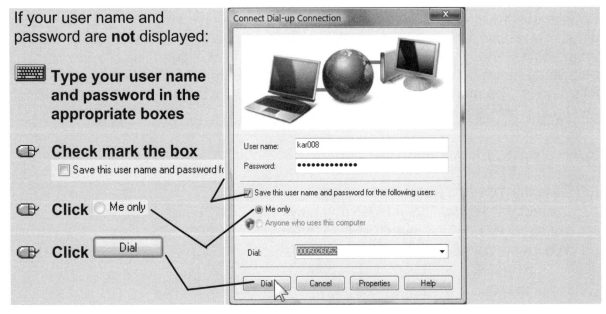

If your user name and password are **not** displayed:

⌨ **Type your user name and password in the appropriate boxes**

⊞ **Check mark the box**
☐ Save this user name and password f(

⊞ **Click** ○ Me only

⊞ **Click** [Dial]

A connection is made to your ISP (*Internet Service Provider*) and you see the home page as it is set up on your computer:

3.2 The Instant Search Box

Internet Explorer offers direct access to the *Microsoft* search engine *Live Search* through the *Instant Search Box*.

You can find the *Instant Search Box* in the top right corner of the *Internet Explorer* window:

In this box you can type one or more words with which you want to base your search. For example, try to find some information about the Dutch painter Rembrandt:

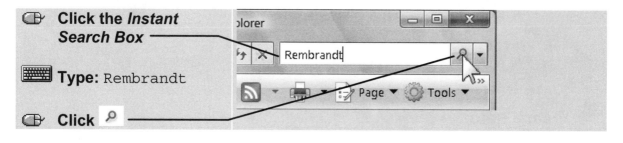

☞ **Click the *Instant Search Box***

⌨ **Type:** Rembrandt

☞ **Click** 🔍

💡 **Tip**

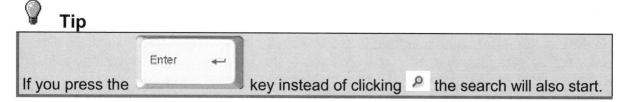

If you press the [Enter ↵] key instead of clicking 🔍 the search will also start.

Within a few seconds, *Live Search* presents the search results:

On top of the page you see some links of SPONSORED SITES, that probably have very little to do with Rembrandt:

Try this search result:

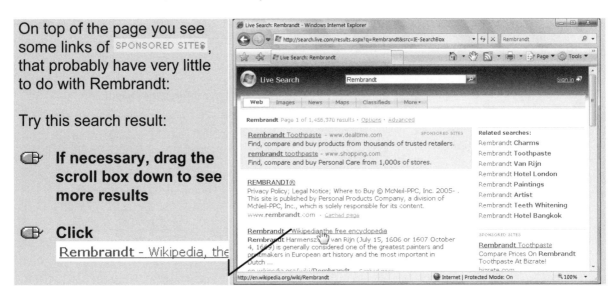

☞ **If necessary, drag the scroll box down to see more results**

☞ **Click**
   <u>Rembrandt - Wikipedia, the</u>

If you can not find this page, you can try to find the page by using the words 'Rembrandt Wikipedia' to search instead of only the word 'Rembrandt'.

You see the *Wikipedia* page for Rembrandt van Rijn:

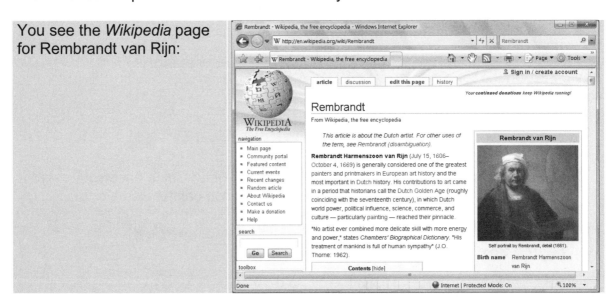

⇨ **Please note:**

Wikipedia is a free encyclopedia collaboratively written by many of its readers from around the world. Each blue word in the text is a link to new article about that word. *Wikipedia* has rapidly grown into one of the largest reference websites on the Internet. New information is added to the *Wikipedia* website regularly. Qualified users may edit existing pages at any time. Therefore, the image you see above may look different from what you see now on your screen.

3.3 Searching for News

Instead of doing a general search, you can also search for news about Rembrandt.

☞ **Go back to the website with the search results** 𝓁𝓁6

⊞ **Click** News

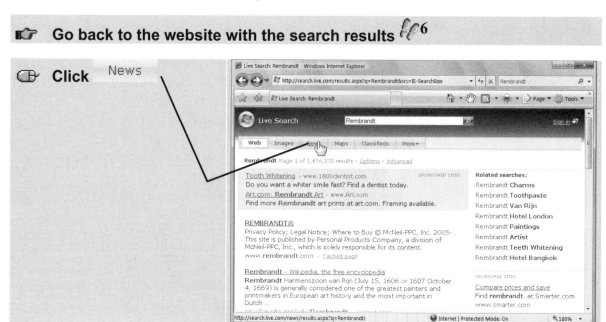

💡 **Tip**

When you press Ctrl while you click, the link opens in a new tab.

You see this site with news topics related to Rembrandt.

Unfortunately, the news is not limited to Rembrandt the painter. There could also be news about a toothpaste or a racehorse named Rembrandt, for example.

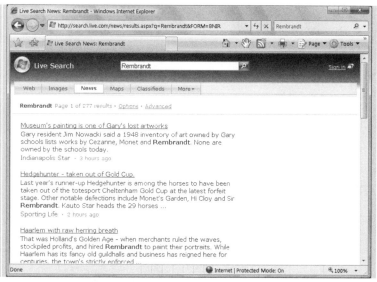

3.4 Changing the Default Search Engine

Live Search is the default search engine in *Internet Explorer*. That is understandable, since *Live Search* is made by *Microsoft*, the maker of *Internet Explorer*. With a few clicks, you can change the default search engine to the very popular *Google Search*:

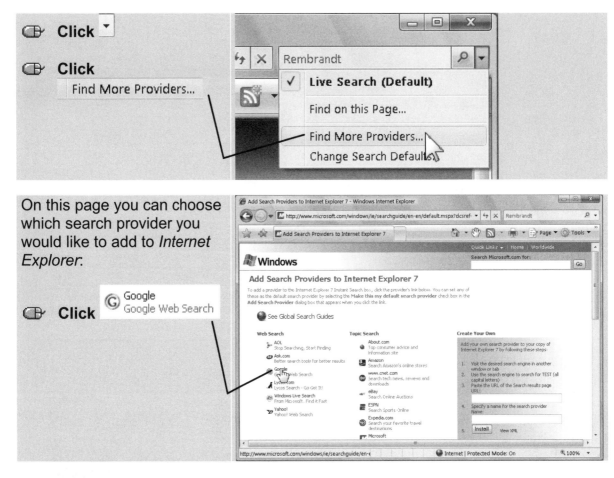

Click ▾

Click
    Find More Providers...

On this page you can choose which search provider you would like to add to *Internet Explorer*:

Click
    Google
    Google Web Search

The window *Add Search Provider* appears.

Here you can choose to make *Google* your default search provider:

Check mark
    ☑ Make this my default search provider

Click Add Provider

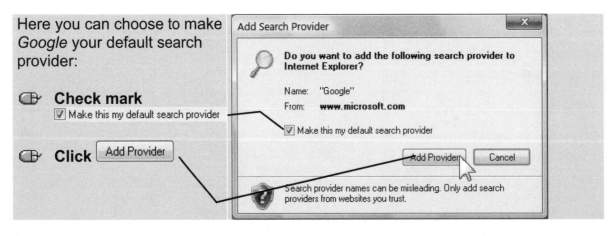

Google has become your default search engine. Here is a quick way to check that:

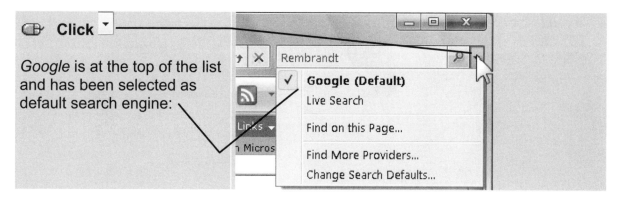

Click

Google is at the top of the list and has been selected as default search engine:

3.5 Searching with Google

Google works pretty much the same as *Live Search,* but without the advertisements. You can start your *Google* search in the *Instant Search Box*. For example, try to find some information about another famous Dutch painter, Vincent Van Gogh:

Click the *Instant Search Box*

Type:
Vincent Van Gogh

Press

 Tip

Display search results in a new tab
To display the results of your search in a new tab you do the following:

Type your search terms in the *Instant Search Box*

Press and hold Alt

Press Enter ←, **then release** Alt

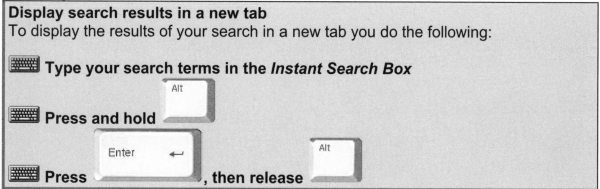

On this *Google* page you see that this search nets over 6 million *hits (*search results).

The first ten of these results are displayed:

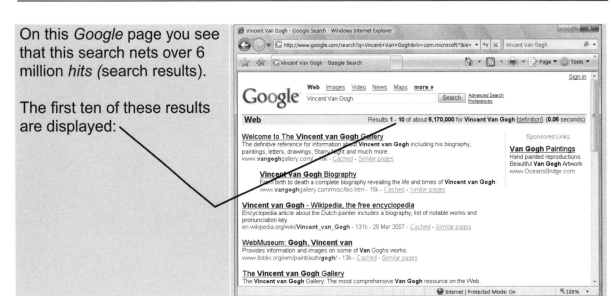

Scroll down to the bottom of the page

At the bottom of the page you see a row of numbers and **Next**.

If you click **Next**, you can view the next ten results.

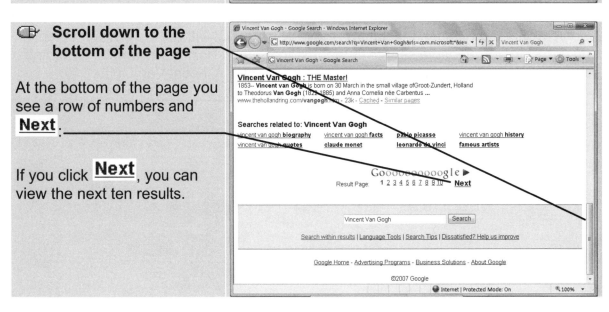

3.6 Narrowing Down the Search Results

It is impossible to go through all these search results and find exactly what you want to know about Vincent Van Gogh. To narrow down your search, you can search within these search results.

Perhaps you would like to find out which museum you can visit to see one of his famous sunflower paintings. Try the following:

Click
Search within results

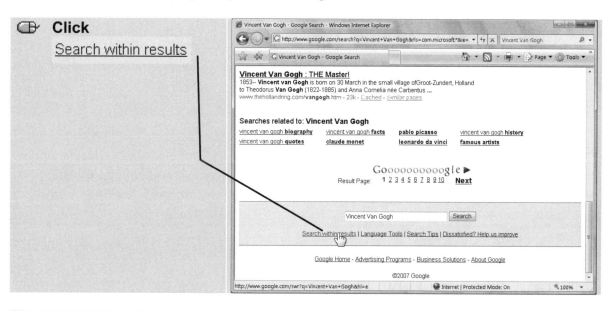

Click the search box on the page

Type:
visit museum
sunflowers

Click
Search within results

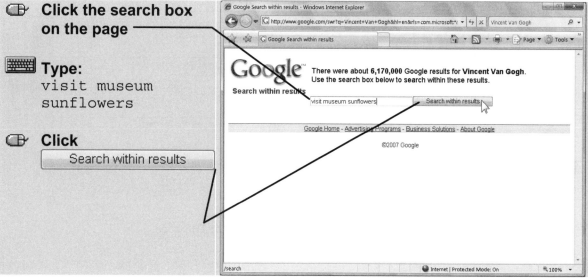

Now the number of hits has been narrowed down to about 55,000: ─────

Most likely, a *Wikipedia* entry appears in the top of the search results. Try another one this time:

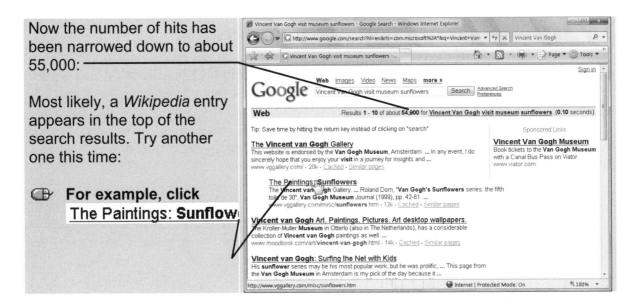

☞ **For example, click The Paintings: Sunflow**

⇨ **Please note:**

The Internet grows and changes all the time. It is possible that the results for this search have changed since this book was published. If you can not find this search result, try another one.

On this webpage of the *Vincent Van Gogh Gallery* you can find the location of all eleven sunflower paintings:

☞ **Use the scroll box to scroll down**

When you are finished reading:

☞ **Click** ⬅

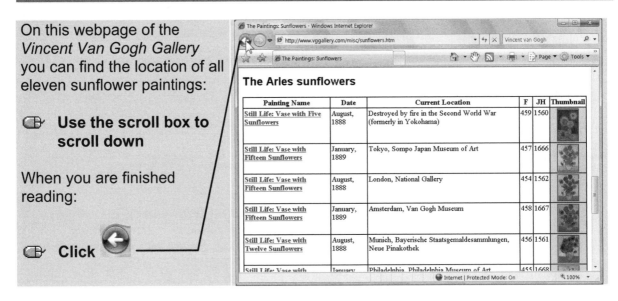

You then return to the webpage with the *Google* search results.

3.7 Advanced Search

Searching and narrowing down the search results is a good way to eventually find what you are looking for. But if you know exactly what you want and more importantly what you do **not** want to find, you are ready to try an *Advanced Search* in *Google*.

Use the scroll box to scroll up

Click Advanced Search

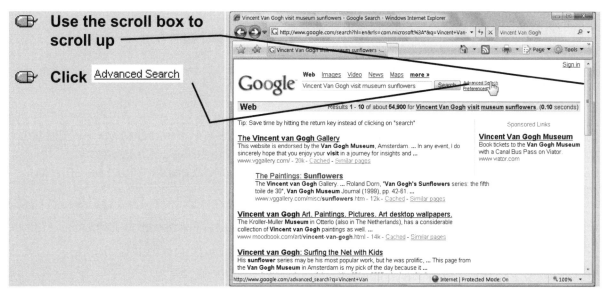

The *Advanced Search* page opens:

The words you used on your last search are entered into one of the boxes:

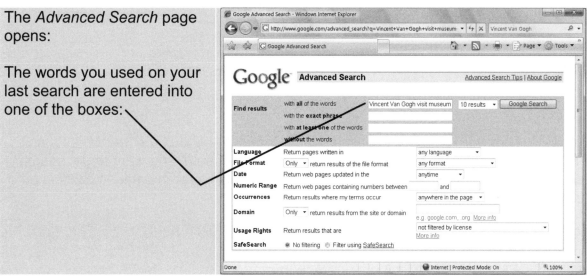

Since you are going to do a different search, you can clear that entry:

Click the box
Vincent Van Gogh visit museum
three times

The entry is selected and turns blue. Now you can delete it:

Press Delete

Say for example, you are going to visit Amsterdam for a weekend and you would like to know when the Rijksmuseum is open for visitors. This museum has many paintings by the Dutch master Rembrandt. The *Advanced Search* might be able to help you out.

First you enter the name and the location of the museum. The search field with **all** of the words will make sure that both of those words are found, but not necessarily in that order.

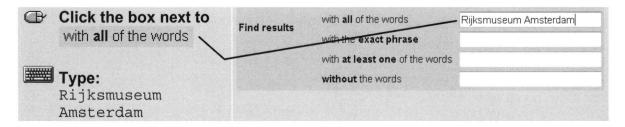

Click the box next to
with **all** of the words

Type:
Rijksmuseum
Amsterdam

In the next box you can enter multiple search terms that should be treated as a unit. Since you are looking for the opening hours of the museum, you want to get search results that contain both words in that exact order. Most search engines call this an "exact phrase".

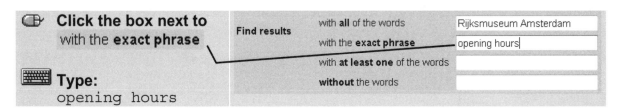

Click the box next to
with the **exact phrase**

Type:
opening hours

You can also enter a few words, one of which should show up in the search results:

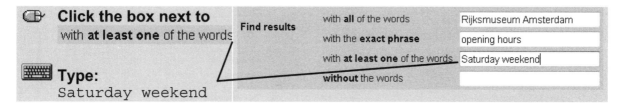

The museum might give the opening hours separately for each day, or combined for weekdays and the weekend. Either way, by using this method you will find out what time the museum opens on Saturday.

You can start the search:

The search results are shown.

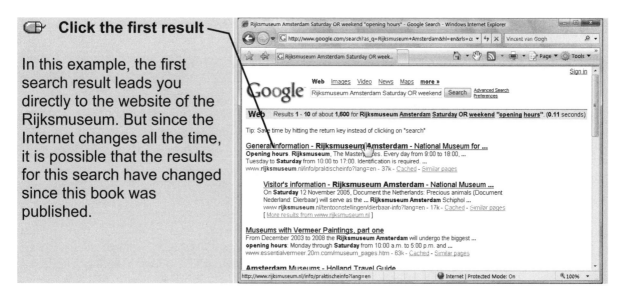

In this example, the first search result leads you directly to the website of the Rijksmuseum. But since the Internet changes all the time, it is possible that the results for this search have changed since this book was published.

The Rijksmuseum's website gives you all the information you need about opening hours and admission fees on their *General Information* web page:

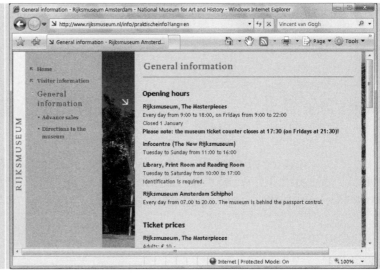

In the next section you will do a specific search for images.

3.8 Searching for Images

It is possible to limit your search to images that have something to do with Vincent Van Gogh:

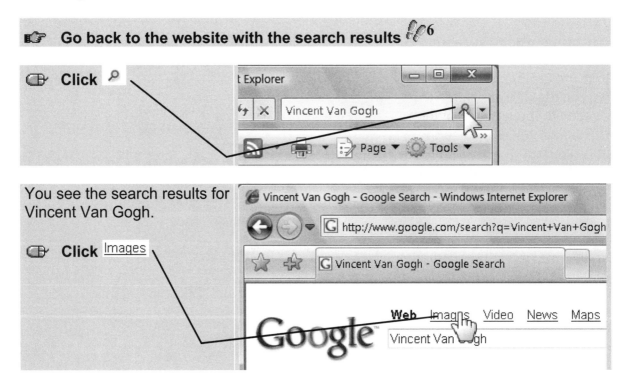

You see the search results with images of Van Gogh's paintings:

👆 **Click one of the images**

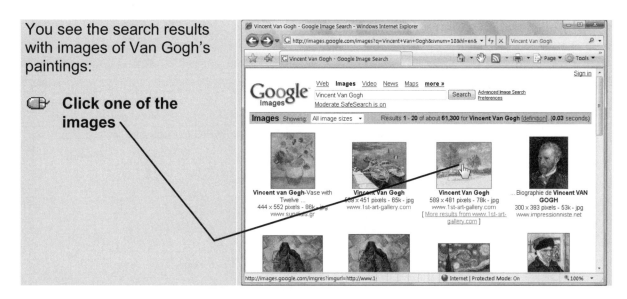

On this page you see a preview of the website where the image has been found.

👆 **Click**
See full-size image.

The image loads into the window. This may take a moment if it is a very large image and you are using a dial-up connection:

👉 **Go back to the previous page** 🖱6

If you want to visit the website where the image has been found you can use the link that is displayed here:

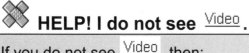 **Go back to the previous page** $\mathscr{CC}^6$

3.9 Searching for Video Clips

In addition to images, you can also use *Google* to look for video clips.

Click Video

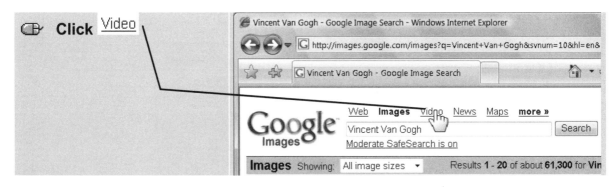

HELP! I do not see Video .

If you do not see Video, then:
- **Click** more »
- **Click** Video / Search for videos
- **In the search box, type:** Vincent Van Gogh

         Enter   ↵

- **Press**

On this page you see a list of videos that have something to do with Vincent Van Gogh. Have a look at the first one:

 Click the first title

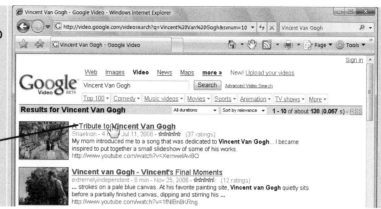

A new page is opened and you can watch the video:

💡 **Tip**

YouTube

YouTube (www.youtube.com) is a free and very popular source for video material. Users can upload, view and share video clips. For each video you can see the average rating and the number of times a video has been watched.

You can search for a video using a search term. The videos are also organized into categories. Use the **Categories** tab to browse through the different categories.

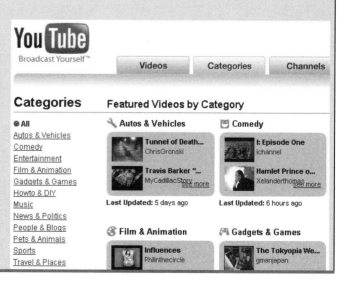

3.10 Directories

In practice, search engines are not always the fastest way to find information about a particular subject. The immense number of pages found in a single search makes it very difficult to find exactly what you need. The reason is simple: the searching is done by computers, not people.

A different way of searching is becoming more popular: the *directory*.
A directory is a website containing a large number of web addresses categorized by subject. This categorizing is done by a large editorial staff who work on the directory by organizing, evaluating and checking websites. This results in a useful summary. That is why many people use this kind of page as their *Internet Explorer* home page.

Another name for a directory is a *portal*. A portal is a useful gateway to the Internet, because you can see in one glance which websites offer what kind of information. America's most extensive portal website is the *Open Directory Project*. There is a link to this directory on the exercise page of this book.

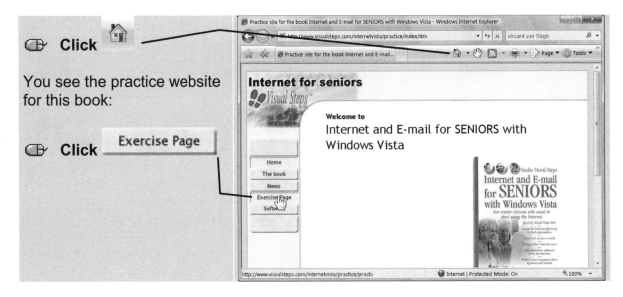

☞ **Click** 🏠

You see the practice website for this book:

☞ **Click** | **Exercise Page** |

On the exercise page you find a link to a page with links to various search engines:

 Click <u>Search engines</u>

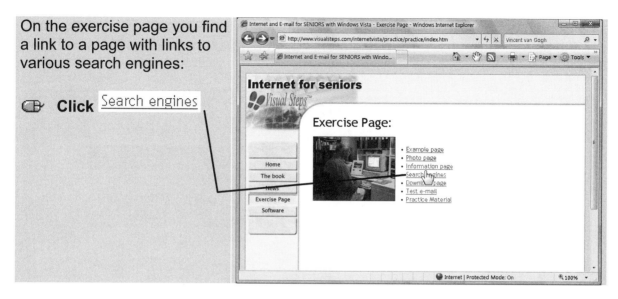

Tip

Visit this page regularly. If important new search features are developed for the Internet, they will most certainly be included on this page.

The link to the *Open Directory Project* can be found near the bottom of the page:

 Drag the scroll box down to see the bottom of the page

 Click http://dmoz.org

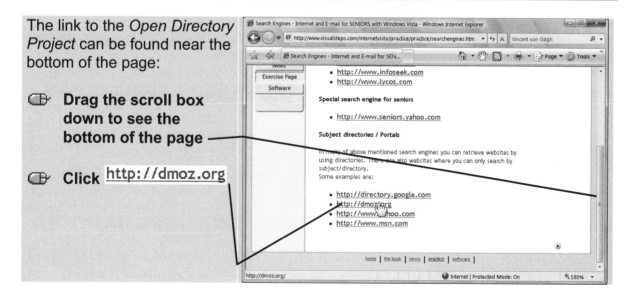

The *Open Directory Project* page opens in a new browser window. Here is how you use the search function on this website to find a restaurant on the tropical island of Bonaire:

Click the text box

Type: Bonaire

Click Search

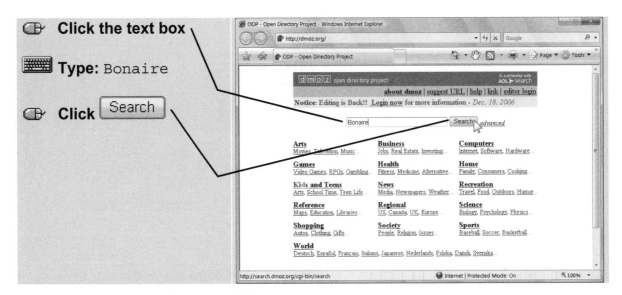

Now it will search for pages containing information about Bonaire.

You see a window with a list of website categories:

Click
1. **Regional: Caribbean:**

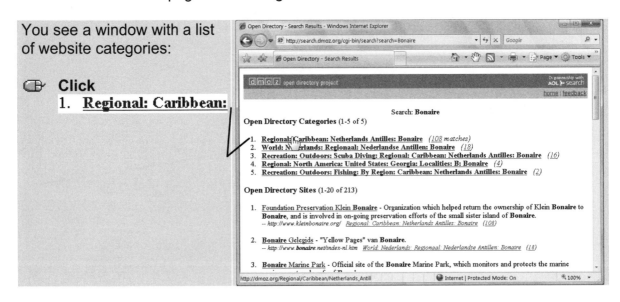

Now you see a page with more categories about Bonaire:

☞ **Click the category**
- **Travel and Tourism**

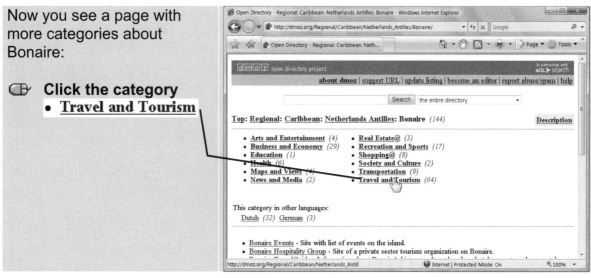

On this page you see various subjects in the category *Travel and Tourism*:

☞ **Click**
- **Restaurants and Bars**

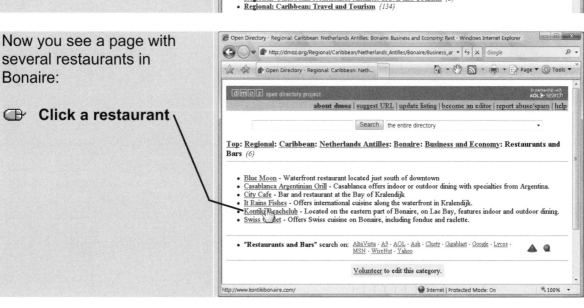

Now you see a page with several restaurants in Bonaire:

☞ **Click a restaurant**

The page for the restaurant opens:

You can close this window now.

☞ Close the window 🐾32

You see the search page for this book again:

👆 **Click** practice

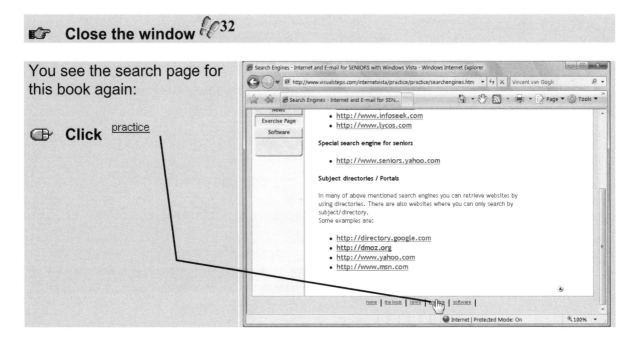

You are back on the exercise page:

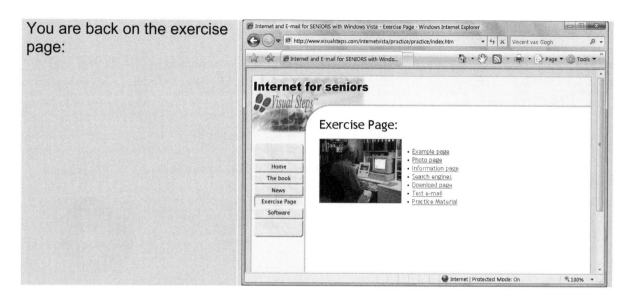

You have seen how to search using a directory. In addition to *www.dmoz.org*, there are many other directory websites.

There is another handy trick in *Internet Explorer* that you can use when you want to search for something on the Internet.

3.11 Searching Within a Page in Internet Explorer

Sometimes a webpage has so much text that it is hard to find your search term. *Internet Explorer* has a solution for that. You can search the text in a window for a particular word or phrase. Here is how you do it:

Click
• Information page

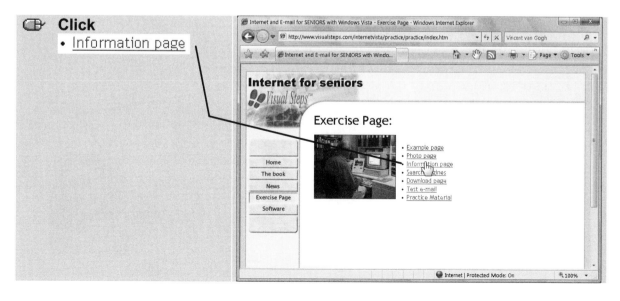

You see a text in the window which tells you the story of Anne Frank.

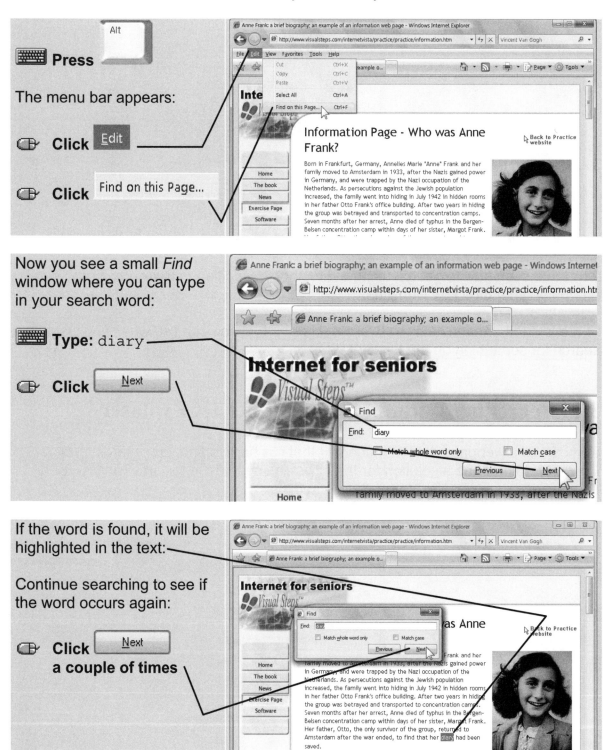

When the search has reached the bottom of the page, it will start again at the top. You can stop the search by closing the *Find* window:

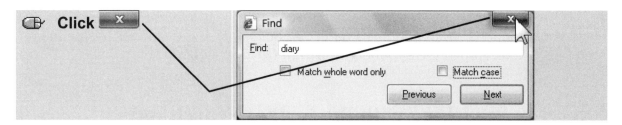

This search function is fairly limited, but can still be very useful.

☞ **Close *Internet Explorer***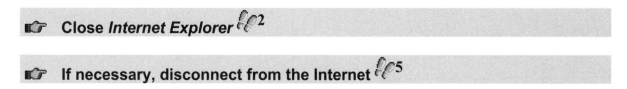

☞ **If necessary, disconnect from the Internet** ℓℓ5

You can practice searching on the Internet in the following exercises.

💡 Tip
Using the Find window

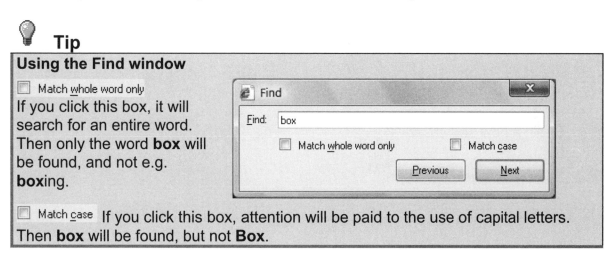

☐ Match whole word only
If you click this box, it will search for an entire word. Then only the word **box** will be found, and not e.g. **box**ing.

☐ Match case If you click this box, attention will be paid to the use of capital letters. Then **box** will be found, but not **Box**.

💡 Tip
Search term not found?
The *Find* window sometimes covers the word you are looking for. To check this, you have to drag the window to a different place on your screen. Here is how to do that:

☞ **Place the mouse pointer on the title bar**

☞ **Drag the window to another area of your screen**

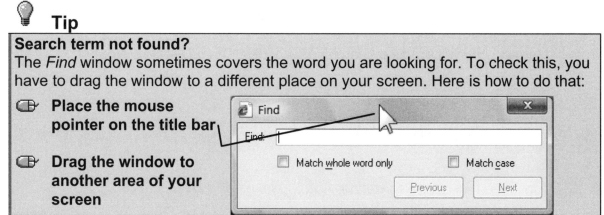

3.12 Exercises

Have you forgotten how to perform a particular action? Use the number beside the footsteps to look it up in the appendix *How Do I Do That Again?*

Exercise: Searching with the Instant Search Box

In this exercise, you will practice searching for information.

✔   Start *Internet Explorer.* [1]

✔   Connect to the Internet if necessary. [3]

✔   Click the *Instant Search Box.* [20]

✔   Search for the word *bridge.* [21]

✔   Take a look at a couple of the websites that were found. [23]

✔   Begin a new search. [22]

✔   Search for *Karel Appel.* [21]

✔   Take a look at a couple of the websites that were found. [23]

Exercise: Searching with a Directory

In this exercise, you will practice searching using the *Open Directory Project.*

✔   Open from History: *dmoz.org* [14]

✔   Search for *Ford.* [21]

✔   Choose the category *Recreation: Autos: Makes and Models: Ford.* [24]

✓ Choose the category *Explorer*. 👣24

✓ Take a look at a couple of the websites that were found. 👣23

Exercise: A Different Search Engine

In this exercise, you will use a different search engine, namely *Lycos*.

✓ Click 🏠

✓ Click ___Exercise Page___ .

✓ Click • Search engines .

✓ Click • http://www.lycos.com .

✓ Click the box next to SEARCH: .

✓ Search for the word *butterflies*. 👣21

✓ Take a look at a couple of the websites that were found. 👣23

✓ Search for *Empire State Building*. 👣21

✓ Take a look at a couple of the websites that were found. 👣23

✓ Close *Internet Explorer*. 👣2

✓ Disconnect from the Internet if necessary. 👣5

3.13 Background Information

Glossary	
Advanced Search	More detailed search, that you can customize for example by adding an exact phrase that should be found, or omitting a word that should not be found in the search results.
Case Sensitive	Words can differ in meaning based on the differing use of uppercase and lowercase letters. Searches performed by *Google* and *Live Search* are not case sensitive.
Default search engine	Search provider that is used by default when using the *Instant Search Box*. You can set your favorite search engine as default search engine.
Directory	An collection of links to other websites, listed by category and sub-category. This categorizing is done by a large editorial staff who work on the directory by organizing, evaluating and checking websites. This results in a useful summary. The *Open Directory Project* is a good example.
Exact Phrase	Search terms that are treated as a unit. To search for an exact phrase, enclose it in quotation marks, for example "Ford Focus".
Google	Popular search engine.
Hits	Search results.
Instant Search Box	Box at the top right of the *Internet Explorer* window that can be used to start a search on the Internet [Google 🔍 ▾].
Live Search	Search engine made by Microsoft.
Search engine	A program that is constantly busy indexing webpages. *Google* and *Live Search* are search engines. You can use the search engine's webpage to search for all the webpages that contain your search terms.
Search terms	A keyword or phrase that is typed into a search engine.
Wikipedia	A multilingual, web-based, free content encyclopedia project. *Wikipedia* is written collaboratively by volunteers, its articles can be edited by anyone with access to the website.
Source: Windows Help and Support	

How does a search engine work?

Search engines are programs that are busy indexing webpages around the clock. This creates an enormous index of search terms. Search engines differ in the method they use to do this. That is why the results from different search engines are often very different. Some search engines index as many words as possible on a webpage. Others only use search terms found in the titles of webpages.

There are also search engines that primarily use key words on webpages. These hidden key words are put in by the web page designer. Sometimes this feature is abused, and particular key words are used intentionally because these words are frequently typed into searches. This can be the reason why you sometimes see webpages in your search results that have very little to do with your search term.

Search engines work like a kind of robot and are therefore fairly limited. No editing or selection is performed on the pages. This limitation becomes particularly evident when you search for words that have multiple meanings. An editor would be able to separate the webpages based upon their content.

All the well-known search engine companies have a department where editing does take place, and hundreds of websites have been organized by subject or category.

There are also websites that specialize in this. These are called *directories* or *portals*.

Usually a website has to be submitted to a search engine in order to be included in its index. Websites that have not been submitted can not be found by the search engine. That might be a reason why you can not find the particular website you were looking for.

3.14 Tips

  Tip

Using search engines
- First, get a lot of practice using a particular search engine such as *Google* and thoroughly investigate all its search options. You can find al lot of information in the search engine's Help pages.

- Once you have some experience, give other search engines a try.
  You will discover through experience which search engines you like best.

- Always begin with the most specific search possible. For example, if you want to find information about the *Epson Stylus Photo 1400* printer, then use this whole phrase as your search term. If you do not get enough results, then try *Epson Stylus*. As a last resort, type just the word *Epson*.

  Tip

Google search tips

- Keep it simple: if you are looking for information on the city of Barcelona, try ***Barcelona***. But remember: this will get you millions of search results.

- Use multiple search terms: if you are looking for a hotel in Barcelona, you will get better results with ***hotel Barcelona*** than with either ***hotel*** or ***Barcelona***.

- *Google* only returns pages that include all of your search terms. To restrict a search further, just include more terms.

- *Google* searches are not case sensitive. All letters will be understood as lower case. For example, searches for ***Rembrandt Van Rijn*** and ***rembrandt van rijn*** will return the same results.

- To find pages that include either of two search terms, add an uppercase OR between the terms. For example, here is how to search for a hotel in either Barcelona or Rome: ***hotel Barcelona OR Rome.***

- When you place the tilde sign (~) immediately in front of your search term, *Google* will also search for synonyms of your search term. For example, a search for ***~milk*** will also produce results for ***dairy***.

Source: Google Search Tips

Tip

Using special symbols

You can also use various symbols in your search, such as **+**, **-**, **"**, *****

If you type: **+Jackson +Browne**
The search engine will search for webpages containing both *Jackson* **and** *Browne*.

If you type: **Jackson –Browne**
The search engine will search for webpages containing *Jackson* **but not** *Browne*.

If you type quotation marks around the words: **"Jackson Browne"**
The search engine will search for webpages containing the phrase *Jackson Browne*.

If you type a star ***** next to a word, for example: **Brown***
This means that any symbol(s) at all can come at the end of the word, and the search engine will find Brown, Browning, Brownies, Brownbag, etc.

If you search for **Jackson Brown***, then you might for example find sites for the singer Jackson Browne, but also for the author H. Jackson Brown.

 Tip

Searching directly by a name
You do not always have to use a search engine to find a particular web address. Brand names and companies are generally easy to find. Usually, if you follow the brand name by .com, you will find the correct address.

For example, if you want to visit the website of the car manufacturer *Ford*, you can type **www.ford.com** in the address bar.

Tip

Searching in the address bar

Internet Explorer has a built-in way to quickly search for something. You usually search for information based on a search term; for example, the word *highway*:

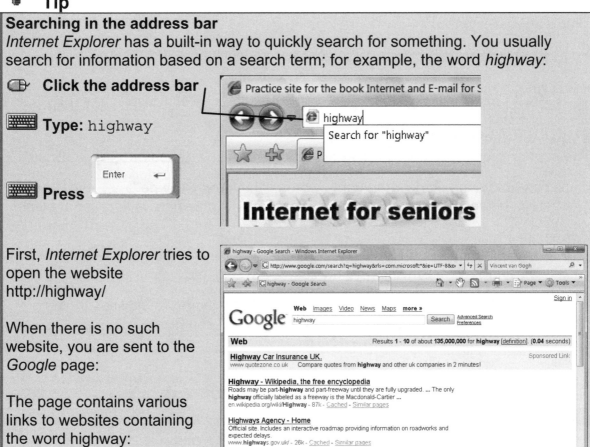

🖱️ **Click the address bar**

⌨️ **Type:** `highway`

⌨️ **Press** Enter ⏎

First, *Internet Explorer* tries to open the website http://highway/

When there is no such website, you are sent to the *Google* page:

The page contains various links to websites containing the word highway:

4. Internet, Your Source of Information

The Internet can be viewed as an enormous library containing all kinds of information: text, photos, drawings, video and music. The most amazing thing is that nearly everything on the Internet that you see on your screen can be saved to your computer's hard drive. Later on, you can use the information that you have stored, for example in your work or for a hobby.

You can copy texts and re-use or edit them in a text-editing program. You can open and edit photos with a photo-editing or drawing program. In this way, the Internet serves as an enormous source of information. In this chapter, you will learn the basic techniques for saving and re-using text and photos on your own computer.

In this chapter, you will learn how to:

- print a page
- select text
- copy and paste text
- copy and paste images
- save an image
- save a webpage
- open a saved webpage in *Internet Explorer*

4.1 Visiting the Practice Website

First, start *Internet Explorer*:

Do you have an external modem?
☞ **Turn on the modem**

☞ **Start *Internet Explorer* ᵍₑ1**

☞ **Connect to the Internet ᵍₑ3**

A connection is made to your ISP (*Internet Service Provider*) and you see the home page as it is set up on your computer:

Do you see a different home page?

☞ **Open the *Internet and E-mail for Seniors* practice website ᵍₑ52**

☞ **Click [Exercise Page]**

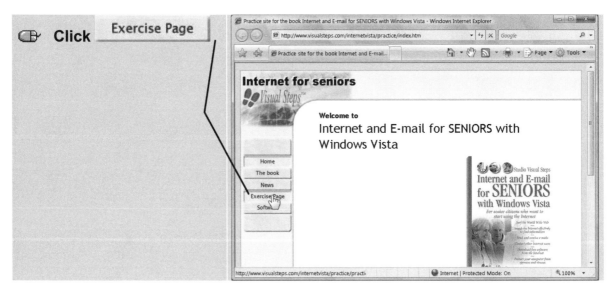

There is a practice page for this chapter on the website. You can open it now:

Click
- Information page

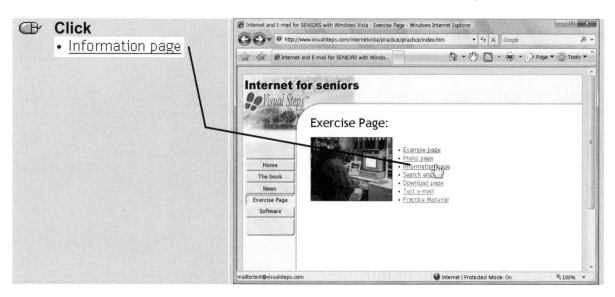

Now you see this information page with text and a photo which you can use for practice:

Do you want to disconnect from the Internet so you can receive calls?
☞ **Wait until the entire page has been loaded**

☞ **Disconnect from the Internet** 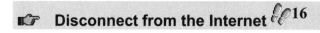16

Now you can take all the time you would like to work through the rest of this chapter.

4.2 Printing a Page

It is not always easy to read a webpage on the screen, particularly if it contains a lot of text.

If you have a printer, you can choose to print the page. You can read the printed version later on at your own pace.

✎ HELP! I do not have a printer.

Then you can simply skip this section.

 First check if the printer is on

Before you print the page, you can take a look at the print preview to see what the print will look like on letter-size paper:

☞ **Click** ▾ **next to** 🖶

☞ **Click** Print Preview...

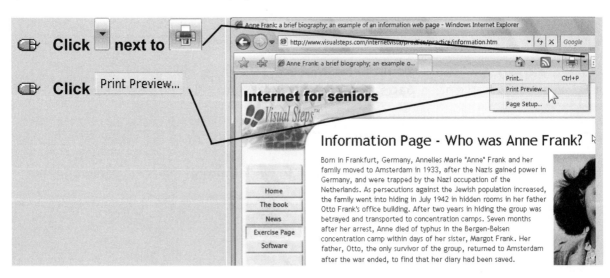

The information page does not fit on one page. At the bottom of the screen you see Page ☐1 of 3 :

This is how you display all pages in the print preview:

☞ **Click** 1 Page View ▼

☞ **Click** 3 Page View

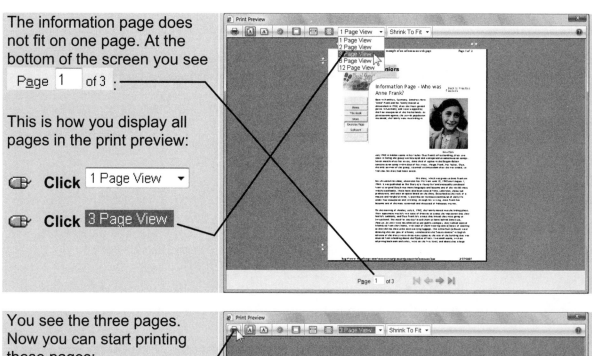

You see the three pages. Now you can start printing these pages:

☞ **Click** 🖶

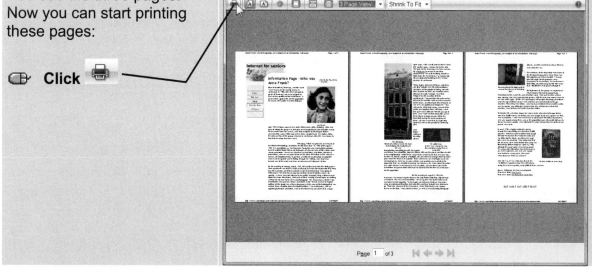

Your printer will start to print the three pages. A little later, a document containing the text and photos from the information page will come out of your printer.

Now you can close the *Print Preview* window:

☞ **Close the *Print Preview* window** 🖙³²

Tip

Other buttons
The other buttons in the *Print Preview* window have the following functions:

Switch between printing the page vertically (*portrait*) or horizontally (*landscape*).

Open the *Page Setup* window.

Turn the *header* and *footer* options on or off.

Zoom the webpage to fit the width of the preview screen (*full width*), or zoom to fit the full webpage (*full page*) in the preview screen.

Adjust margins (only in ⌷1 Page View ▼⌷): drag the horizontal or vertical markers to change how the content fits on the printed page.

Stretch or shrink the page size by a percentage to fill the printed page. Increasing the print size to for example 150%, makes the text and images look larger on the print. However, you will need more pages to print the website.

 Tip

Printing a webpage with frames
When a webpage you want to print consists of multiple frames, you will see an extra option in the *Print Preview* window:

Click ▼

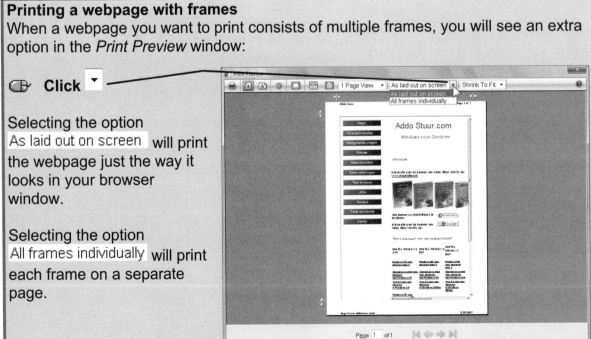

Selecting the option
⌷As laid out on screen⌷ will print the webpage just the way it looks in your browser window.

Selecting the option
⌷All frames individually⌷ will print each frame on a separate page.

4.3 Selecting Text

You can save a text you have read on the Internet on your computer and edit it later, perhaps using it in a text of your own. For example, you could copy information and use it in a club newsletter. To do this, you copy the text and paste it into another (text-editing) program.

First make sure the menu bar is displayed in the *Internet Explorer* window:

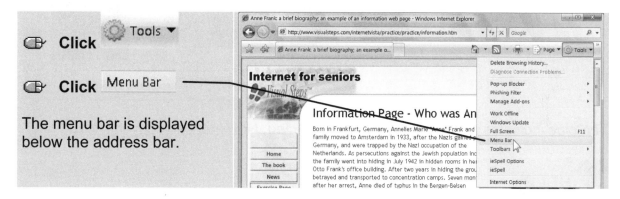

☞ **Click** ⚙ Tools ▼

☞ **Click** Menu Bar

The menu bar is displayed below the address bar.

For practice, you are going to copy a portion of text and paste it into the *WordPad* program. Before you can copy something, you have to *select* it first. In *Windows*, you do this by *clicking and dragging* the mouse.

 HELP! I do not know how to drag.

Read page 44 to find out how to drag.

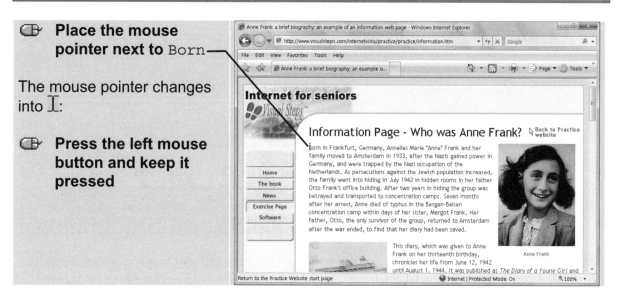

☞ **Place the mouse pointer next to** Born

The mouse pointer changes into I:

☞ **Press the left mouse button and keep it pressed**

Slide the mouse down and to the right

You see that the first few lines of text turn blue:

 Release the mouse button

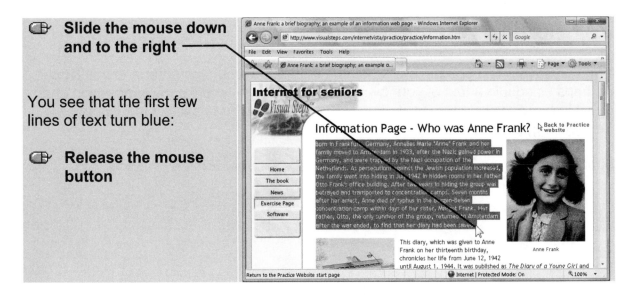

The blue indicates that the text has been selected. Now you can copy this text.

⚜ HELP!

Having trouble selecting exactly the right text? It does not matter for this exercise. The important thing is that some part of the text has been selected.

4.4 Copying Text

Once the text has been selected, you can copy it:

 Click Edit

 Click Copy

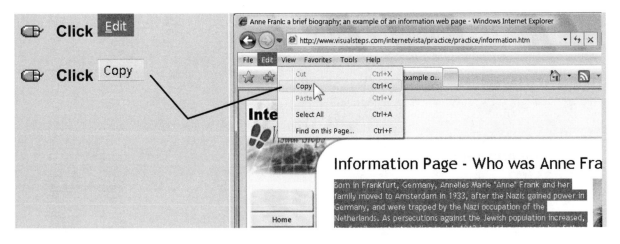

Although you did not see anything happen, the text has indeed been copied. Now you can paste it into another program. You can paste it into a text-editing program such as *WordPad* or *MS Word*, an e-mail message, or a drawing program.

4.5 Pasting Text into WordPad

For practice, you are going to paste the copied text into the text editor *WordPad*. *WordPad* is a simple text-editing program that comes standard with *Windows*. This is how to open it:

☞ **Click**

☞ **Click** ▶ **All Programs**

☞ **Click** Accessories

☞ **Click** WordPad

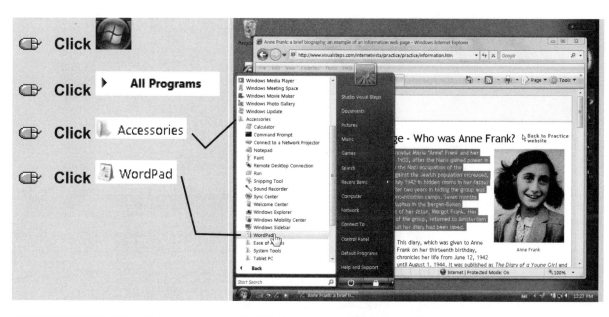

You see the *WordPad* window:

At the top left, you see a small blinking line. This is called the *cursor*.

The text will be pasted at the location of the cursor.

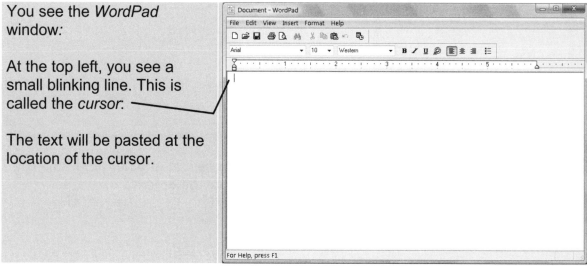

Now you can give the command to paste the text:

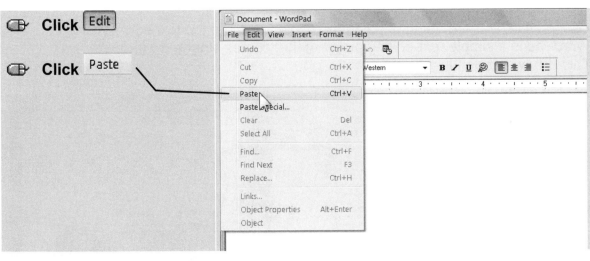

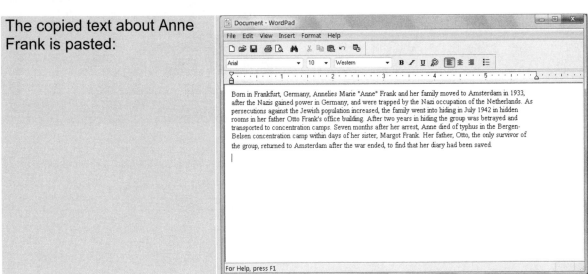

The copied text about Anne Frank is pasted:

In this way, you can copy any text on the Internet and use it in another program. You can edit and save this text on your computer just like any other text.

You can also select the entire text all at once from a webpage and then paste it. To see how, first minimize the *WordPad* window:

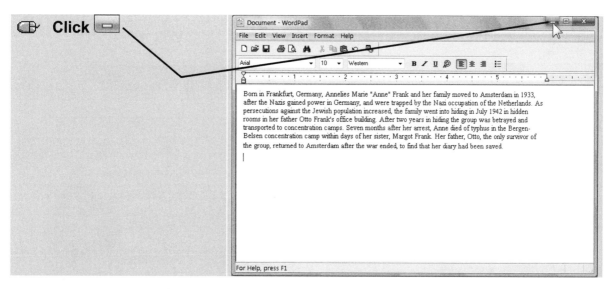

Click [—]

You see the *Internet Explorer* window containing the information page again:

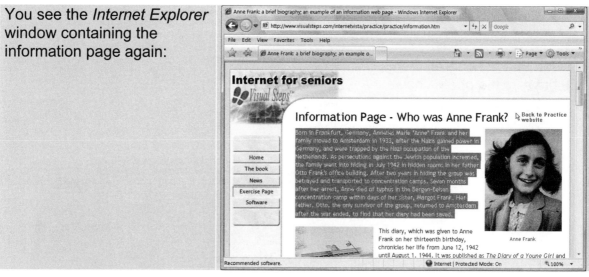

It is not always practical to select a text by dragging the mouse. There is another method you can use.

4.6 Select All

You can select all the text and images on a webpage with a single command. This is useful if you want to work quickly while you are surfing. Here is how you do it:

Click Edit

Click Select All

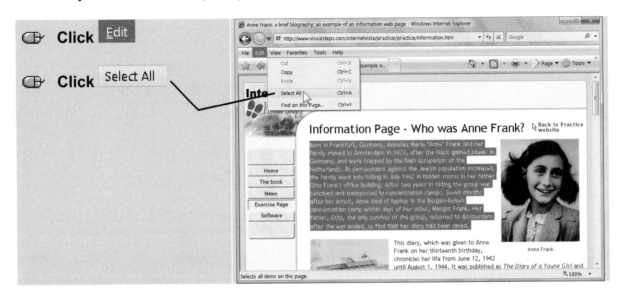

You see that not only all the text, but also the photos have been selected:

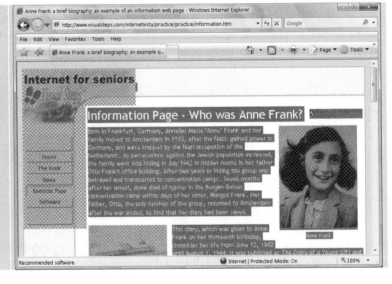

You can copy the text and pictures:

☞ **Click** Edit

☞ **Click** Copy

The entire page has been copied, and you can open the *WordPad* window again.

☞ **Click**

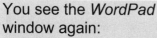

on the taskbar

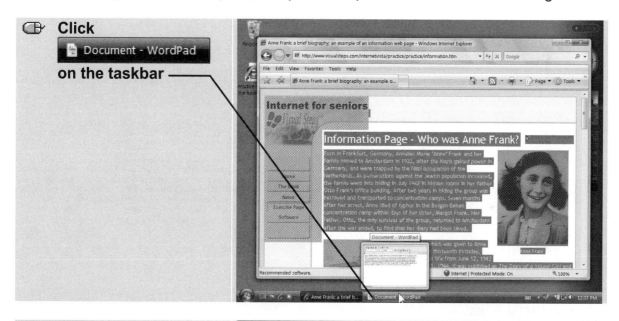

You see the *WordPad*
window again:

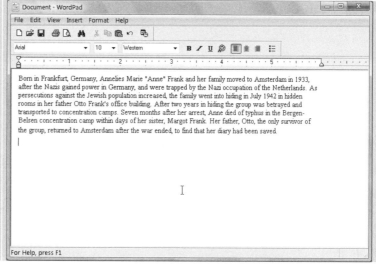

Now you want to put the cursor (the blinking line) at the very top. The text will then be pasted there:

Click before the first line

The cursor is blinking now on the left of the first line.

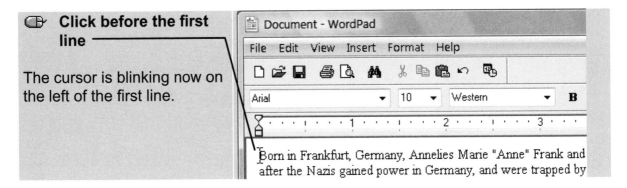

Now you can paste the text:

Click Edit

Click Paste

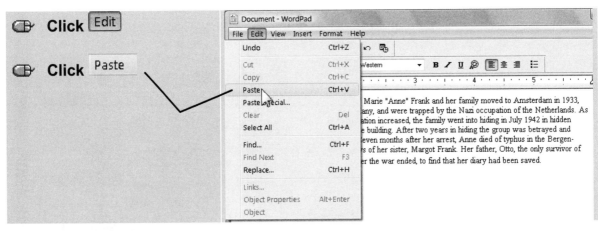

You see that the text has been pasted:

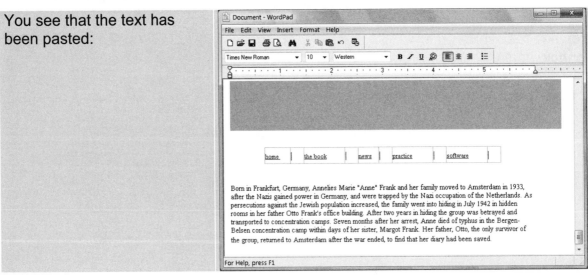

HELP! I do not see any pictures.

The *WordPad* program does not display pictures.
If you paste this webpage into a document in *Microsoft Word* or into an e-mail message in *Windows Mail*, it does work properly. The technique for doing this using one of these programs is exactly the same as described above.

4.7 Closing WordPad

Now you can close *WordPad*. You do not need to save the text. Here is how to close:

Click File

Click Exit

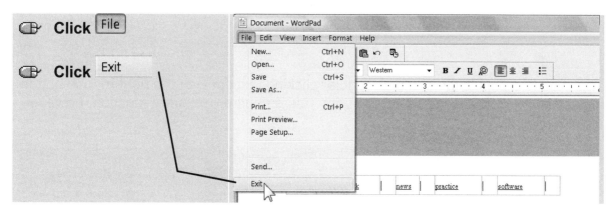

WordPad asks if the text should be saved. This is not necessary, so:

Click Don't Save

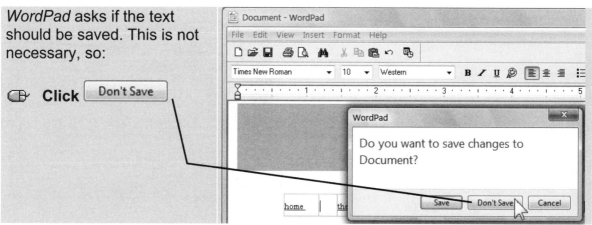

 Tip

Text or image?
Some text on the Internet is in fact an image. For example, the text on the button Exercise Page is an image. You can not copy the text on an image like this and paste it into a text-editing program or an e-mail program. You can, however, copy and paste the entire image. You will read how to do that later on in this chapter.

4.8 "Grabbing" Images from the Screen

You are bound to come across an interesting photo, image or drawing on the Internet that you want to save or even print. You can copy and save almost all the graphic material that appears on your screen, to use or print at a later time.

You can save an image by right-clicking it. Here is how you right-click:

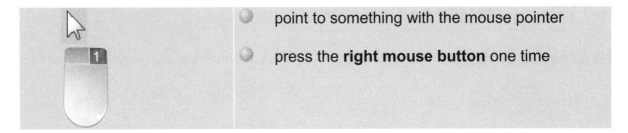

point to something with the mouse pointer

press the **right mouse button** one time

This mouse action is the same as regular clicking, except with the right mouse button instead of the left. The right mouse button has an entirely different function, however, as you will see.

Click in the text on the webpage

Use the scroll box to scroll down to the second photo

Now you can select the photo, like this:

Point to the photo

While the pointer rests on the photo, click with the <u>right</u> mouse button

A menu with a list of various commands appears:

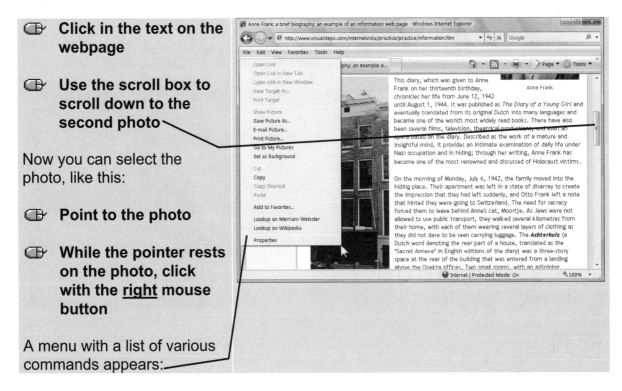

You can choose one of these commands. Use the left mouse button again to do that.

4.9 Copying an Image

First you are going to copy the image. Then you can use it in another program, such as a drawing program.

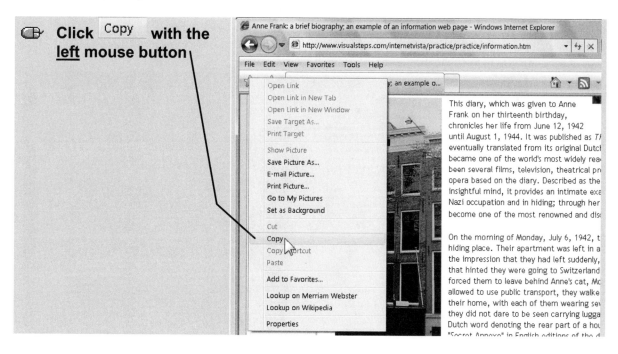

You did not see anything happen, but you can be certain that the image has indeed been copied.

4.10 Pasting an Image into Paint

You can paste the image not only into a text-editing program like *WordPad* or *MS Word*, but also into a program for photo editing or a drawing program.
For practice, you are going to paste the image into the drawing program *Paint*. *Paint* is a simple drawing program that comes standard with *Windows*.
Here is how you start this program:

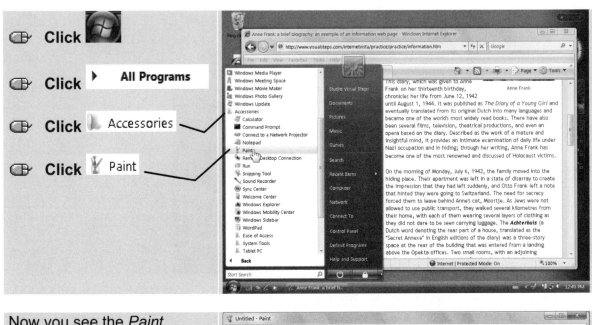

Now you see the *Paint* window:

There is a vertical bar containing all kinds of tools on the left-hand side:

At the top, you see a bar containing colors:

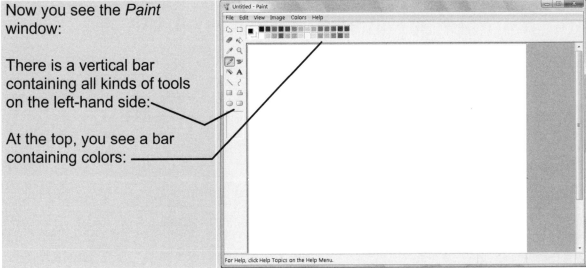

There is a large white surface in the middle of the page on which you can draw. This is the piece of paper, so to speak. You can paste the image onto it.

Click Edit

Click Paste

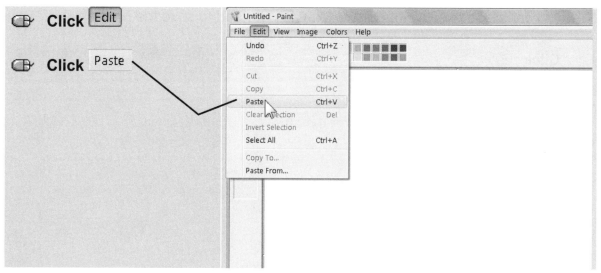

You see that the photo of the house has been pasted:

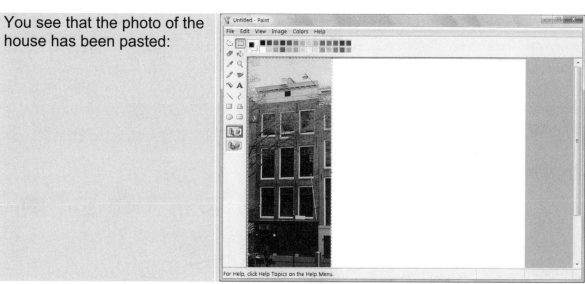

You can use *Paint* to edit, save, or print the photo.

Now you can close the *Paint* program. You do not need to save the photo:

Click File

Click Exit

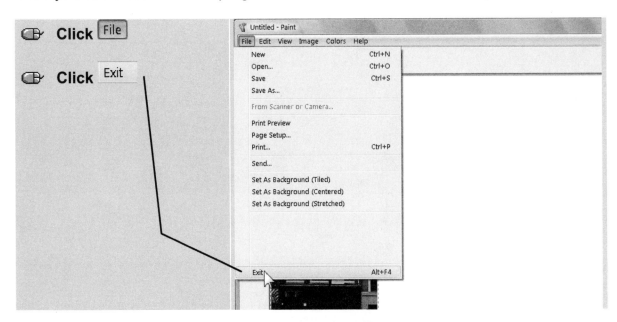

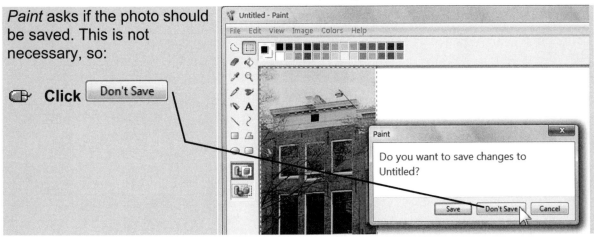

Paint asks if the photo should be saved. This is not necessary, so:

Click Don't Save

 Tip

You can use this method to paste an image into a *Microsoft Word* document or an e-mail message in *Windows Mail*. In fact, you can paste it into a document in almost any program.

4.11 Saving an Image

You can also save an image directly to your computer, without having to paste it into a drawing program. Then you can use your favorite program at any time to open it. This is how:

Point to the photo of the house and click with the <u>right</u> mouse button

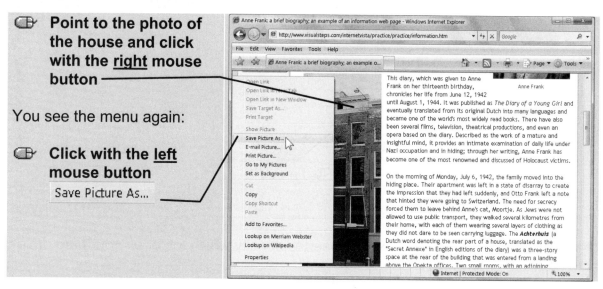

You see the menu again:

Click with the <u>left</u> mouse button

Save Picture As...

Now you see this window where you can specify the folder on your hard drive to be used for saving the photo:

The photo already has a name:
AnneFrankHouseAmsterdam

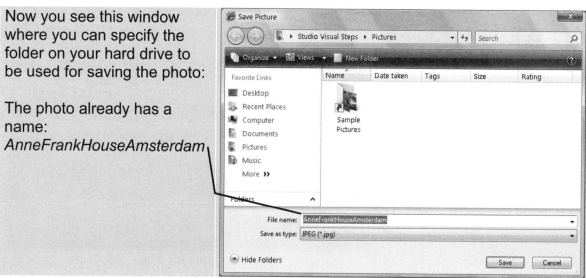

 HELP! My window looks different.

If you do not see the folders on the left side of the window, then:

Click

You can give this photo a different name if you would like. For example, you can choose a name that tells you this is a photo.

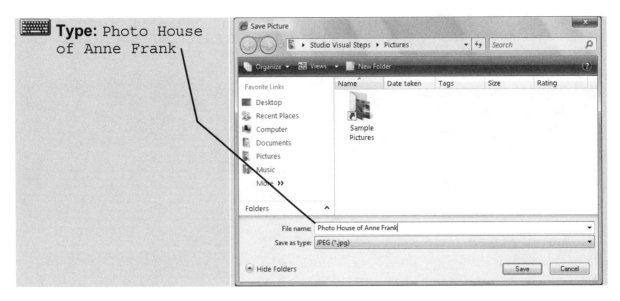

Now the photo has a name. Next you need to specify which folder on your hard drive is to be used for saving the photo.

4.12 Where to Save?

It is important to pay attention to where you save the photo. It is a good idea to always save to the same folder. That makes it easier to find things later and helps keep you from forgetting where things are. By default, images in *Windows Vista* are saved in the folder ▸ Pictures . You can find this folder in your *Personal* folder.

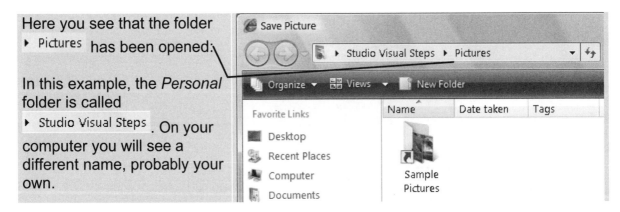

Here you see that the folder ▸ Pictures has been opened.

In this example, the *Personal* folder is called ▸ Studio Visual Steps . On your computer you will see a different name, probably your own.

The folder ▸ Pictures is intended for saving image files, for example drawings or photos. You can save the photo Anne Frank's house in the folder ▸ Pictures .

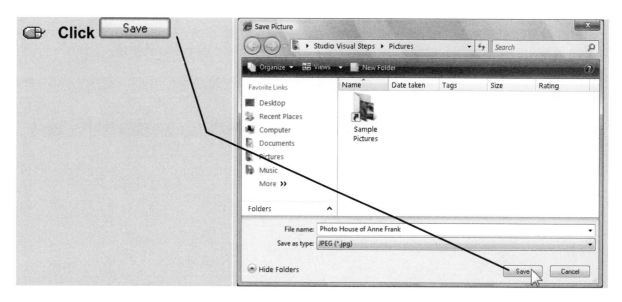

The photo has now been permanently stored on your hard drive. You can open it again later and use it in a different program, or even send it to someone in an e-mail.

4.13 Saving a Webpage

You can also save an entire webpage, including all its text and images. The page will be saved as a webpage on your hard drive. You can open it again later in *Internet Explorer*. This can be useful, for example, if you find an interesting webpage and want to look at it again later without having to connect to the Internet. Here is how you save a webpage:

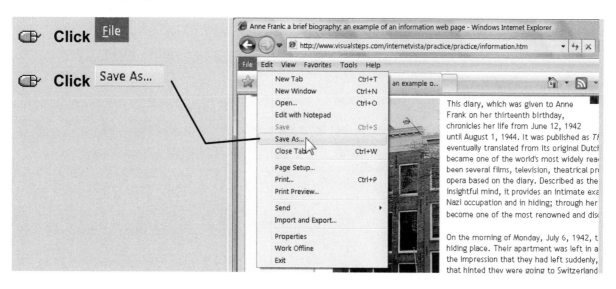

Instead of the folder ▸ Pictures , save the webpage in the folder *Documents*. That is a folder in your *Personal* folder intended for saving all kinds of documents.

Click 📄 Documents

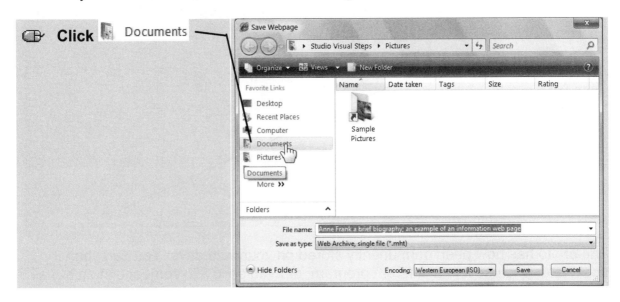

It is a good idea to choose a new name for the webpage – one that describes the content better:

The filename is already blue which indicates that it has been selected. You can type the new filename right away:

⌨ **Type:**
Information on
Anne Frank

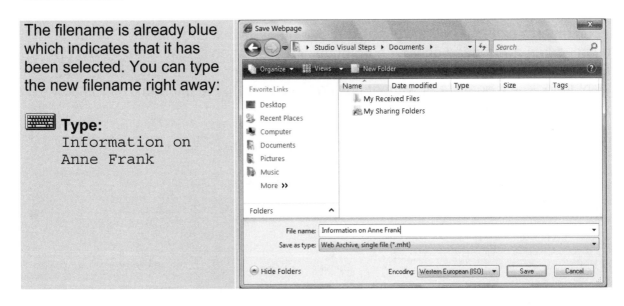

Now you need to make sure the entire webpage will be saved. Then you can save the webpage:

Beside Save as type: , make sure the setting is
Web Archive, single file (*.mht) .

If this is not the case, then:

☞ **Click** ▾ **after**
Save as type:

☞ **Click**
Web Archive, single file (*.mht)

☞ **Click** Save

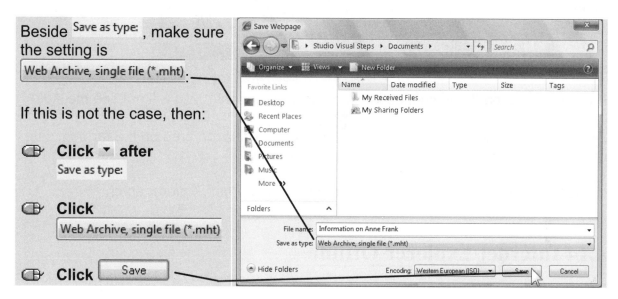

The webpage has now been saved to your hard drive in the folder ▸ Documents . You can open the page again any time you like.

You can close *Internet Explorer* now. You do that by using a window button:

☞ **Click** ✕

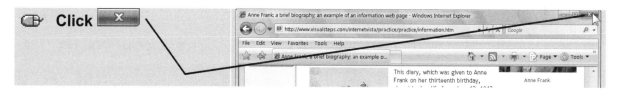

If you have a dial-up connection, you see the *Auto Disconnect* window:

☞ **Click** Disconnect Now

The connection has been broken.

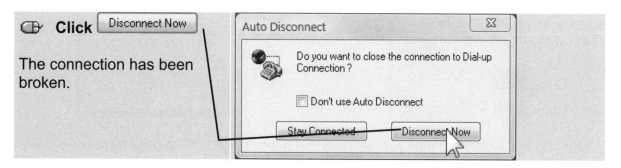

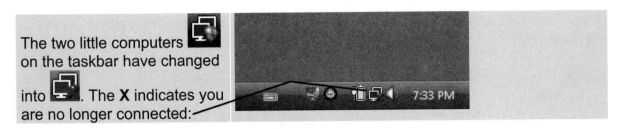

The two little computers on the taskbar have changed into [icon]. The **X** indicates you are no longer connected:

If you have a broadband connection such as DSL or cable, you will not see the *Auto Disconnect* window. You will still see [icon] in the notification area on the far right side of the taskbar because you are continuously online.

In the following section, you will start the program *Internet Explorer* again.

4.14 Internet Explorer Offline

You are going to start *Internet Explorer* once more, but this time you do not need to connect to the Internet. This is called *working offline*.

☞ **Start *Internet Explorer*** ❧1

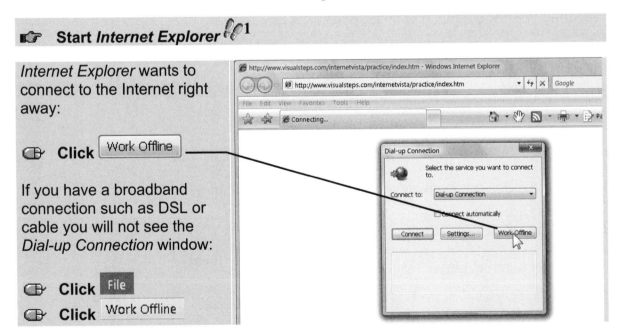

Internet Explorer wants to connect to the Internet right away:

☞ **Click** Work Offline

If you have a broadband connection such as DSL or cable you will not see the *Dial-up Connection* window:

☞ **Click** File
☞ **Click** Work Offline

When you are working offline, sometimes the home page will be read from memory ("cache"). It might seem like you are connected to the Internet but you are not.

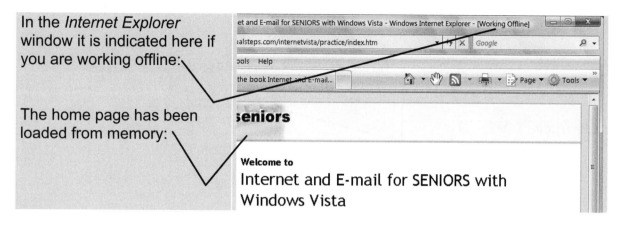

In the *Internet Explorer* window it is indicated here if you are working offline:

The home page has been loaded from memory:

Now that you have started *Internet Explorer* in offline mode you can open the saved page.

4.15 Opening the Webpage

The webpage can be opened from the folder *Documents* like this:

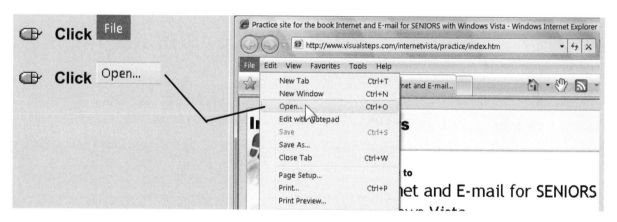

☞ **Click** File

☞ **Click** Open...

First you have to find the folder where you saved the webpage. You do this by "browsing" through the folders on your hard drive.

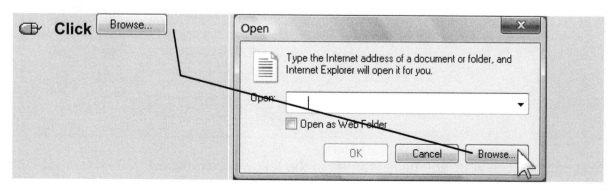

☞ **Click** Browse...

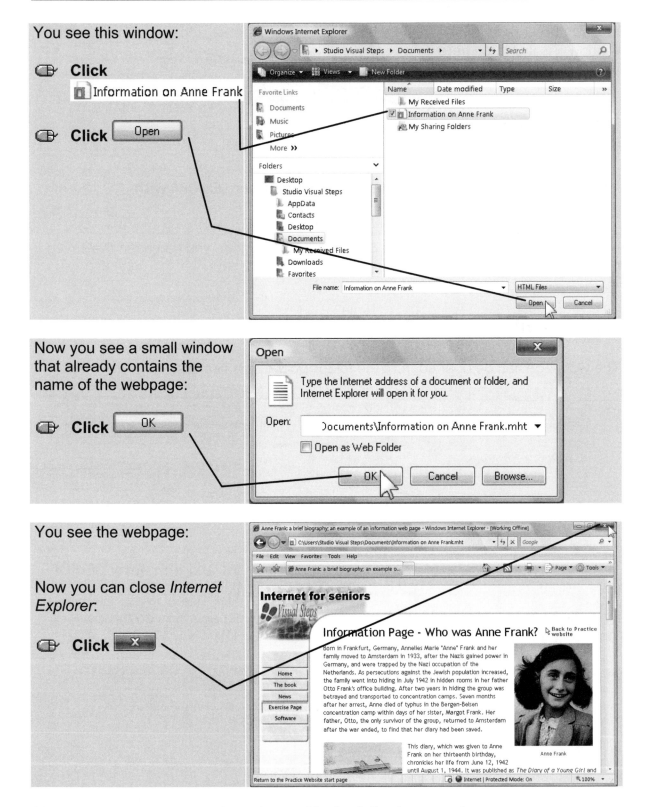

You see this window:

☞ **Click**
    🔲 Information on Anne Frank

☞ **Click** Open

Now you see a small window that already contains the name of the webpage:

☞ **Click** OK

You see the webpage:

Now you can close *Internet Explorer*:

☞ **Click** x

You can practice what you have learned in the following exercises.

4.16 Exercises

Have you forgotten how to perform a particular action? Use the number beside the footsteps to look it up in the appendix *How Do I Do That Again?*

Exercise: Copying Text

In this exercise, you will practice copying text.
You do not need to open the information page on the Internet, because this webpage has been saved to your computer.

✓ Start *Internet Explorer,* but stay offline. ₡₡²⁵

✓ Open the webpage *Information on Anne Frank.* ₡₡²⁶

✓ Go to the last line of the text. ₡₡⁹

✓ Select the last line of the text. ₡₡²⁷

✓ Copy the text. ₡₡²⁸

✓ Minimize the *Internet Explorer* window. ₡₡¹¹

✓ Start *WordPad.* ₡₡²⁹

✓ Paste the text. ₡₡³⁰

✓ Close the *WordPad* window without saving the text. ₡₡³¹

Exercise: Saving an Image

In this exercise, you will practice saving an image.

✔ Open the *Internet Explorer* window on the taskbar. 🦶¹²

✔ Click with the right mouse button on the photo of Anne Frank's Diary:

✔ Save the photo. 🦶³³

✔ Give the photo the name *Diary*. 🦶³⁴

✔ Close *Internet Explorer*. 🦶²

Exercise: Saving a Page

✔ Start *Internet Explorer*. 🦶¹

✔ Connect to the Internet if necessary. 🦶³

✔ Open the *Internet and E-mail for Seniors* practice website. 🦶⁵²

✔ Click ⌞ Exercise Page ⌟.

✔ Click • Search engines .

✔ Save this page. 🦶⁵³

✔ Close *Internet Explorer*. 🦶²

✔ Disconnect from the Internet if necessary. 🦶⁵

4.17 Background Information

Glossary

Cursor	A flashing vertical line that indicates where the next text that you type or paste will appear.
Footer	Text at the bottom of a printed webpage.
Frame	An independent section on a webpage. Each frame is actually a separate webpage and can have its own scroll bars.
Grabbing	Popular term for copying images or text from a webpage.
Header	Text at the top of a printed webpage.
Orientation	The way your document is positioned on the paper. There are two orientation options: portrait and landscape. Portrait orients the page for vertical viewing, landscape orients the page for horizontal viewing.
Paint	*Paint* is a program used to draw, color, and edit pictures.
Personal folder	A folder containing your most frequently used folders (such as *Documents*, *Pictures*, *Music*, *Favorites*, *Contacts*, and other folders that are specific to your user account). The *Personal* folder is labeled with the name you use to log on to your computer and is located at the top of the *Start* menu.
Printer	Device that prints text and graphics from your computer onto paper.
Print Preview	You can use *Print Preview* to see how a printed webpage will look and to adjust page orientation, scaling, and margins.
Web Archive	A saved webpage can be saved as a web archive. A web archive is saved in the Multipurpose Internet Mail Extension HTML (MHTML) format. Web archives can be recognized by the .MHT file extension. The .MHT file can be viewed using *Internet Explorer*.
WordPad	*WordPad* is a simple word processor that is included in *Windows*. A word processor is a computer program that you can use to create, edit, view, and print text documents.

Source: Windows Help and Support

Photos
You might be wondering how to get a photo onto a computer. There are different ways of doing this.

You can copy a printed photo with a *scanner*.

The photo is placed in the scanner, which is then closed. The computer then "scans" the picture. This is also called *digitizing*.

It is also possible to scan photo negatives with a special kind of scanner, or to have a camera store place your photos directly onto a CD when you have them developed.

Scanner

The newest method is to take photos without using a roll of film or photo paper. The photos you take are stored digitally from the start. You can do this using a *digital camera*.
The photos are stored in the camera on a small memory card. You can connect the camera to your computer with a cable when you want to transfer your photos to the PC.

Digital camera

Photo editing

Paint is a very simple drawing program that provides a few photo editing capabilities. Special photo editing programs contain many more features. In these programs, you can increase and decrease a photo's size, or crop it into a particular shape. You can also change the colors or sharpen the contrast. You have access to a complete digital darkroom.

Many programs have additional options for framing your photos or placing them in albums. Sometimes you can even create special webpages that you can upload to the Internet. In short, you can enjoy endless possibilities of using your computer with digital photography.

On the webpage www.visualsteps.com/info_downloads you can download a free guide: **A Short Guide to Digital Photo Editing**. This useful guide gives you background information about photo editing, digital cameras and scanners. You do not necessarily need a digital camera for this interesting hobby, by the way. A scanner or a photo CD-ROM is enough. The free booklet is in PDF format. You can open this file and print it by using the free program *Adobe Reader*.

Free Short Guide to Digital Photo Editing - see www.visualsteps.com/info_downloads

Photo editing programs and the Internet
Photo editing programs are increasingly becoming specialized for Internet applications. Photos can be optimized for use on the Internet. Even with digital photos, the size, file type and color may have to be adjusted for the specific requirements of the Internet. Modern photo editing programs offer a variety of tools for making these kinds of technical modifications.

Easy photo editing and organizing in ArcSoft PhotoStudio

With the help of one of these programs you, too, can place your photos or photo albums on the Internet and share them with others. You can make a family album, for example, that is immediately accessible to anyone in your family around the world.

Some photo printing centers offer web space where you can put your photos online. Your photos are immediately available to family members all over the world. One useful option is that other people can order prints of your photos (if you specify that). This is often a paid service.

Pixels

Computer images (drawings or photos) are made out of dots. These dots are called *pixels*. If you zoom in on one of these photos, you will see a grid of colored dots. In computer terminology, this grid is called a *bitmap*:

Each pixel can have a different color. The more colors that are used, the more information that can be stored in the photo. This is called the *color depth*. The more information that has to be saved, the larger the file. The standard files are called *bitmap files* and are denoted by the file extension *.bmp*.

The quality of a photo depends upon the number of pixels it contains. If the photo contains a lot of pixels, it will be sharp. As the number of pixels decreases, the photo becomes fuzzier. In addition, the quality is affected by the number of colors used. The more colors, the more realistic the photo. At present, 16 million colors are the standard on a normal PC. For professional photos much larger numbers are used.

Color Depth	Number of Colors Possible	File Size BMP
1-bit	2 colors	59 KB
4-bit	16 colors	235 KB
8-bit	256 colors	470 KB
24-bit	millions of colors	1407 KB

BMP files with sizes like this are impractical for use on the Internet. They are too big and take far too long to load. This is why two file types have been developed that give good results, but still maintain a reasonable file size.

The first file type, *GIF,* is often used for colorful images like drawings. GIF files have the extension *.gif*. A photo with 256 colors and a file size of 470 KB in the BMP format needs only 3 KB when converted to GIF format.

The other file type, *JPEG*, is mainly used for photos and is recognizable by the extension *.jpg*.

Copyright
By copyright, we mean the rights of the creator of an original work. That work might be a book, an article, a composition, a painting or a CD recording. Someone who has created one of these things is entitled to call it his or her "intellectual property". It is obvious that this person also has the right to a reasonable compensation. That is why the law forbids copying another person's "intellectual property". The symbol © is often used to indicate that a work is protected by copyright. Even if there is no © symbol, the work may not be copied without permission.

This law clearly extends to the Internet. A good rule of thumb is to assume that nothing may be copied unless clearly stated otherwise, and under what conditions. The Internet contains countless websites offering all kinds of material for free: images, photos, sounds, midi files (music), text, computer programs or complete music CDs.

On these websites, copying is permitted or even encouraged, sometimes on the condition that the source is identified – for example, if you copy a photo to put on your own website.

Sometimes website owners solicit material for which they do not own the copyright. In this case, both the offering and the copying are illegal activities strongly contested by the rightful copyright holders.

Making your own website
Most *Internet Service Providers* allow you to put your own website on the Internet. They give you a certain amount of space (in MB) on their hard drive for this. Creating webpages is not all that terribly difficult, particularly if you use a special program. This kind of program is called a *web editor*.

Creating webpages is a lot like creating any kind of text: you write the text, add images and then add hyperlinks to your text. When your website is ready, you send the pages to your ISP's server. Your ISP gives you the web address where everyone can find your website.

The Internet keyboard

In recent years, the computer has been increasingly adapted for use with the Internet. One important component of this is the keyboard.

This keyboard has special Internet related buttons, which make it a snap to start your Internet browser, begin a search, go to your *Favorites* or open your e-mail.

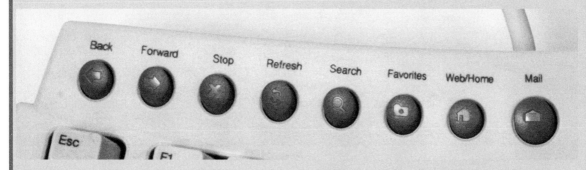

Here you see buttons for browsing forward and back, refreshing a page, searching on the Internet and opening your favorites. There is also a button for opening your home page. Another button opens your e-mail program.

4.18 Tips

 Tip

Zooming in
If you want to view the pixels in a photo in *Paint*, you will need to zoom in:

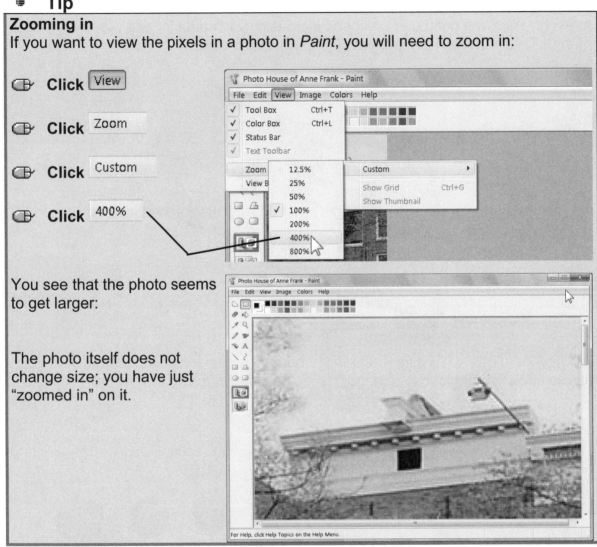

Click View

Click Zoom

Click Custom

Click 400%

You see that the photo seems to get larger:

The photo itself does not change size; you have just "zoomed in" on it.

 Tip

Want to know more?
Would you like to know more about the program *WordPad*, for example: how to edit and format text?
You can read about that in the book *Windows Vista for Seniors*.
Have a look at **www.visualsteps.com/vista**

5. E-mail, Your Electronic Mail

One of the most widely used Internet applications is electronic mail, or e-mail. E-mail uses no pen, paper, envelope or stamp. You type your message into the computer and it is sent via the Internet.

If you have an Internet service subscription, you will automatically be assigned an *e-mail address*. This e-mail address can be used to send and receive mail. Your *Internet Service Provider* (ISP) has a kind of post office, also called a *mail server*. Like with regular mail, this electronic post office handles all the daily mail traffic.

In order to send an e-mail to someone, the addressee must have an e-mail address of course. But it does not matter where that person lives. Sending an e-mail to someone in Australia takes the same amount of time and money as sending an e-mail to your next-door neighbor. There are no direct costs to you for sending an e-mail other than your Internet service subscription. There is also no limit on the number of messages you may send or receive.

E-mail is used a great deal by people who work with computers. It is fast: the message usually arrives at its destination within 60 seconds.

Windows Vista has a simple program, *Windows Mail*, that you can use to simply and quickly send and receive electronic "letters". You will be using this program in this chapter.

In this chapter, you will learn how to:

- open *Windows Mail*
- create an e-mail message
- send and receive e-mail
- read e-mail

 Please note:

In order to work through this chapter, you need to have an e-mail address, and your e-mail program must be properly installed. If this is not the case, contact your ISP for help. You also need the user name and password provided by your ISP.

5.1 Opening Windows Mail

Windows Vista has a program that you can use to send and receive electronic mail. It is called *Windows Mail.* Here is how you open the program *Windows Mail*:

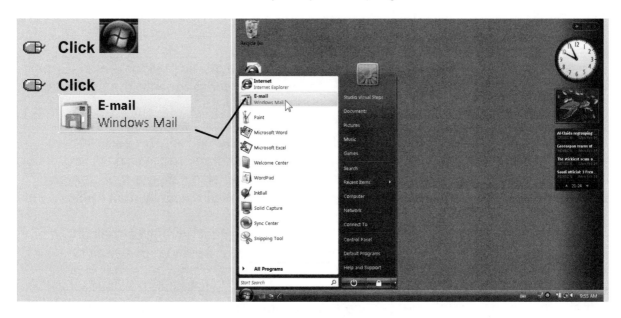

Windows Mail will immediately determine whether you are connected to the internet (*online*). If you are *offline*, you see a small window like below. You might want to work offline if you want to reduce the amount of time you spend online, either because your *Internet Service Provider* (ISP) charges you by the hour, or because you have only one phone line and you are not using a broadband connection.

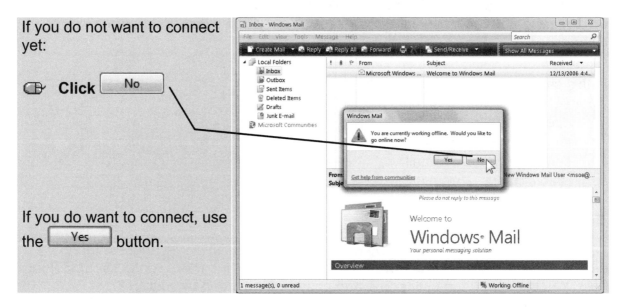

If you are using *Windows Mail* for the first time and you are online, you will see a window like this:

Type your user name ⎯

Type your password ⎯

The user name and password are provided by your ISP (*Internet Service Provider*).

☞ **Click** [OK]

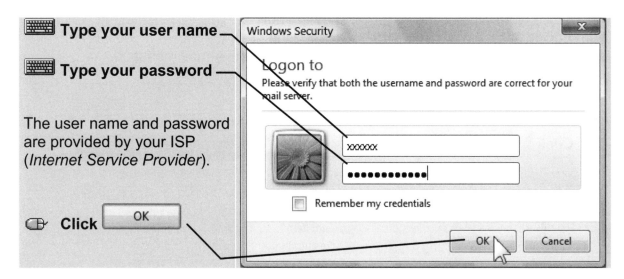

Next you will see the *Windows Mail* start-up window.

On the left there is a folder list: ⎯⎯⎯

On the right you see a message list with headers:

Here is the *Preview Pane*:

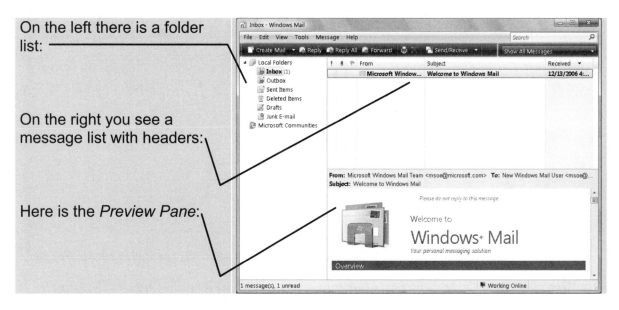

If you are the first user of *Windows Mail*, you will see a *Welcome to Windows Mail* message in the message list and *Preview Pane*.

 HELP! My window looks entirely different.

When someone else already used the program, the window may look different. This does not matter. Just continue reading.

5.2 The E-mail Address

To practice, you will be sending a message to yourself. This is an excellent way to learn how to send e-mail. Since the message is sent straight to you, you will also learn how to receive e-mail. This is how to create a new e-mail message:

At the top left of the window:

☞ **Click**

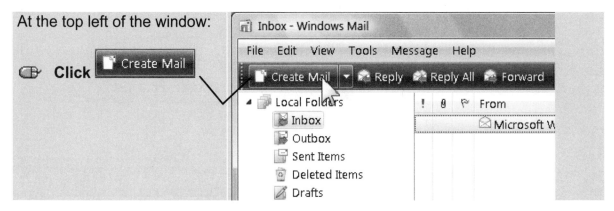

Now you see the window *New Message* on top of the program window:

In this window you can create a new e-mail message:

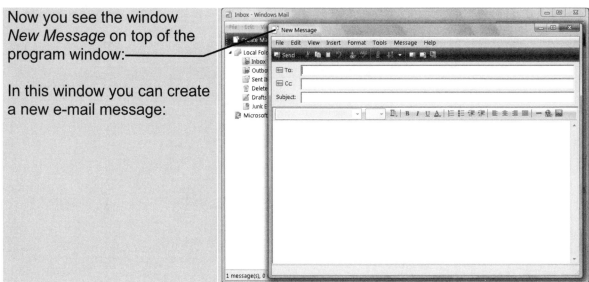

The first thing to do is to address your message using an e-mail address. Every e-mail address consists of a number of words, with the familiar symbol @ somewhere in the middle. For example:

name@provider.com

The name of the addressee is located in front of the @. Behind it, the address usually contains the name of the *Internet Service Provider* from which you received the e-mail address.

Please note:

> **E-mail addresses may not contain spaces.**
> This is why names or words are sometimes separated by a dot (**.**). These dots are extremely important. If you forget one in the address, your message will never arrive. Your mailman may understand what the sender means if the address is not completely correct. But a computer does not.

5.3 Creating an E-mail Message

The best way to test that your electronic mail works as it should is to send an e-mail message.

In the line marked
To: **type your own e-mail address**

Every e-mail is also given a subject:

Click in the box next to Subject:

Type: test

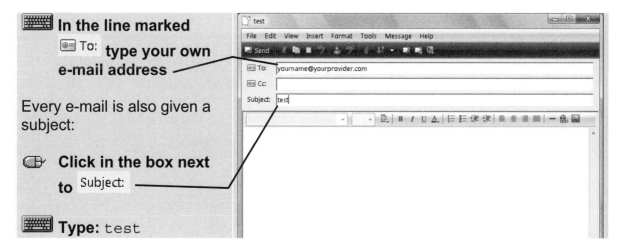

 Tip

> **Entering more e-mail addresses**
> An e-mail can be sent to multiple recipients. If you want to send your e-mail to more than one e-mail address, you must type a semicolon (;) or comma between the addresses.

Click in the main message window

You can type the message here.

Type:
This is a first
e-mail as a test.

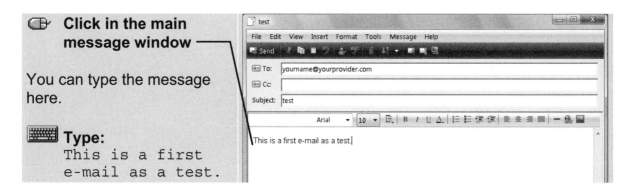

Writing a message in this window works just the same way as a text-editing program such as *WordPad*. To change font type, size, style, and to add effects such as color, use the *formatting bar* 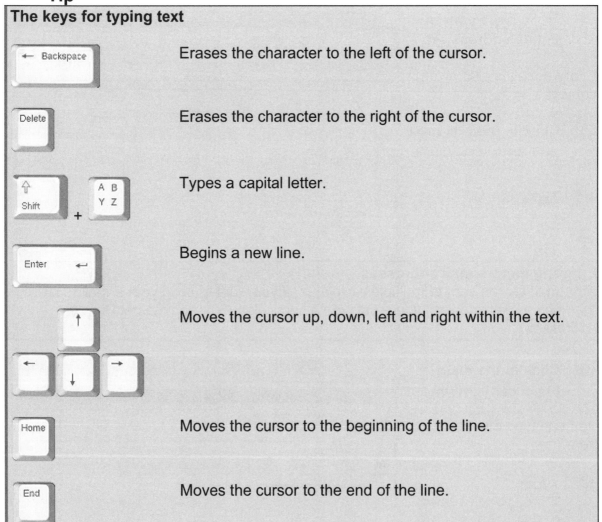 just like in *WordPad*.

 Tip

Would you like to know more?
Would you like to know more about typing and formatting text in *Windows*? Then read the Visual Steps book *Windows Vista for Seniors*. See **www.visualsteps.com/vista** for more information.

The most important keys for editing and correcting text are shown below.

 Tip

The keys for typing text

Backspace — Erases the character to the left of the cursor.

Delete — Erases the character to the right of the cursor.

Shift + — Types a capital letter.

Enter — Begins a new line.

— Moves the cursor up, down, left and right within the text.

Home — Moves the cursor to the beginning of the line.

End — Moves the cursor to the end of the line.

5.4 Sending E-mail

When you have finished the e-mail, you can send it.

At the top left of the window:

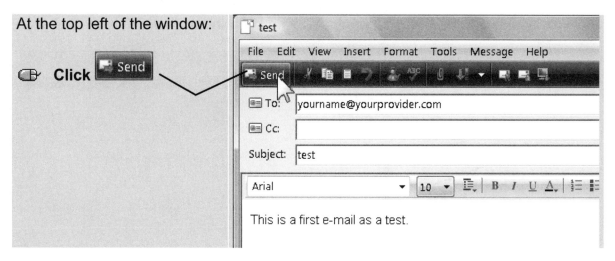

☞ **Click** ⊞ Send

When you work offline, the program reminds you that the message is placed in the *Outbox* first:

☞ **Click** OK

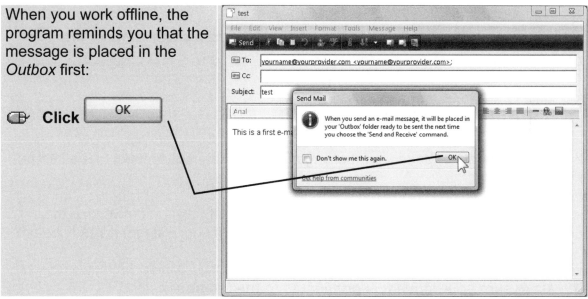

 HELP! No reminder.

If you do not see the reminder about the *Outbox* on your screen then you are probably using a broadband connection, for example a DSL line. This means that *Windows Mail* has a different setting and your e-mail is mailed immediately. If this is the case, skip the following section and continue at **5.7 Reading an E-mail.**

5.5 The Outbox

When you work offline, all of the e-mails you write are collected in the *Outbox* first. Your message will not be sent until you connect to the Internet. This means that you can write as many e-mails as you want, and then send them all at one time.

Now you see the *Windows Mail* window again.

There is one message in the 📤 **Outbox** (1):

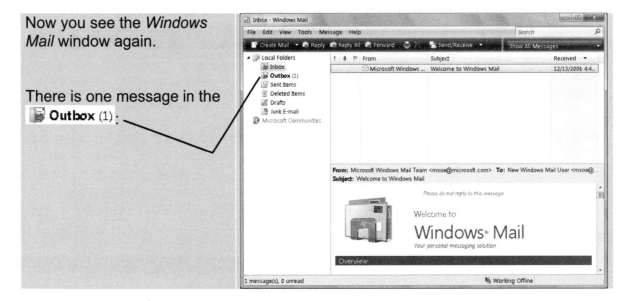

5.6 Sending and Receiving

Now you can manually send your message. The program will connect to the Internet to send it.

Sending and receiving manually is useful if you are using dial-up networking to connect to the Internet. In that case, be sure to check if your modem is ready before you try to connect.

☞ **Make sure your modem is connected to the telephone line**

Do you have an external modem?
☞ **If so, turn the modem on**

Do you have an internal modem?
☞ **Then you do not need to do anything**

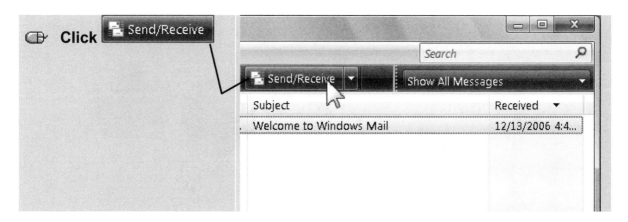

When you work offline, *Windows Mail* will tell you that you are still offline and asks whether you want to go online.

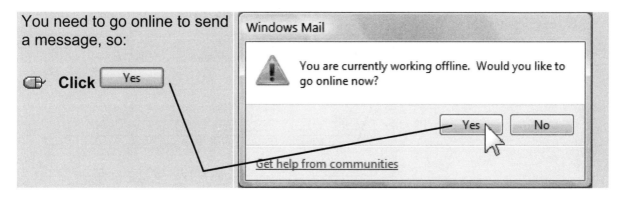

If you are using dial-up networking to connect to the Internet, you will see a *Dial-up Connection* window. It probably looks like this one:

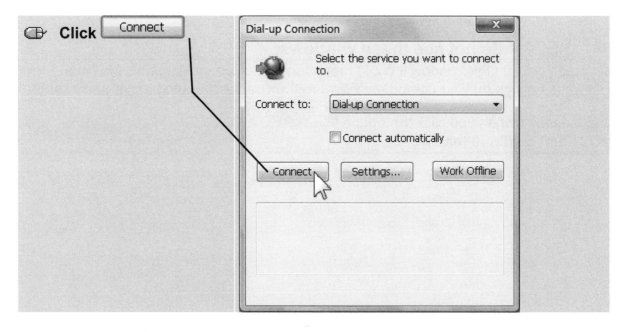

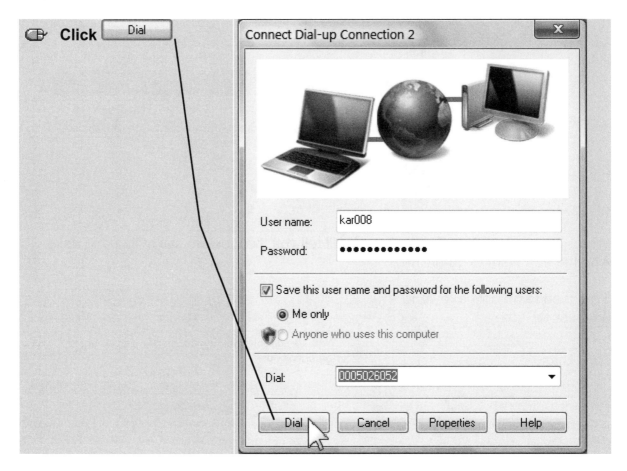

☞ **Click** [Dial]

A connection is made to your ISP (*Internet Service Provider*). Next your e-mail message is sent. The program also automatically checks to see if you have any new e-mail messages.

 HELP! I do not see these windows.

If you do not see this window it could mean that the program *Windows Mail* has different settings on your computer. Your program connects automatically and sends

the message when you click the button .

☞ **Just continue reading**

You can follow this process as it proceeds in a window like this:

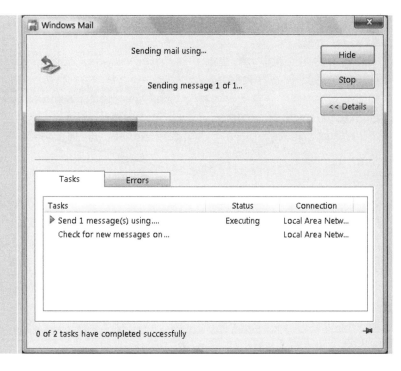

If everything went as it should, your test message was immediately sent to you. Then it is put in the *Inbox*.

5.7 Reading an E-mail

All e-mail messages you receive are placed in a separate folder called the *Inbox*.

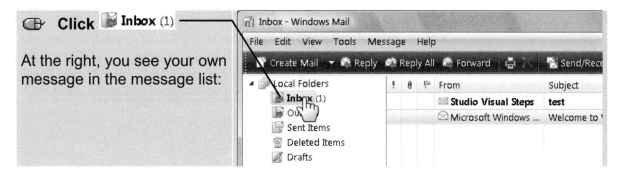

At the right, you see your own message in the message list:

 HELP! I do not have any mail.

Is there no message in your *Inbox*?
Perhaps it has not yet been received. Try again later to receive the message:

Click Send/Receive

You can open the message in a new window and then read it:

In the message list you see the header of your message:

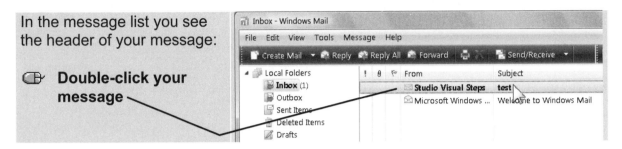

 Double-click your message

💡 Tip

Are you having trouble double-clicking?
You can also use the following trick:

 Click the message

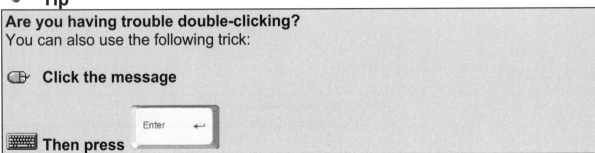

⌨ **Then press**

💡 Tip

A better view
You can best read an e-mail if you temporarily maximize its window:

In the top right corner:

 Click 🗖

You see how much easier it is to read your e-mail message when the window is fully maximized.

Now go ahead and close this window:

 Click ❌

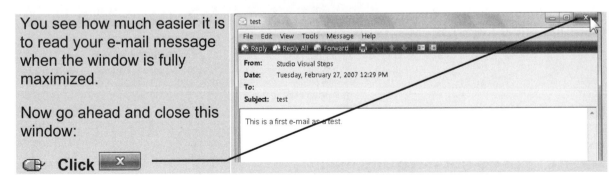

5.8 The Folders

Windows Mail has a sophisticated system of folders for organizing your e-mail messages. In addition to the *Inbox* and the *Outbox*, there are three other folders. *Windows Mail* saves all the e-mail messages you have sent in a separate folder called *Sent Items*.
You can delete messages you do not want to keep. These will be stored in the folder *Deleted Items*.
Last but not least, there is a folder for messages that are not yet finished. These are placed in the folder *Drafts*.

The 🗒 Sent Items folder contains copies of the e-mails you have sent:

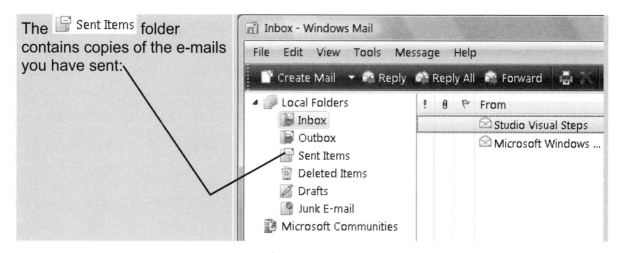

The message you just sent to yourself should be in there.

👉 **Click** 🗒 Sent Items

Your first e-mail is indeed in this folder:

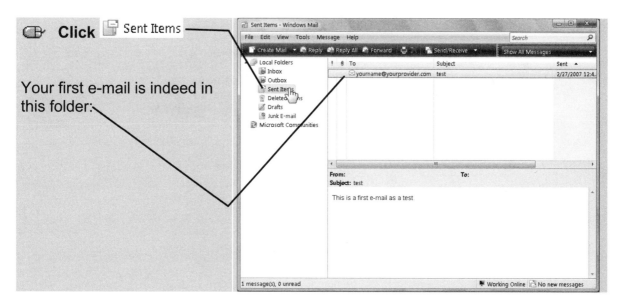

You can delete this e-mail message now.

5.9 Deleting E-mail Messages

Many people use the folders *Inbox* and *Sent Items* as a kind of archive. All of your correspondence is stored neatly, and you can easily retrieve your e-mail messages. There is no limit on the number of e-mail messages you can store.
In practice however, you will want to regularly delete unnecessary messages to keep your folders from becoming too cluttered. You can delete the test message now.

Before you can delete an e-mail, you have to select it:

Click the e-mail message

The message is now light blue, indicating that it is selected:

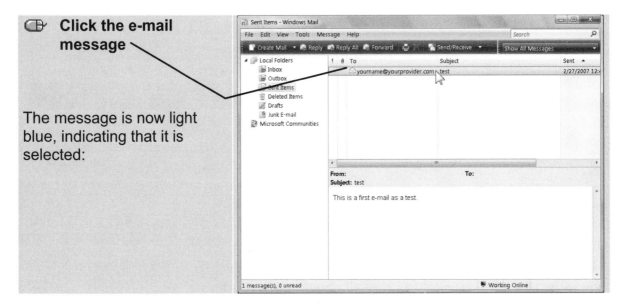

Now you can tell *Windows Mail* to delete the message.

Click

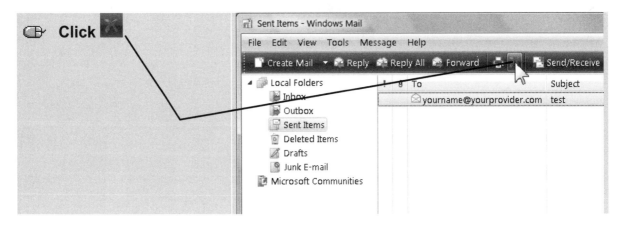

The folder Sent Items is now empty:

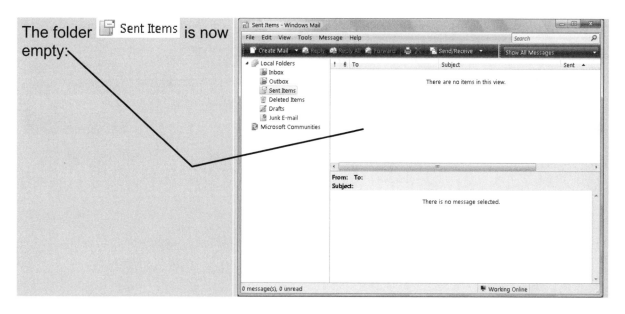

A message that you have deleted in this manner, is not actually gone forever. *Windows Mail* saves all the e-mail messages you have deleted in a separate folder called *Deleted Items*. This is actually a safety feature. You can retrieve a message out of this folder if you put it there by mistake. In the next step you will learn how to permanently delete the message.

Click Deleted Items

Now you see your test mail here:

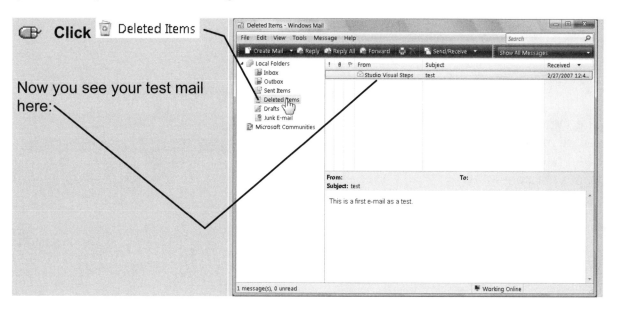

When you are ready to permanently delete the e-mails you have thrown away, you can empty the 🗑 Deleted Items folder. This is how you do that:

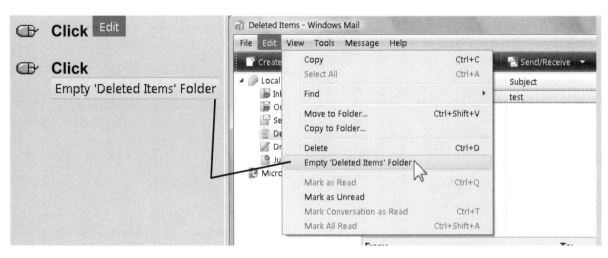

Click Edit

Click

    Empty 'Deleted Items' Folder

Windows Mail asks you to confirm, just to be sure:

Click Yes

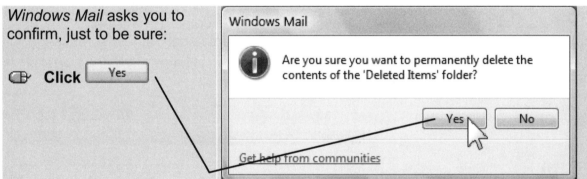

The folder is now empty. The e-mail messages have now been permanently removed from your computer:

5.10 A Second Test Message

In order to practice receiving, answering and forwarding e-mails, you can send a test message to a special e-mail address. You will get an automated e-mail reply back. First you create a new e-mail.

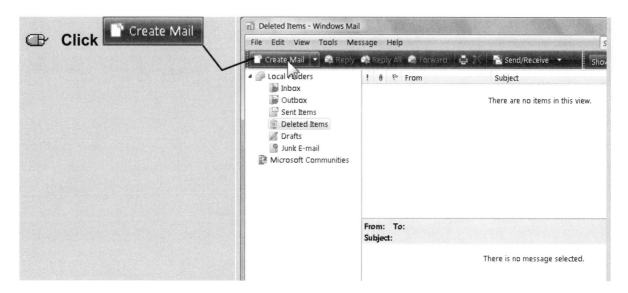

The e-mail address for the test message is: **test@visualsteps.com**

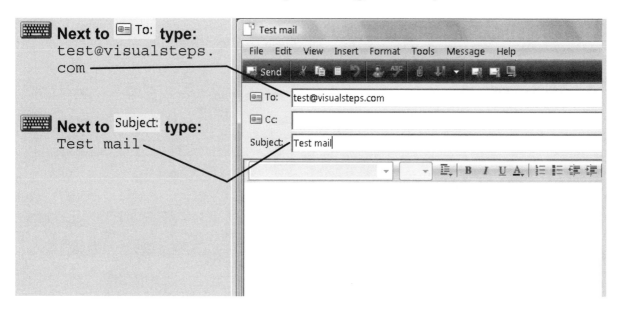

The test message is ready. You are not going to send this message immediately. Instead, you are going to save it in the Drafts folder first.

5.11 The Drafts Folder

Sometimes you do not want to send a message immediately, perhaps because you want to think about the content a little longer. In that case, you can save the e-mail in the ✎ Drafts folder.

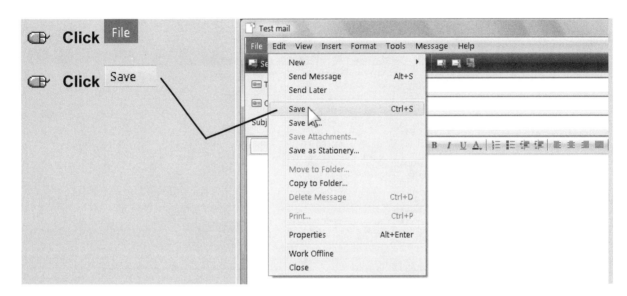

Click File

Click Save

Windows Mail tells you the e-mail has been saved in ✎ Drafts:

Click OK

Now you can close the window containing the e-mail.

Click X

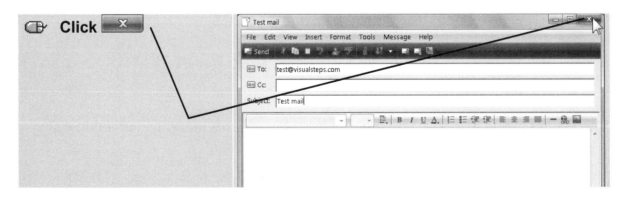

The letters in the word
Drafts (1) are in bold, and
the number 1 is displayed.
That means there is one
message in the folder:

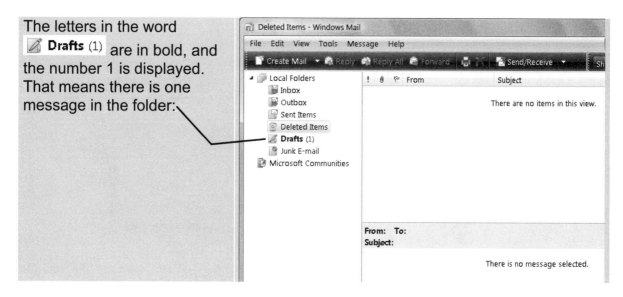

You can leave the message in this folder even if you close *Windows Mail.* Later on,
you can simply open this message again and continue working on it:

Click *Drafts* (1)

Double-click the message

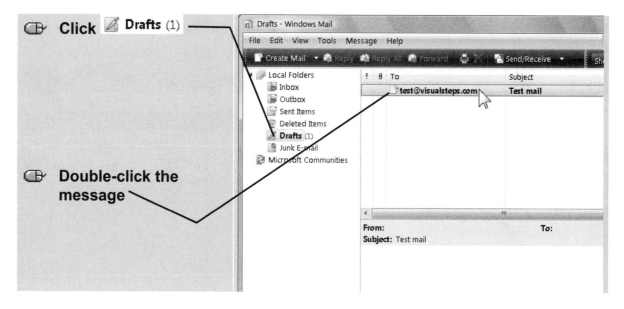

The message is opened. Now you can send it:

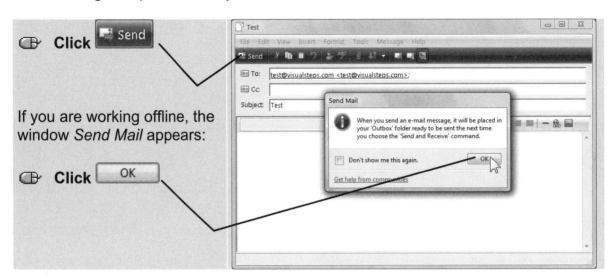

☞ **Click** 📨 Send

If you are working offline, the window *Send Mail* appears:

☞ **Click** OK

If you are using a broadband connection like DSL or cable, you are continuously online and your message is sent immediately. If you are working offline, or if your *Windows Mail* settings have been set up to do so, your message has been placed in the *Outbox*.

You can see this by the bold letters and the number at the end 📨**Outbox** (1) :

You can send your test e-mail.

☞ **Click** 📨 Send/Receive

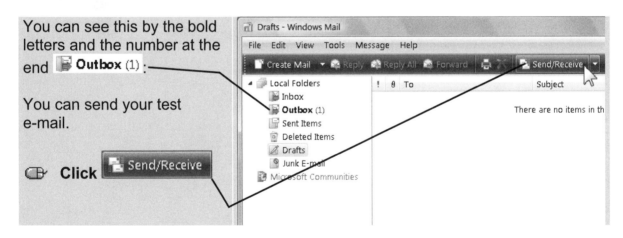

👉 **If necessary, connect to the Internet** 👣³

Your message is sent, and *Windows Mail* checks if you have received any mail.

➡ **Please note:**

It might take a little while before you receive a reply to your test mail.
Wait about fifteen minutes and try again:

☞ **Click**  Send/Receive

HELP! I see a message about junk mail.

Do you see this window?

⊕ **Click** [Close]

This message means that the response to your test mail has been moved to the folder 🔒 Junk E-mail. *Windows Mail* automatically identifies what looks like unsolicited commercial e-mail messages and moves them to this folder.

You can open the folder *Junk E-mail*:

⊕ **Click** 🔒 **Junk E-mail** (1)

The folder is opened and you see the message:

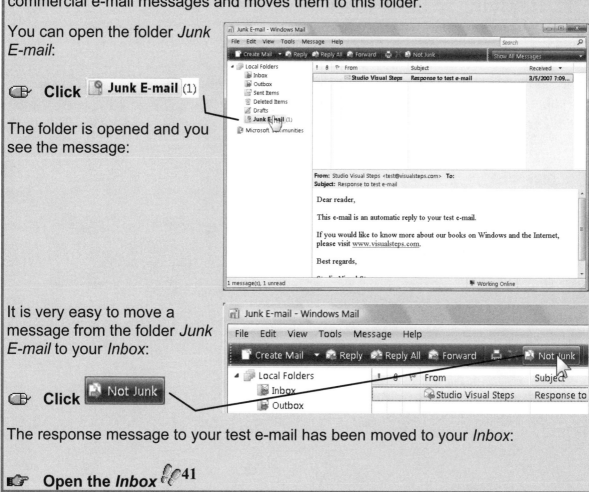

It is very easy to move a message from the folder *Junk E-mail* to your *Inbox*:

⊕ **Click** [📄 Not Junk]

The response message to your test e-mail has been moved to your *Inbox*:

☞ **Open the *Inbox*** 🦶⁴¹

Please note:

Windows Mail unfortunately does not see the difference at times between a harmless test e-mail and unwanted commercial e-mail (also called *spam*). E-mail from your friends or family could also end up in the folder Junk E-mail.

Check this folder regularly to make sure you do not miss any e-mails that you do want to receive!

💡 **Tip**

Read more about the Junk Mail Filter
In Chapter 9 you can read more about the *Junk Mail Filter* and how to customize the settings for this filter.

5.12 Replying to an E-mail

Is the response message to your test mail in your *Inbox*?

Then you see a message with the subject *Response to test e-mail:*

☞ **Click the e-mail message**

In the *Preview Pane*, you see the text of the message:

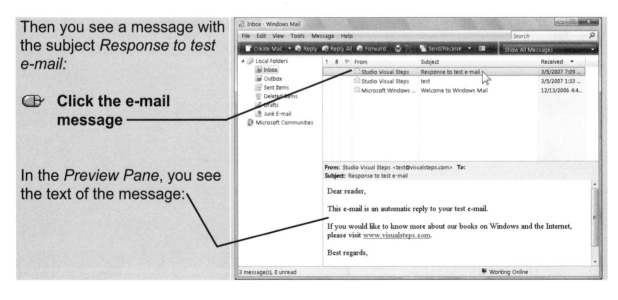

If you have received an e-mail, you do not have to type in the e-mail address again in order to reply to it. *Windows Mail* has various buttons for replying to this e-mail. There is a toolbar for this, containing the following buttons:

Reply	**Reply** Reply to sender, the "to" portion already contains the correct e-mail address.
Reply All	**Reply All** An e-mail message can be sent to more than one person. This button is used to send a reply to everyone to whom the original e-mail was addressed. The original e-mail message is included.
Forward	**Forward** A new e-mail is made from the original message that can be sent to someone else. The original e-mail message is included.

In most cases, you will just want to reply to a message. Give it a try:

In the top left corner:

☞ **Click** Reply

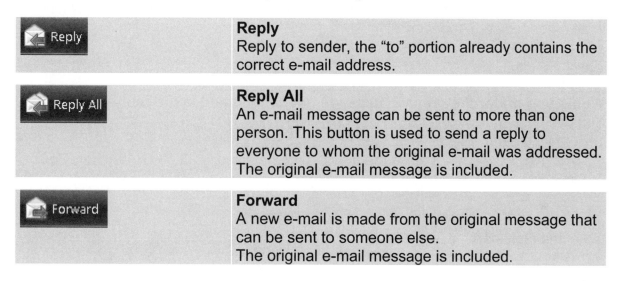

Now you see this window:

The e-mail address has already been entered in the right place:

The subject has been copied with *Re:* at the beginning of it. That stands for *Regarding*:

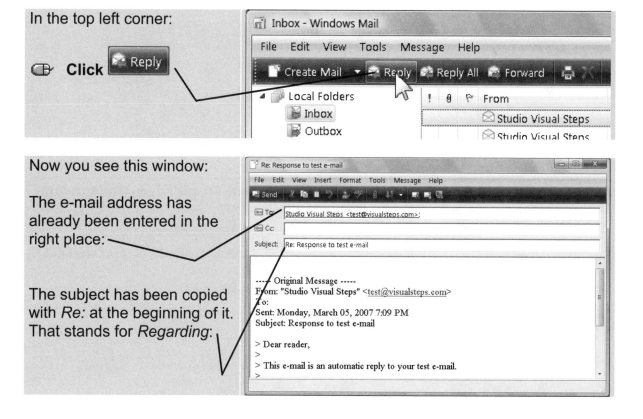

The text of the original message is automatically included in the reply message. You can see it under *-----Original Message-----*.
This is very useful: the person to whom you are replying can immediately see what the message was about. On the other hand, the message just gets longer and longer in an extended correspondence.

  Tip

Would you prefer the original message not be included in the reply?
You can prevent its inclusion by:
- creating a new message instead of using the *Reply* button
- setting up *Windows Mail* differently; see the next section **5.13 Optimizing Your Windows Mail Settings**

You can type your reply at the top of the message:

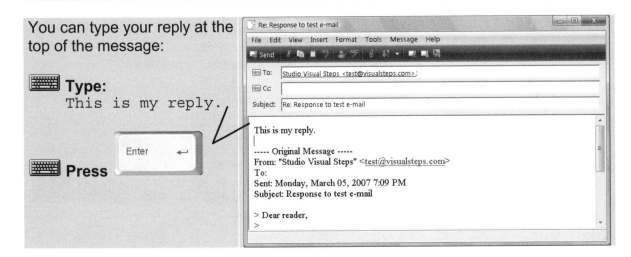

Type:
   This is my reply.

Press Enter ↵

➡️ **Please note:**

You will only get one reply a week to e-mail you send to test@visualsteps.com.
The reply message is automatically sent by our ISP's computer. The limitation to one message per week has been made so that two computers do not become overwhelmed sending automated messages back and forth.

Now you can send this message, but you will not get a reply to it.

☞ **Send the message to the *Outbox*** 🦶³⁷

If you are working offline:

☞ **Send and receive your e-mail** 🦶³⁹

☞ **If necessary, connect to the Internet** 🦶³

5.13 Optimizing Your Windows Mail Settings

You can adjust various things in *Windows Mail* such as:

- your mail delivery
- the way in which your e-mail messages are sent
- your e-mail account information

5.14 Mail Delivery

Windows Mail can be set up in one of two ways:

- Automatic connection - It connects automatically to the Internet and sends and receives mail when it opens.
- Manual connection - It does <u>not</u> connect automatically to the Internet. You must manually give the command to send and receive.

It is a matter of personal preference which setting you decide to use.

You can adjust the settings as follows:

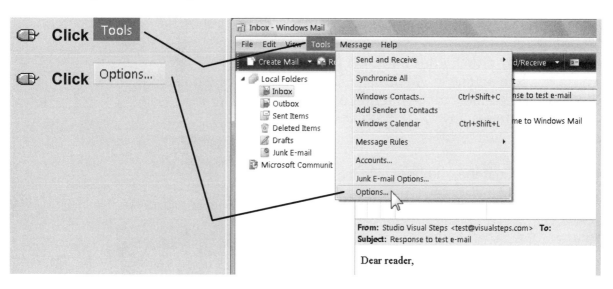

Click `Tools`

Click `Options...`

Now you see this window with a large number of settings:

See if the box beside

☑ Send and receive messages at startup

has been checked:

Do you want to send and receive mail immediately at startup?

 Make sure this box is checked

If you do <u>not</u> want to automatically connect to the Internet when it opens:

 Make sure this box is not checked

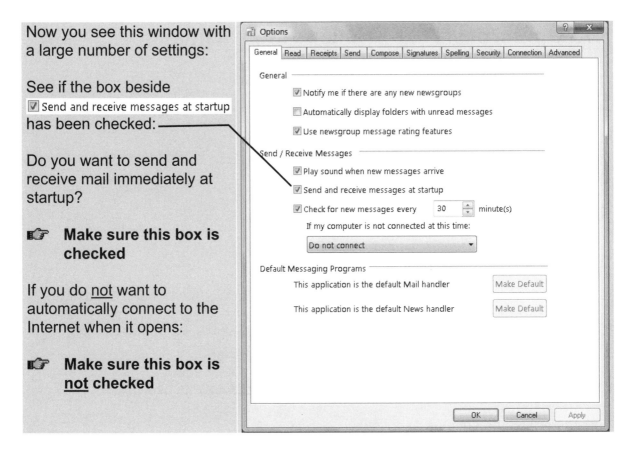

💡 **Tip**

Automatically check your e-mail
There is also a setting in *Windows Mail* to determine **how often** you want to automatically connect to the Internet and check your e-mail.

You can turn this on by checking this box:

Here you can set the number of minutes:

Here you can specify what should happen if you are not already connected:

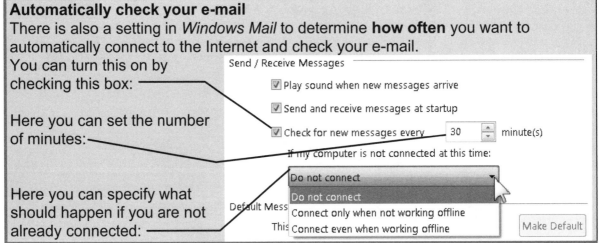

5.15 Send Options

Windows Mail has several settings for answering your e-mail. You can view these as follows:

 Click the tab Send

You see several check boxes:

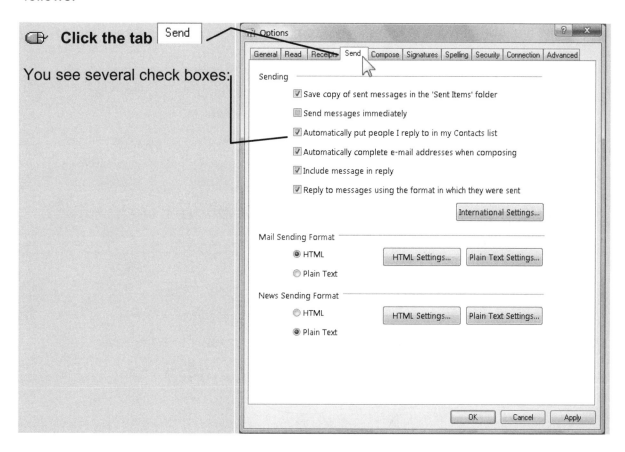

Not all these settings are equally important; they are often a matter of personal preference. For that reason, we are only going to discuss the most important ones here:

- sending your mail immediately, instead of putting it in the *Outbox* first
- not including the original message in your replies

You can try out all the other options if you would like. These kinds of changes are easy to undo.

5.16 No Outbox

You can choose not to use the *Outbox*. When you have written an e-mail message and you click the *Send* button, you will connect automatically to the Internet. This does however, have a slight disadvantage. You can not write all your e-mail messages first and then send them all at the same time.

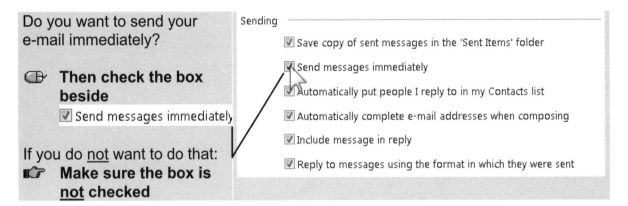

Do you want to send your
e-mail immediately?

☞ **Then check the box
beside**

☑ Send messages immediately

If you do <u>not</u> want to do that:
☞ **Make sure the box is
<u>not</u> checked**

5.17 Your Reply

You can choose to include the original message in your reply to an e-mail.

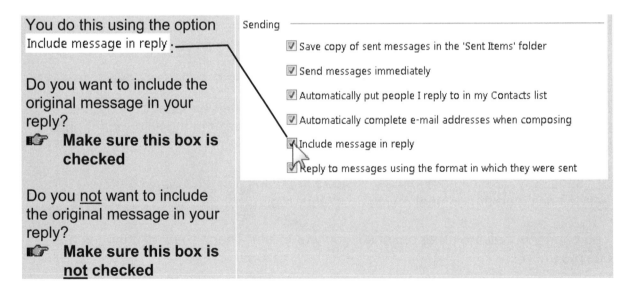

You do this using the option
Include message in reply :

Do you want to include the
original message in your
reply?
☞ **Make sure this box is
checked**

Do you <u>not</u> want to include
the original message in your
reply?
☞ **Make sure this box is
<u>not</u> checked**

If you do not check this box, you will begin with an empty message and the original message will not be shown.

You can save the settings
and then close the window.

Click OK

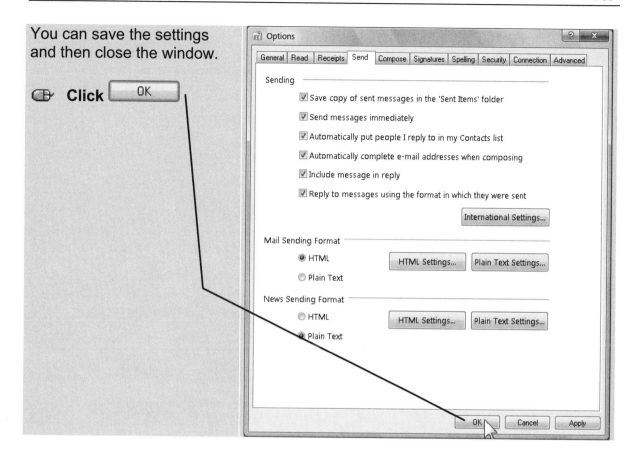

5.18 Checking Your E-mail Account

By *e-mail account*, we mean your mailbox at your ISP. It is a good idea to check the settings of your e-mail account information from time to time.
Here is how you do it:

Click Tools

Click Accounts...

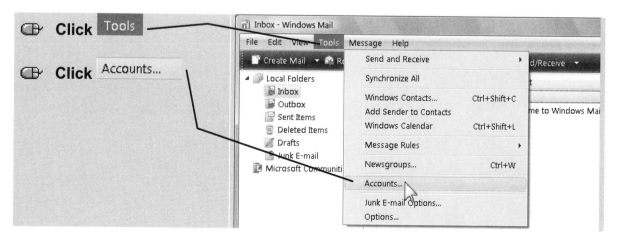

You see this window with the
name(s) of your e-mail
account(s):

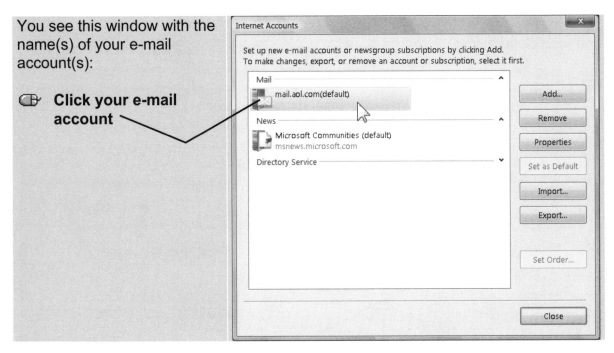

☞ **Click your e-mail**
   account

☞ **Click** Properties

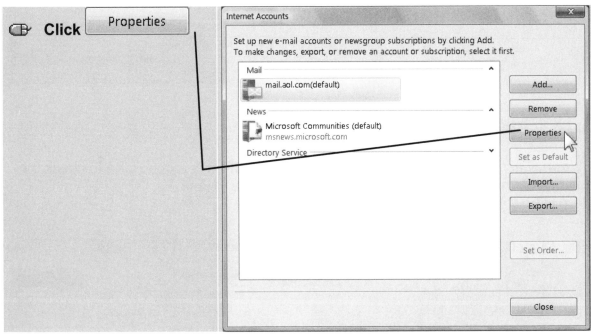

5.19 Checking Your Name

When you were setting up your e-mail account, you probably entered a name. That name is used as the name of the sender for each e-mail you send. You might want to change or edit this name. You can do that in the window below:

☞ Check your name

If you are not satisfied, you can change the name.

If you have multiple e-mail addresses, you can also use one of these other addresses as your reply e-mail address. You can use this box:

☞ Click   OK

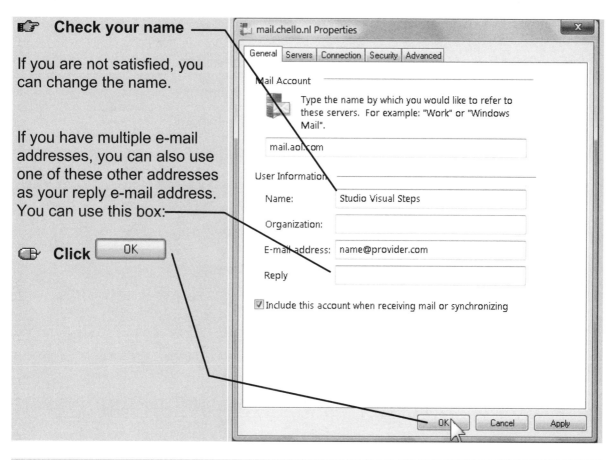

☞ Close the *Internet Accounts* window *32

☞ Close *Windows Mail* *43

In the following exercises, you can practice sending and receiving e-mails.

5.20 Exercises

Have you forgotten how to perform a particular action? Use the number beside the footsteps to look it up in the appendix *How Do I Do That Again?*

Exercise: Creating an E-mail

In this exercise, you are going to write a new e-mail message.

✔   Open *Windows Mail*. 𝓁𝓁 35

✔   Create a new e-mail message addressed to yourself. 𝓁𝓁 36

✔   Send it. 𝓁𝓁 37

✔   Check if your e-mail is in the *Outbox*. 𝓁𝓁 38

✔   Send and receive your e-mail. 𝓁𝓁 39

✔   Check if you have received e-mail in the *Inbox*. 𝓁𝓁 41

✔   Read your e-mail message. 𝓁𝓁 42

✔   Close *Windows Mail*. 𝓁𝓁 43

Exercise: Do You Have Mail?

In this exercise, you are just going to check if you have any new e-mail messages.

✔   Open *Windows Mail*. 𝓁𝓁 35

✔   Send and receive your e-mail. 𝓁𝓁 39

✔   Check if you have received e-mail in the *Inbox*. 𝓁𝓁 41

✔   Close *Windows Mail*. 𝓁𝓁 43

Exercise: Deleting an E-mail

✓ Open *Windows Mail.* 🐾35

✓ Send and receive your e-mail. 🐾39

✓ Look in the *Inbox.* 🐾41

✓ Delete your test e-mail. 🐾44

✓ Close *Windows Mail.* 🐾43

Exercise: E-mail in the Drafts Folder

✓ Open *Windows Mail.* 🐾35

✓ Create a new e-mail message addressed to yourself. 🐾36

✓ Save it. 🐾45

✓ Close the window containing the new e-mail. 🐾32

✓ Check if your e-mail is in the *Drafts* folder. 🐾46

✓ Delete your new e-mail. 🐾44

✓ Close *Windows Mail.* 🐾43

5.21 Background Information

Glossary	
Deleted Items	Deleted e-mails are moved to the *Deleted Items* folder. To permanently remove a deleted item from your computer: delete the message in the *Deleted Items* folder.
Drafts	An e-mail that you write and save instead of sending it right away, is placed in the *Drafts* folder.
DSL	A type of high-speed Internet connection using existing copper telephone wires. Also referred to as a broadband connection.
E-mail	Short for electronic mail. Messages sent via the Internet.
E-mail account	The server name, user name, password, and e-mail address used by *Windows Mail* to connect to an e-mail service. You create the e-mail account in *Windows Vista* by using information provided by your *Internet Service Provider* (ISP).
E-mail header	Information included at the top of an e-mail message: name of the sender and recipient, subject, date, and other information.
Inbox	The *Inbox* is where all of the e-mail messages that you receive are placed.
ISP	*Internet Service Provider* - A company that provides Internet access. An ISP provides a telephone number, a user name, a password, and other connection information so that users can access the Internet through the ISP's computers.
Junk e-mail	Unsolicited commercial e-mail, also known as spam.
Junk E-mail Folder	*Windows Mail* filters obvious unsolicited commercial e-mail messages and moves them to a special folder called *Junk E-mail*.
Message list	List of messages in various folders in *Windows Mail*.
Outbox	When you manually send e-mail and you finish writing a message and click the *Send* button, the message will be placed in your *Outbox* folder. Messages in the *Outbox* folder will be sent when you click the *Send/Receive* button.

-Continue reading on the next page-

Preview Pane	Here you can view the message's contents without opening the message in a separate window. To view an e-mail message in the *Preview Pane*, click the message in the message list.
Sent Items	A copy of every message you send is saved in the *Sent Items* folder, just in case you need it later.
Spam	Unsolicited commercial e-mail, also known as junk e-mail.

Source: Windows Help and Support

The parts of the Windows Mail window
You can display or hide the following parts of the window.

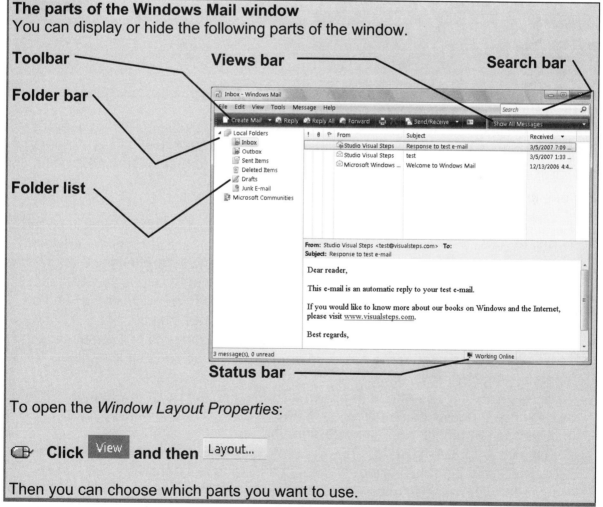

To open the *Window Layout Properties*:

Click View and then Layout...

Then you can choose which parts you want to use.

How does e-mail work?

All e-mail messages are delivered to a *mail server*. This is a computer at your ISP (*Internet Service Provider*) that is dedicated to processing electronic mail.

If you have written to someone and the e-mail has been sent, then it is transported by your ISP's mail server until – after passing through a number of intermediate stations – it reaches the mail server at the addressee's ISP and is stored there.

It works the same way in reverse. E-mail for you is saved on your ISP's mail server until you pick it up with *Windows Mail*.

Netiquette

The word *netiquette* is an abbreviation of the phrase "*Internet etiquette*". It denotes a collection of rules that people who use e-mail are advised to follow. It is particularly advisable for *newbies* (beginners on the digital highway) to take note of netiquette.

For effective communication, follow these guidelines:

- Be careful with humor and emotion. E-mail does not convey emotion well, so the recipient might not understand your intended tone. Sarcastic humor is particularly risky because the recipient might interpret it literally and take offense.
- Think before you send. Writing and sending an e-mail message is fast and easy. Make sure you have thought out your message first, and avoid writing when you are angry. Once you send the message, you can not get it back.
- Use a clear and concise subject line. Summarize the contents of the message in a few words. People who receive a large amount of e-mail can use the subject to prioritize the message.
- Keep messages short. Although an e-mail message can be of any length, e-mail is designed for quick communication. Many people do not have the time or patience to read more than a few paragraphs.
- Avoid using ALL CAPITAL LETTERS. Many people perceive sentences written in all uppercase letters as "yelling" and find it annoying or offensive.
- Be careful with sensitive or confidential information. The addressee might share his or her computer and e-mail program with other persons. Any recipient can forward your message to others—either intentionally or accidentally.

Unwelcome e-mails and spam

There are two kinds of unwelcome e-mails that you may receive.

The first are e-mails from businesses you know that are trying to sell you something. This can happen, for example, after you e-mailed them asking for information about a product or ordered something from them before. By doing that, you could have ended up on their mailing list.

The second group of e-mails seems to "fall out of nowhere" and you have no idea how such a company has gotten your e-mail address. This type of unsolicited commercial e-mail is called *spam*. There is a thriving trade in e-mail addresses, and you may have ended up on such a list. Usually, these spam e-mails offer things like cheap medication, university degrees, stock advice and "get rich quick"-schemes.

What can you do?

- If the e-mails come from a company you know, you can follow the instructions in the e-mail to unsubscribe from their mailing list. This can be done by clicking a link, or by sending an e-mail with a subject or text consisting of a particular sentence or command. This command is processed by a computer without any human intervention. There is often no other way to unsubscribe.

- But be careful: **NEVER** respond to a spam e-mail and **NEVER** click on an unsubscribe-link in such an e-mail. Also: **NEVER** order something that is offered in an spam e-mail. By doing any of these things, you confirm to the company that your e-mail address is a real address. The only result will be that you are flooded with ten times as much spam!

- If you can not stop the messages by the above method, you can think about filtering them out. Most ISPs offer spam filters that stop spam at their mail server, even before it enters you mailbox. Some ISPs allow you to change the settings for the spam filter.

- *Windows Mail* includes a *Junk E-mail Filter* that analyzes the content of messages sent to you and moves suspicious messages to the special *Junk E-mail* folder, where you can view or delete them at any time.

- Some anti-virus programs contain a spam filter. Consult the program's *Help* function to find out how to install this spam filter.

5.22 Tips

 Tip

Larger buttons
If you think the buttons in the *Windows Mail* and message windows are too small, you can enlarge them like this:

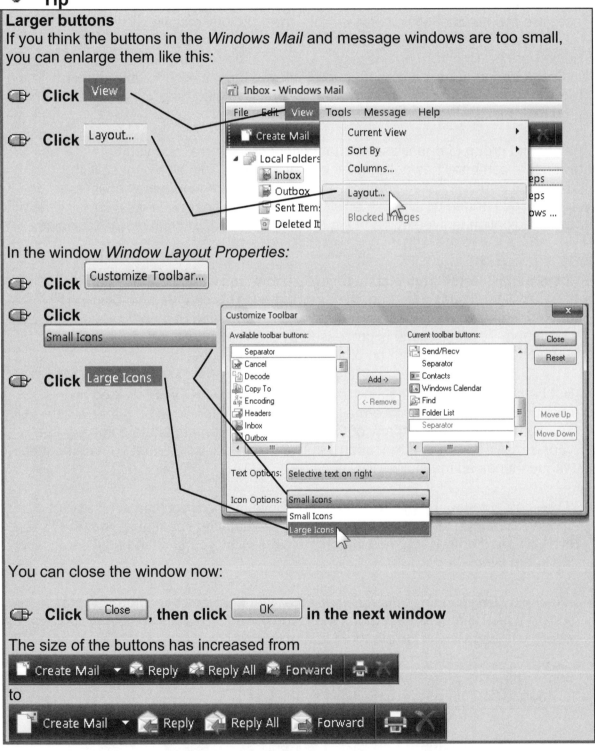

☞ **Click** View

☞ **Click** Layout...

In the window *Window Layout Properties:*

☞ **Click** Customize Toolbar...

☞ **Click**

Small Icons

☞ **Click** Large Icons

You can close the window now:

☞ **Click** Close , **then click** OK **in the next window**

The size of the buttons has increased from

to

Tip

Larger text
If you have trouble reading e-mail messages, you can increase the text size.

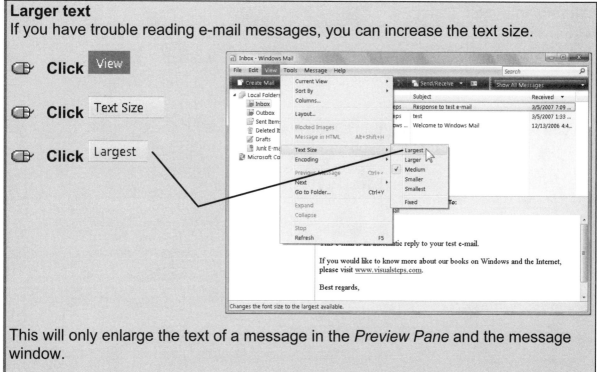

⊂⊐ **Click** View

⊂⊐ **Click** Text Size

⊂⊐ **Click** Largest

This will only enlarge the text of a message in the *Preview Pane* and the message window.

The size of the text in the e-mail headers and the folder names will not be changed.

 Tip

Tired of entering your user name and password every time?
Do you have to enter your password every time in this window? You can change the settings by doing the following:

⌨ **Type your user name**

⌨ **Type your password**

⊂⊐ **Check the box**
☑ Remember my credentials

⊂⊐ **Then click** OK

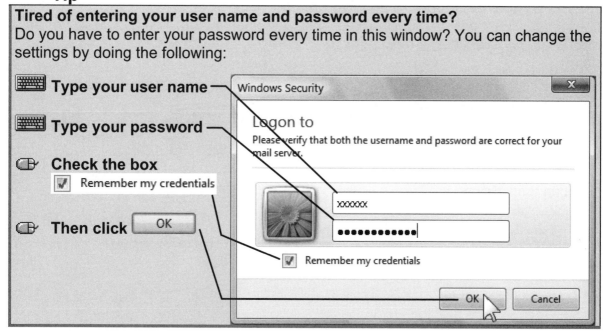

Tip

Printing an e-mail

 Use this button on the toolbar if you want to print an e-mail message.

 Tip

Do you want to avoid seeing this window again?
You see this window every time you send a new e-mail message:

☞ **Check the box**
☑ Don't show me this again.

☞ **Then click** OK

The window will not appear again.

 Tip

Do you want to send only, or receive only?
By default, all e-mails are sent and received at the same time. You can, however, tell *Windows Mail* to only send messages, or only receive messages. Here is how you do it:

☞ **Click** ▼ **next to**
🗒 Send/Receive

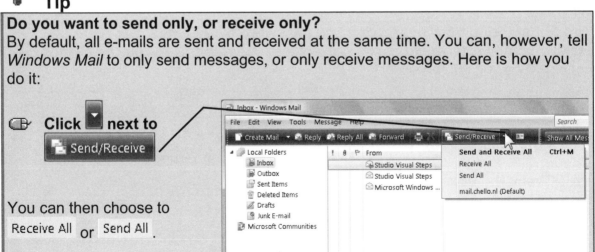

You can then choose to
Receive All or Send All .

6. Addresses, E-mails and Attachments

In the 1970s, people thought the computer would come to occupy such a central position that a paperless society would arise. All information would be read on (portable) monitors. Paper would become superfluous. In reality, things have turned out differently. In fact, more paper than ever is being used. After all, it is very easy to print out an e-mail message, and people do it quite often.

Nonetheless, the rise of the Internet has contributed to a change in communication. E-mail is slowly replacing the function of the telephone, the letter and the fax. This is in part a result of the fact that, not only short messages but all kinds of other information can be sent by e-mail, such as photographs or drawings.

The speed of communication has also increased dramatically: An e-mail can arrive within seconds. A photo can be sent in minutes. Extensive exchange of e-mails also occurs in work environments. The increase in e-mail usage has led to an increased importance of its management. The computer is being used more and more as an archive for our correspondence.

In this chapter, you will learn how to organize your e-mail messages. You will also learn how to save your e-mail addresses in your *Contacts* folder, and how to keep them organized so you can quickly retrieve them. You will learn how to send an attachment with an e-mail message. This will enable you to exchange photos with family and friends, wherever in the world they may be.

In this chapter, you will learn:

- how to use the *Contacts* folder
- how to add information and a picture to a contact
- how to add a new contact
- what happens with a bad e-mail address
- how to use a signature in your e-mails
- how to sort your e-mails
- how to search within your e-mails
- how to send, view, open and save an attachment

6.1 Opening Windows Mail

First, open the program *Windows Mail*:

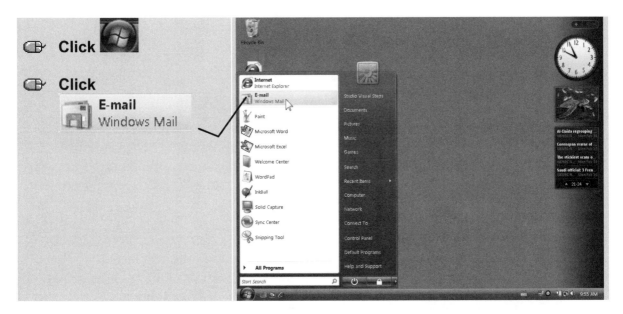

⊕ **Click**

⊕ **Click**

    E-mail
    Windows Mail

In this chapter, *Windows Mail* does not need to connect to the Internet right away. Of course, you can check your e-mail if you would like.

You see the *Windows Mail* window:

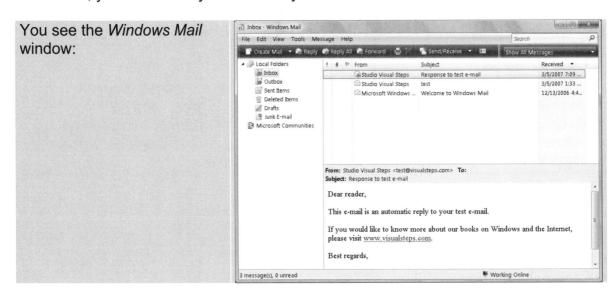

6.2 The Contacts Folder

Windows Vista contains a folder called *Contacts*. This folder is one of the folders in your *Personal* folder. The *Contacts* folder functions as the address book for *Windows Mail*. By default, *Windows Mail* saves all the e-mail addresses from e-mails you have replied to in this folder. Here is how you view the *Contacts* folder:

In the previous chapter, you replied to the test mail from test@visualsteps.com. This e-mail address should have been stored in your *Contacts* folder.

You see the *Contacts* folder window.

The folder Contacts is stored in the *Personal* folder that has your name. You see that here

Studio Visual Steps ▸ Contacts .

If everything has gone well, there should be at least one address here, the address of test@visualsteps.com:

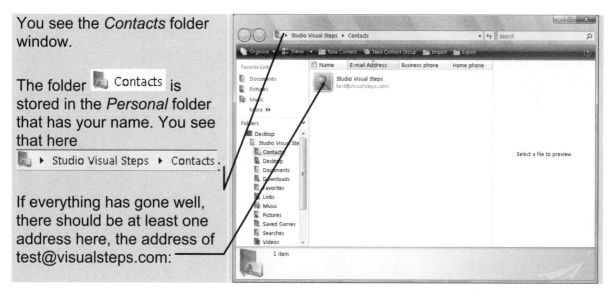

HELP! There are not any addresses.

If you do not see the address in the window above then you did not answer the e-mail in the previous chapter, or your *Windows Mail* is set up differently.
☞ **Just keep reading up to the section *6.6 Adding a New E-mail Address***

6.3 Adding Information to a Contact

Each listing in your *Contacts* folder contains at least an e-mail address. More information such as name, address or telephone number can be added.
You can open and edit the e-mail address information as follows:

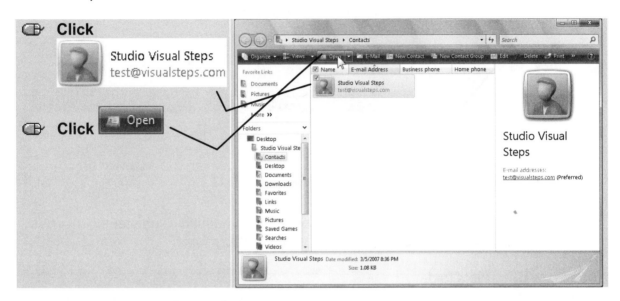

Now you see the window with the properties of this e-mail address:

The first and last names have already been filled in by the program, but they will not be right in this case. You can fix that yourself.

First erase the first name; it is already selected:

Press Delete

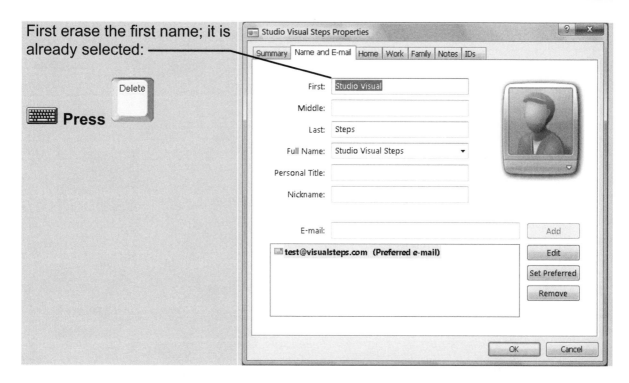

Now you can change the last name. You can move quickly to that field using a key.

Press Tab **twice**

Now the last name is selected:

Press Delete

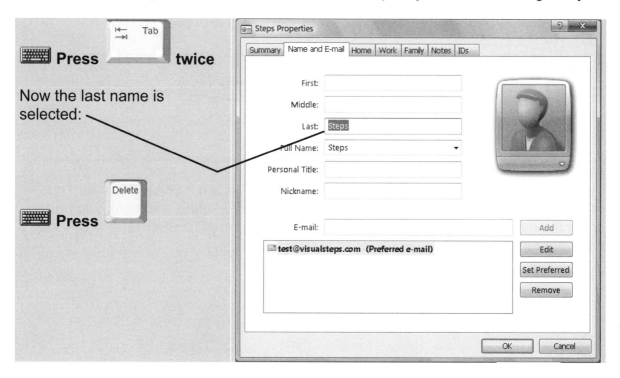

The last name has been deleted, and you can type in a different name:

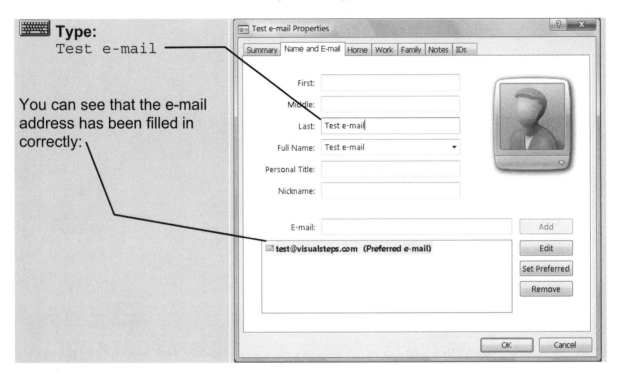

 Type:
Test e-mail

You can see that the e-mail address has been filled in correctly:

💡 **Tip**

Do you want to change the e-mail address?

Then click the [Edit] button:

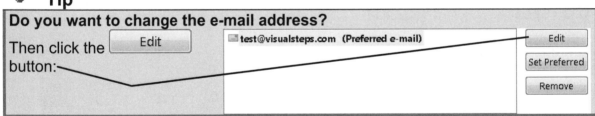

The e-mail address is usually stored correctly when it is automatically saved. The other information may need to be modified or expanded. In this example, you have given the e-mail address a made-up last name (*Test e-mail*), but in general this will be the name of an existing person or organization.

6.4 Adding a Picture to a Contact

You can add a picture to personalize a contact. This is a fun way to easily identify your contact. It also helps you keep the *Contacts* folder more organized.

Below the default image:

Click

Click Change picture...

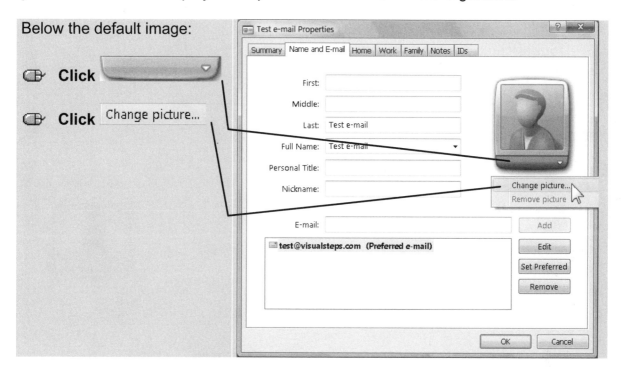

The folder ▸ Pictures is opened. Here you have saved a photo of Anne Frank's house:

Click Photo House of Anne Frank

Click Set

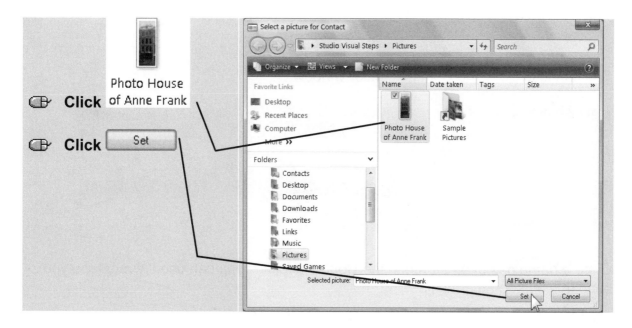

HELP! I do not have that photo in my Pictures folder.

Then you can choose one of your own pictures, or:

Sample Pictures

☞ **Double-click** Pictures
☞ **Click one of the sample pictures**
☞ **Click** Set

The photo of Anne Frank's house has been added as the picture for this contact.

You can close this window now:

☞ **Click** OK

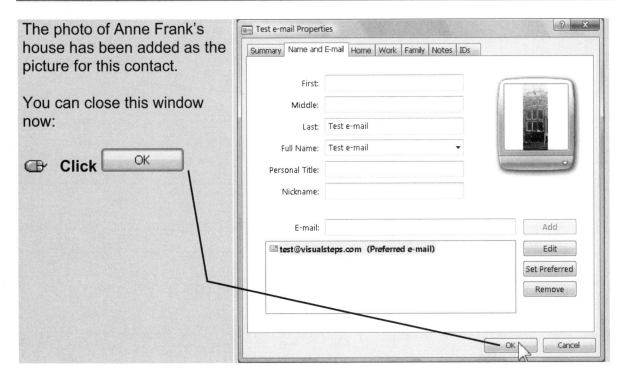

You can also close the *Contacts* folder window:

☞ **Click** ✕

Once a name has been stored in the *Contacts* folder, you can use it every time you send this person an e-mail.

6.5 Using an Address

Now that the e-mail address has been saved in the *Contacts* folder, you can easily use it to create a new e-mail message:

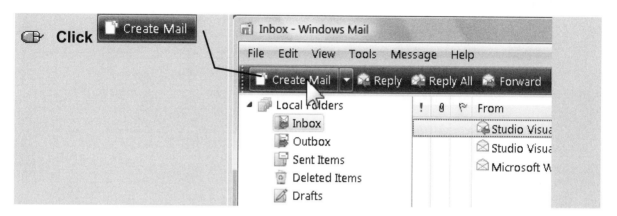

Here is how you choose an address from the *Contacts* folder:

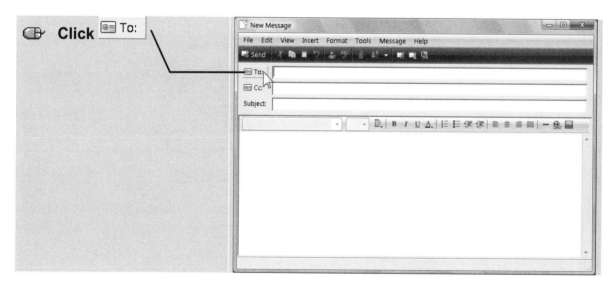

Now you see this window. First choose a name from the list on the left-hand side:

Click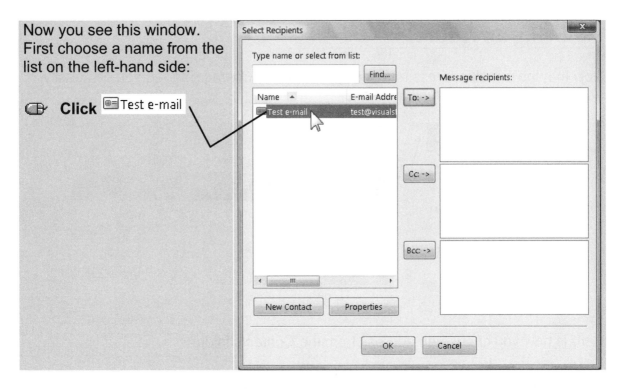

Then you can add the address to the *Message recipients* box:

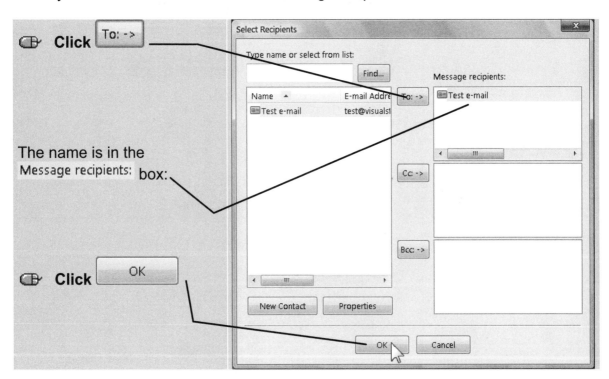

Click `To: ->`

The name is in the
Message recipients: box:

Click `OK`

Tip

Multiple addresses?
You can also use this window to send the same e-mail to multiple addresses. You do this by selecting the names in the left-hand list in the *Select Recipients* window, and clicking the [To: ->] button.

You see that the name has been entered next to ⊞ To: :

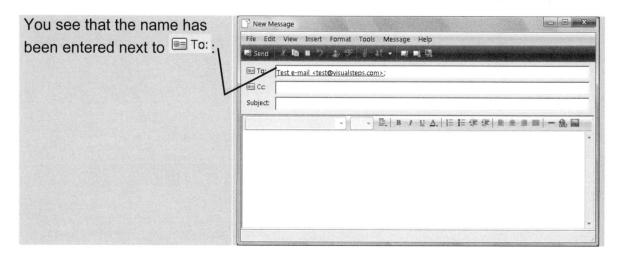

You do not actually have to send this e-mail. You can close the window without saving the e-mail message:

☞ **Click** [X]

☞ **Click** [No]

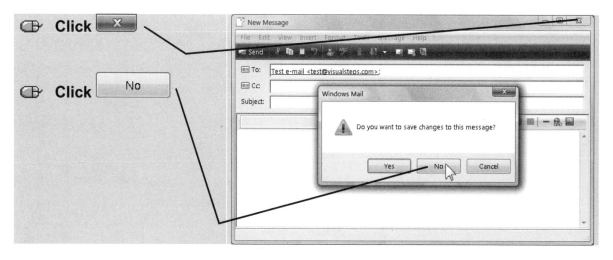

Now you have seen how you can use an e-mail address from the *Contacts* folder.

In *Windows Mail*, the e-mail address of every person to whom you have sent a reply is automatically stored. Of course, you do not have to wait until you get an e-mail from someone. You can add an e-mail address to the *Contacts* folder at any time.

6.6 Adding a New E-mail Address

You can manually add the e-mail addresses of your family, friends and acquaintances to the *Contacts* folder. This is how:

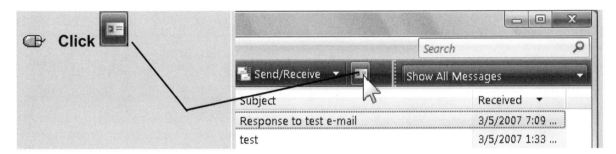

Once the *Contacts* folder is opened, you can add a new contact:

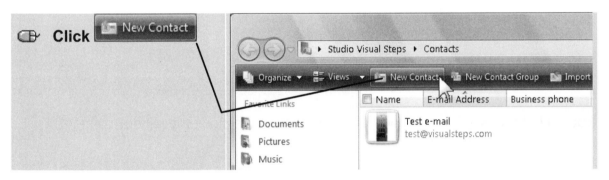

You see this window again for entering the name and e-mail address:

6.7 A Wrong E-mail Address

There is a good chance that once in a while you will use a wrong e-mail address. People frequently change their *Internet Service Provider*, and ISPs themselves go out of business or change their names. Furthermore, you can always make a typing error. A single letter or dot in the wrong place means the e-mail will never arrive. It is a good exercise to send an e-mail to a wrong address and see what happens:

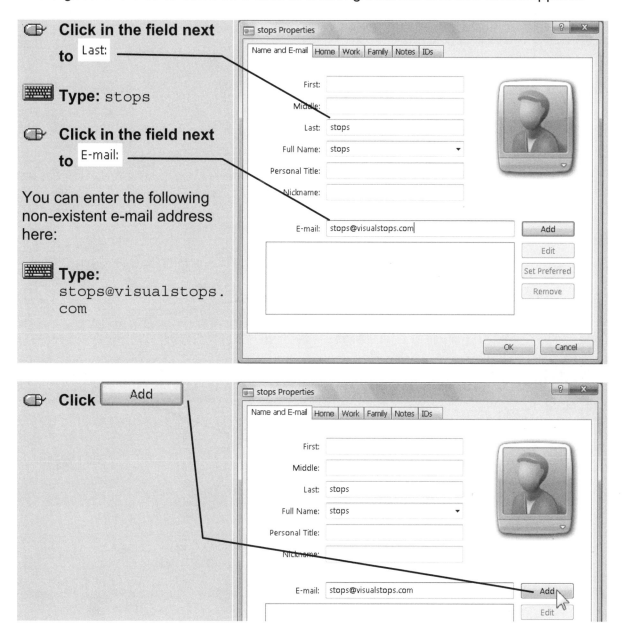

☞ **Click in the field next to** Last:

⌨ **Type:** stops

☞ **Click in the field next to** E-mail:

You can enter the following non-existent e-mail address here:

⌨ **Type:**
stops@visualstops.
com

☞ **Click** Add

Tip

Multiple addresses?
The *Contacts* folder has been designed so that a person can have multiple e-mail addresses, for example, a private address and one for work. You can add multiple e-mail addresses for one person.

You see that the e-mail address has been moved here:——

☞ **Click** OK

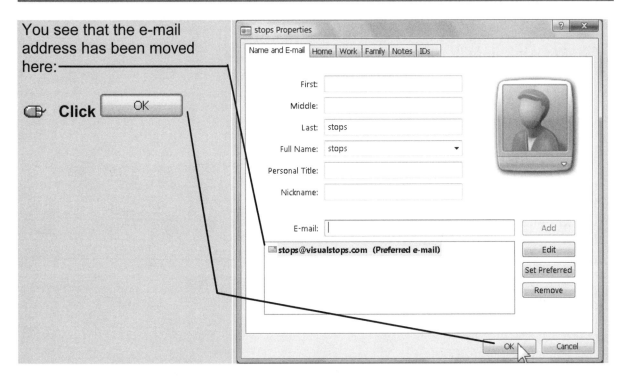

The name has been added to your *Contacts* folder, now you can close it:

☞ **Click** X

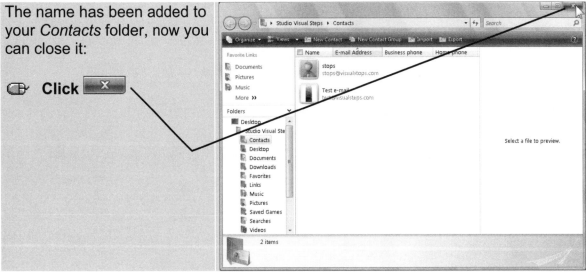

You can create a test mail and send it to the wrong address *stops@visualstops.com*. Then you can see what happens:

☞ **Create a new message** 🦶³⁶

☞ **Choose from the *Contacts* folder:** `stops (stops@visualstops.com)` 🦶⁵⁴

☞ **Type for the subject:** `Wrong address`

☞ **Type for the body:** `This is an e-mail to a wrong address.`

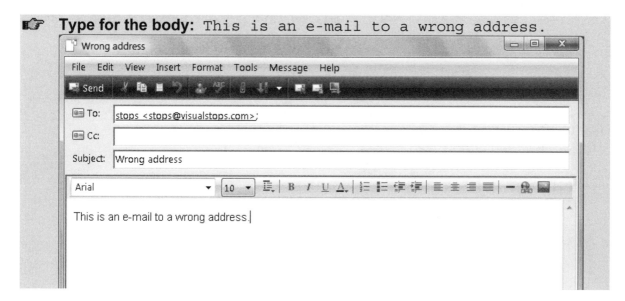

☞ **Send your e-mail to the *Outbox*** 🦶³⁷

☞ **Send and receive your e-mail** 🦶³⁹

☞ **If necessary, connect to the Internet** 🦶³

After a while, you will automatically receive a message about this wrongly addressed e-mail. This occurs quickly with some ISPs, and takes a bit longer with others.

☞ **Check your mail later in the *Inbox*** 🦶³⁹

HELP! I did not receive any mail.

Is there no message in your Inbox?
Maybe it has not been received yet. Try again later. If necessary, continue on with the next section and check again tomorrow.

☞   **Check your received e-mail again later** ⫝⫝39

Once you have received mail, you should have an automatic message from a *Mail Administrator* or a *Mail Delivery Subsystem*.

For example, a message like this:

The technical terms describe what went wrong during delivery. In this case, the destination computer was not found:

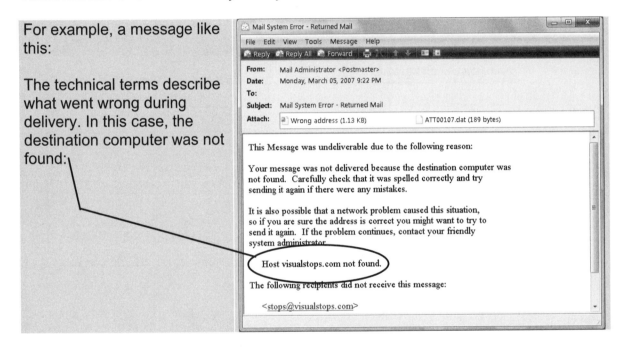

When you get this kind of error message, check in the *Sent Items* folder to see if the e-mail address you used is correct. Check:

- Are there any spaces in the e-mail address?
- Are all the dots in the right places?
- Is there a typing error in the e-mail address?

 Tip

Type it over?
You do not have to retype an e-mail that has been addressed incorrectly. You can select the text and copy it. Then you can paste it into a new message, and send this to the right e-mail address.

6.8 Your Signature

In some cases, e-mail will replace your regular correspondence. Just as in every letter, your full name and address information should appear in these messages. You do not have to type these in with every new message. You only have to type them once, into a "signature". Here is how you create a signature:

Click Tools

Click Options...

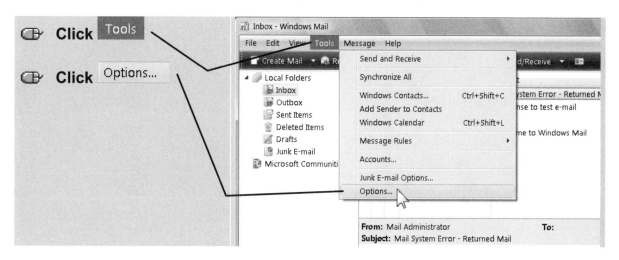

Click the tab Signatures

Now you see the window where you can type your signature.

Click New

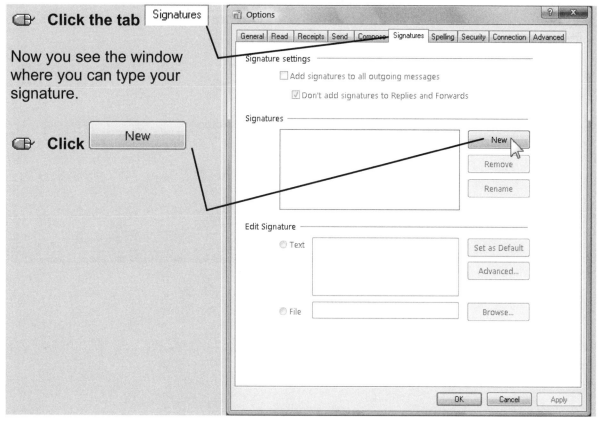

In *Windows Mail*, you can create and save multiple signatures.

You see that Signature #1 has been created:

In the box next to ● Text you can type your information:

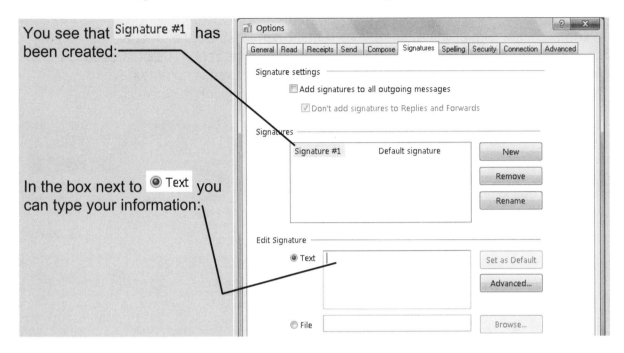

The signature does not look like a signature you would write with a pen. This signature consists solely of text and contains your address. Now you can type your information:

Type your full name and address

Click Apply

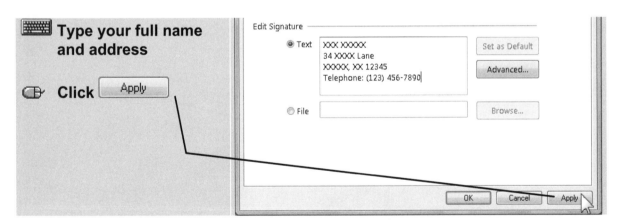

You can also decide whether you want the signature to appear automatically at the bottom of every new e-mail.

You do this by checking this box: —————————

If you would rather add your signature manually make sure the box is <u>not</u> checked.

In this example, you will add the signature manually:

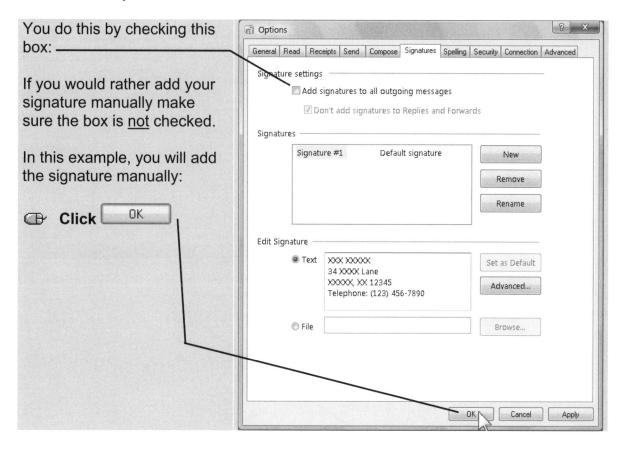

⌐☞ **Click** [OK]

Now you can add your signature to any e-mail message. First, create a new e-mail message.

☞ **Create a new e-mail message** ✐✐³⁶

⌐☞ **Click in the body of the message** —————

You can add the signature at the location of the cursor.

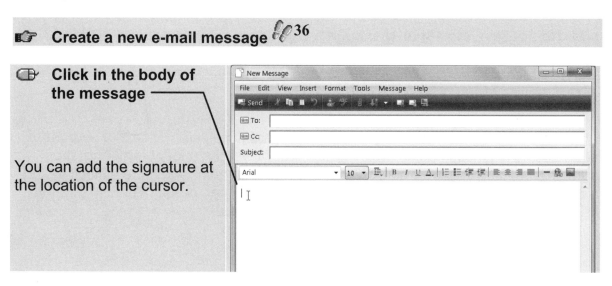

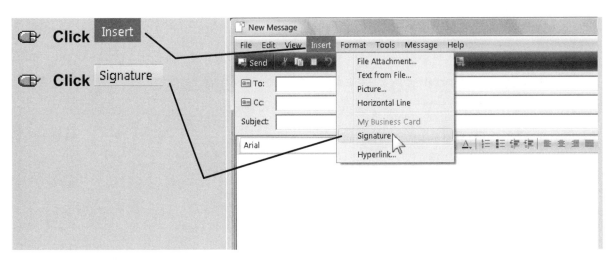

Click Insert

Click Signature

You see that your signature has been inserted:

You do not need to save this message.

Click X

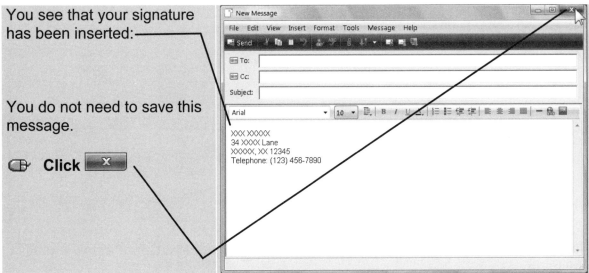

☞ **Do not save the e-mail message** 🦶55

6.9 The Inbox, Your Archive

All the messages you receive are saved in the *Inbox*. You will notice that your *Inbox* soon begins to function as an archive. Especially if you do a lot of e-mailing, the number of e-mails will grow quickly and it will become more and more difficult to find a particular message. There are two ways you can find an e-mail. You can *sort* the list of e-mails, or you can *search* through the messages.

6.10 Sorting E-mails

Your e-mail messages are usually sorted by date received.
You can sort them differently, however, such as by the sender's name. Here is how you do that:

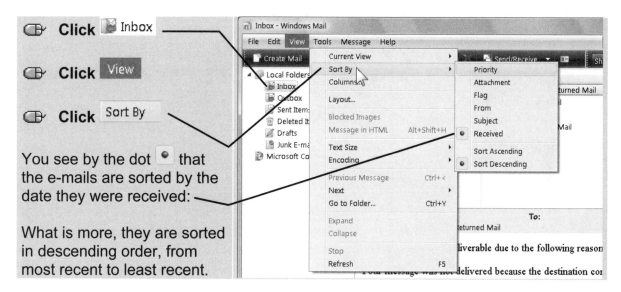

You see by the dot ● that the e-mails are sorted by the date they were received:

What is more, they are sorted in descending order, from most recent to least recent.

Now you can sort them by the sender's name. The name is in the *From* field:

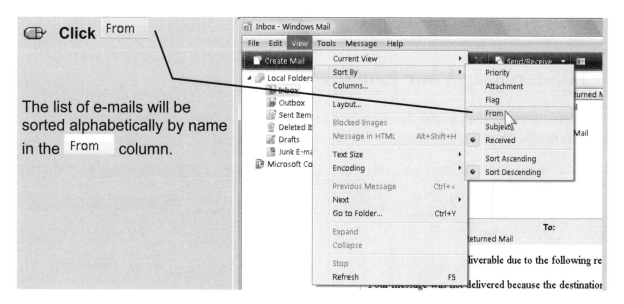

The list of e-mails will be sorted alphabetically by name in the From column.

If your e-mails are sorted alphabetically by the sender, it is easier to find an e-mail from a particular person. All e-mails from the same person will be together.

Please note:

The default setting is to sort on date received, with the most recently received e-mails at the top. That is quite useful, so you can restore the old setting:

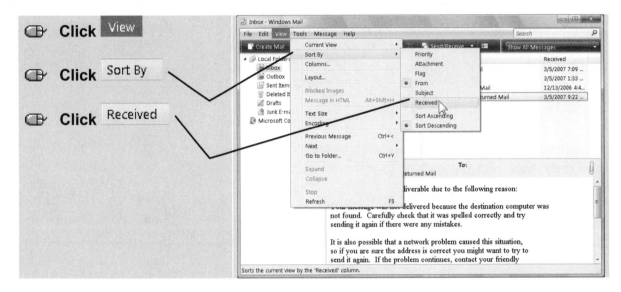

Click View

Click Sort By

Click Received

The e-mails will again be sorted by date received.

6.11 Searching Your E-mails

Windows Mail has an extensive search function that you can use to search through your e-mails. Here is how you start:

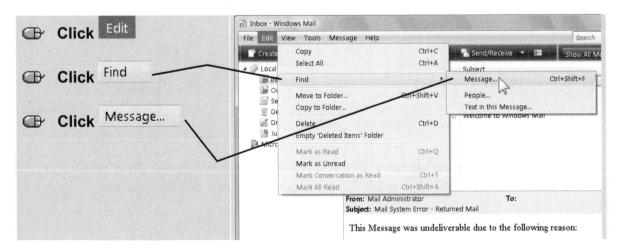

Click Edit

Click Find

Click Message...

Now you see this window with various fields:

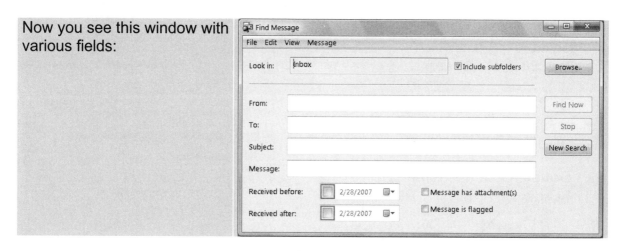

You can search every part of an e-mail message: *From*, *To*, the *Subject* or within the body of the *Message* itself. In addition, you can refine the search, such as specifying the date of receipt.

If you know what the content of the e-mail message is, you can search for it by using a search term. For example, you can use the word "Internet"; that word should be in a test mail you received earlier.

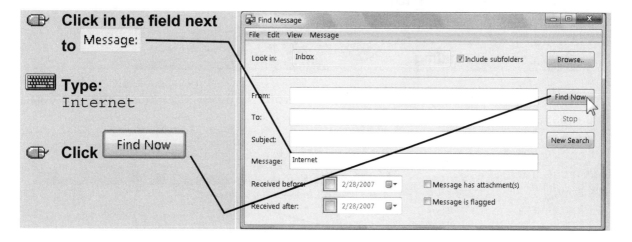

Click in the field next to Message:

Type:
Internet

Click Find Now

At the bottom of the window, you see the e-mails in which the word "Internet" appears:

To view one of these e-mails:

 Double-click the e-mail header

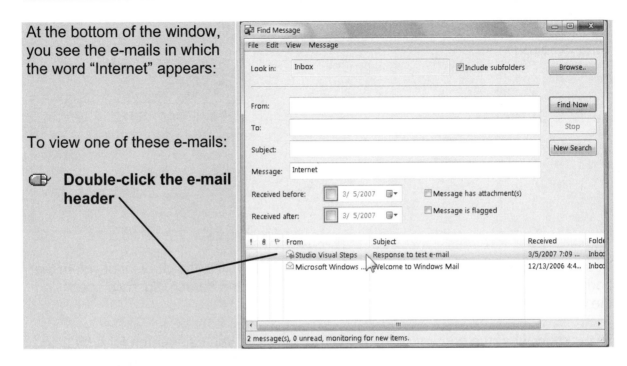

HELP! I do not see any e-mails.

If you do not see any e-mails in the above window, then you may not have received the test mail in the previous chapter.

☞ **Just continue reading**

The message opens and you can read it. The word "Internet" appears somewhere in this message.

When you are finished, you can close the message window.

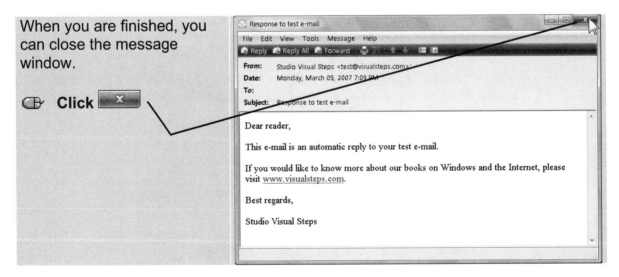

 Click [X]

Dear reader,

This e-mail is an automatic reply to your test e-mail.

If you would like to know more about our books on Windows and the Internet, please visit www.visualsteps.com.

Best regards,

Studio Visual Steps

You can also close the *Find Message* window:

☞ **Click** [X]

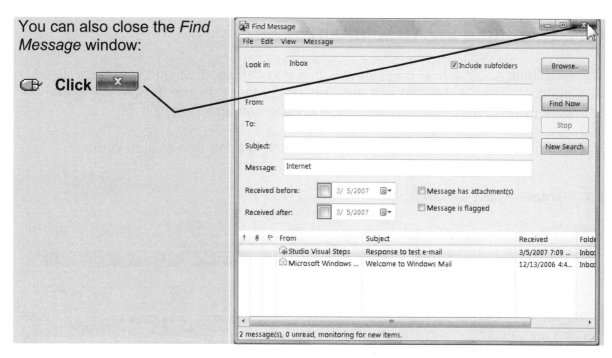

💡 **Tip**

Quick search using the Search Box
In the top right corner of the *Windows Mail* window you see the *Search Box*:

Using this *Search Box* you can search an entire folder for a particular search term. When you type a search term in the *Search Box*, not only the body of the messages, but also the e-mail headers and the names of senders and addressees are searched.

☞ **Click the folder you want to search**

☞ **Click the Search Box**

⌨ **Type your search term**

While you type, the message list is filtered so that it only shows messages containing your search term:

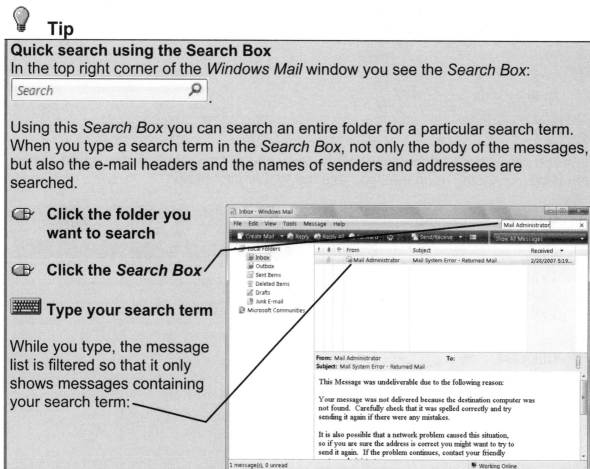

6.12 Including an Attachment

The nice thing about e-mail messages is that you can send all kinds of things along with them. You can add a photo, a drawing, or another document. Something that you want to send with an e-mail message is called an *attachment*.

You can practice sending an attachment by sending another e-mail to yourself.

☞   Create a new e-mail ℒℒ**36**

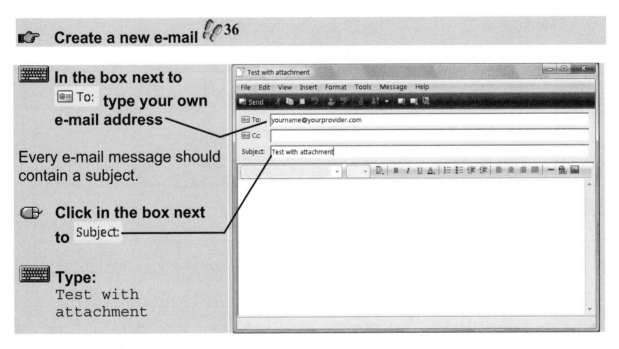

⌨ **In the box next to**
▣ To: type your own
e-mail address

Every e-mail message should contain a subject.

🖰 **Click in the box next**
to Subject:

⌨ **Type:**
Test with
attachment

Now you can add the attachment: in this case, one of the sample pictures that comes with *Windows Vista*. To do that, you use the "paper clip" button:

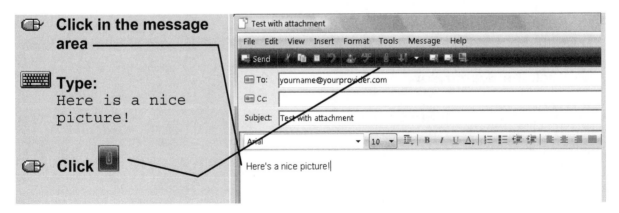

🖰 **Click in the message**
area

⌨ **Type:**
Here is a nice
picture!

🖰 **Click** 📎

Now you see this folder window. By default, the folder *Documents* will be opened.

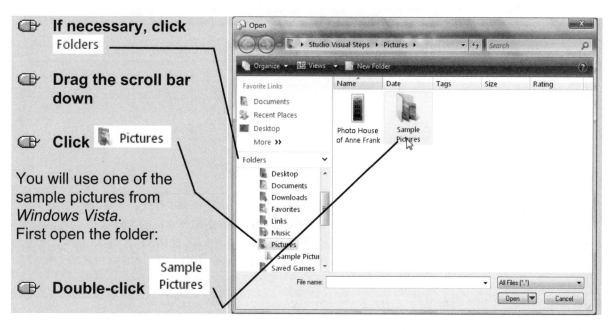

☞ **If necessary, click** Folders

☞ **Drag the scroll bar down**

☞ **Click** 🖼 Pictures

You will use one of the sample pictures from *Windows Vista*.
First open the folder:

☞ **Double-click** Sample Pictures

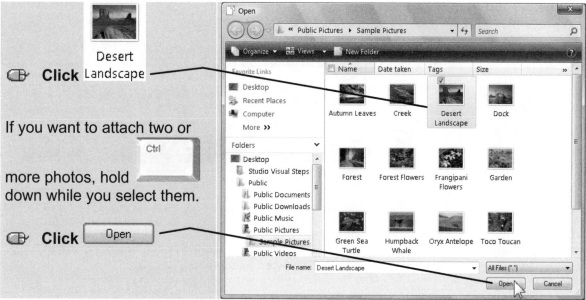

☞ **Click** Desert Landscape

If you want to attach two or more photos, hold Ctrl down while you select them.

☞ **Click** Open

The attachment is added to
your message: ――――――

The size of the attachment is
shown: (223 KB)

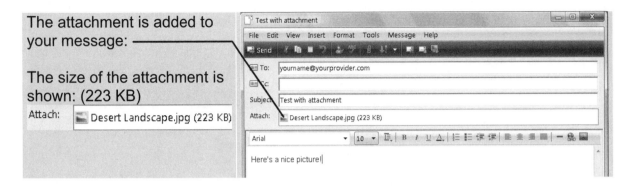

⇨ Please note:

Sending an e-mail with an attachment takes more time than sending and receiving a
"bare" e-mail message, especially if you or the addressee are using dial-up
networking to connect to the Internet. Sending pictures takes a particularly long time.
You may decide for yourself whether or not you really want to send this message.

If you do not want to send it:

☞ **Close the message window**
The program will ask whether you want to save the changes:

☞ **Click** No

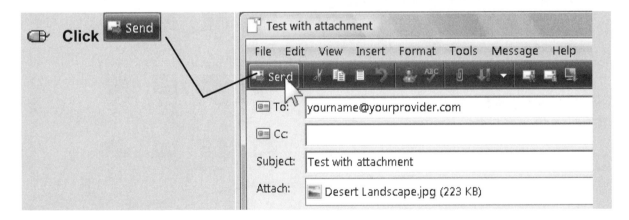

If your message is placed in the *Outbox*, you can send it now manually. If your mail is
sent immediately, you do not have to send it manually.

☞ **Send and receive your e-mail** ℓℓ³⁹

⇨ Please note:

Sending this e-mail will take some time if you are using dial-up networking.

6.13 Opening an Attachment

Once your e-mail is sent, it should arrive very quickly. You can see this in the *Inbox*:

If necessary, click
Inbox (1)

Click the message
with the attachment

Here you see the preview of
your own message:

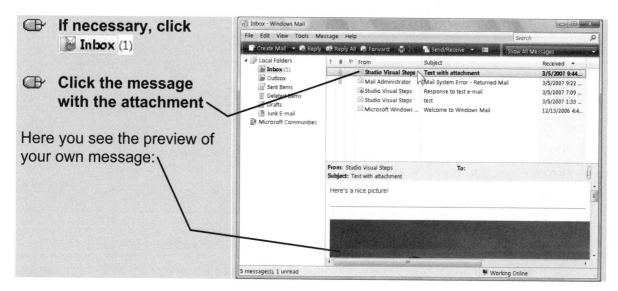

 HELP! I do not have any mail.

Is there no new message in your Inbox?
Perhaps it has not yet been received. Try again later:

Click

In one of the first columns in
the message list, a small
paper clip 🖇 indicates that an
attachment has been
included:

Double-click your new
message

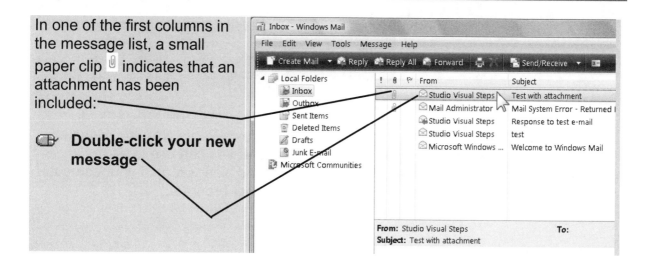

Tip

In *Windows Mail*, there is an icon next to every e-mail. Here is what they represent:

- an unread message
- a message you have already read
- a message you have already answered
- a message you have forwarded

- the message contains an attachment
- a message you have marked ("flagged")
- a message marked as important by the sender

You see your message in a separate window:

The window is too small to show the whole picture. Using the scroll box you can see the picture:

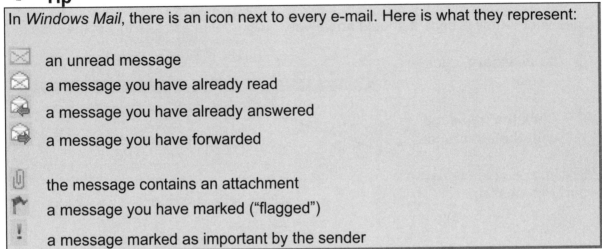

☞ **Double-click**
   Desert Landscape.jpg (229 KB)

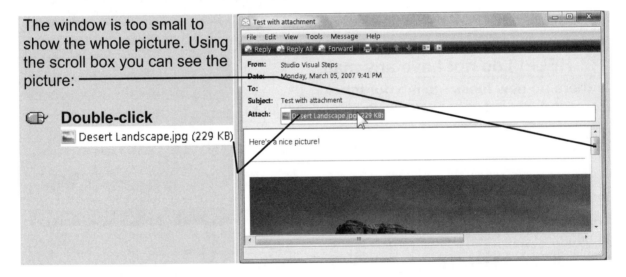

The default program to view the picture is called *Windows Photo Gallery*. *Windows Photo Gallery* is a tool included with *Windows Vista* that you can use to view, organize, edit, share, and print your digital pictures (and videos too). If your computer is set up differently, the picture may be shown in another program.

After you have seen the
picture, you can close the
program window:

CB **Click** [×]

You see the message window again.

6.14 Saving an Attachment

After you have saved an attachment such as a photo, you can use it again in various
ways. For example, you can open it in a program like *Paint* or another photo editing
program. There you can edit and change the photo. Maybe you want to use the
photo in a club newsletter you have written in *WordPad* or *MS Word.* You can also
send the photo by e-mail to someone else.

An e-mail can contain various attachments. The easiest way to save attachments is
as follows:

CB **Click** File

CB **Click** Save Attachments...

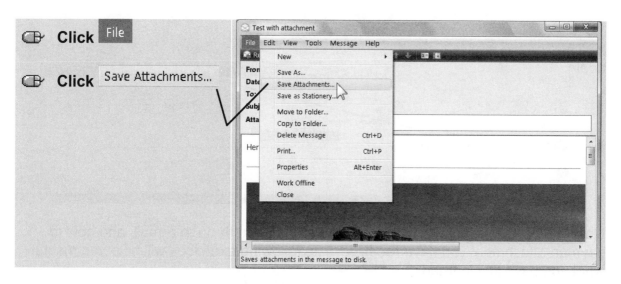

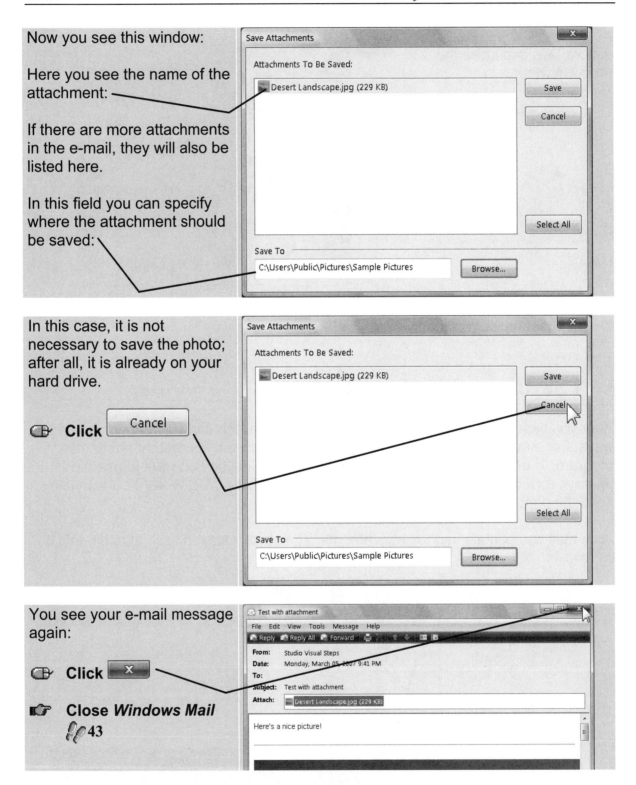

Now you see this window:

Here you see the name of the attachment: ──

If there are more attachments in the e-mail, they will also be listed here.

In this field you can specify where the attachment should be saved:

In this case, it is not necessary to save the photo; after all, it is already on your hard drive.

☞ **Click** Cancel

You see your e-mail message again:

☞ **Click** X

☞ **Close** *Windows Mail*
    𝄞 43

Now you have seen how you can send an attachment through e-mail, and how to save an attachment you have received. The following exercises will help you master what you have just learned.

6.15 Exercises

Have you forgotten how to do something? Use the number beside the footsteps to look it up in the appendix *How Do I Do That Again?*

Exercise: Sending an Attachment

In this exercise, you will practice writing a new e-mail message with an attachment.

✔ Open *Windows Mail*. $\ell\ell$ 35

✔ Create a new e-mail message addressed to yourself. $\ell\ell$ 36

✔ Add the photo of Anne Frank's house (from Chapter 4) as an attachment. $\ell\ell$ 40

✔ Send the e-mail message to the *Outbox*. $\ell\ell$ 37

✔ Send and receive your e-mail. $\ell\ell$ 39

Exercise: Viewing an Attachment

✔ Open *Windows Mail*. $\ell\ell$ 35

✔ Check your mail. $\ell\ell$ 39

✔ See if you have new mail in your *Inbox*. $\ell\ell$ 41

✔ Open your e-mail message. $\ell\ell$ 42

✔ View the attachment. $\ell\ell$ 57

✔ Close the e-mail message window. $\ell\ell$ 32

6.16 Background Information

Glossary	
Attachment	Documents, images, and other files can be sent as attachments to an e-mail message. Messages that contain attachments are indicated by a paper clip icon in the attachment column of the message list. For security reasons many e-mail programs (including *Windows Mail*) prevent recipients from opening executable file attachments, such as those with .exe, .bat and .inf file name extensions.
Contacts folder	You can use *Windows Vista* to keep track of people and organizations by creating contacts for them in your *Contacts* folder. Each contact contains the information for one person or organization: name, address, telephone number, e-mail address and even a picture. The *Contacts* folder functions as the address book for *Windows Mail*.
Search Box	*Windows Mail* includes the *Search Box*, which makes it easy to find specific e-mail messages. Using the *Search Box*, you can quickly filter your message list so that it only shows messages containing specific words, characters, or e-mail addresses.
Signature	A signature can contain your name, e-mail address, phone number, and any other information that you want to include at the bottom of your e-mail messages.
Virus	A piece of code or program designed to cause damage to a computer system (by erasing or corrupting data) or annoying users (by printing messages or altering what is displayed on the computer screen).

Source: Windows Help and Support

Risks involved in opening attachments

Opening an attachment received with an e-mail could possibly infect your computer with a computer virus. A computer virus is a very small program that can copy itself to another computer. Once present on a computer system, it can do a lot of damage. Not all viruses are equally dangerous. Because the virus arrives together with another file, you can not tell without using a special program whether or not you have been infected.

If an e-mail with an attachment was sent by someone with whom you frequently correspond, the risks are smaller than if it comes from someone you do not know. Nonetheless, caution is always advisable.

☞ **Never open an attachment if you are suspicious.**
   If necessary, send your acquaintance an e-mail requesting clarification.

☞ **If you are suspicious of an unknown sender: Delete the e-mail and its attachment immediately without opening.**
   If the attachment did not contain a virus, that is too bad, but the sender should have been more clear about his subject. In situations like these, the sender can always send the e-mail again.

☞ **If you receive a "strange" e-mail from a known sender: Delete the e-mail without opening it.**
   If necessary, ask for clarification from the sender.

☞ **Do not forget to empty the *Deleted Items* folder.**
   Only then is the e-mail permanently deleted from your computer.

Viruses like the infamous "I love you" virus not only do great damage, but also read your entire *Contacts* folder and send an e-mail containing a copy of themselves to all the contacts inside. This is also the reason why you can not always trust e-mail from people you know.

In any event, if you regularly use the Internet be sure you use a good **anti-virus software**. This software will give a warning in most cases before the virus can do its work. It is very important that you keep this software up-to-date. Consult the software's documentation for this.

In **Chapter 9 Security and Privacy** you can read more about viruses and anti-virus software.

The smaller, the faster
On the Internet, there is one golden rule: the smaller the message is, the faster it is sent. The same applies to attachments. If you send a small attachment, such as a small photograph, the transmission will only take a few seconds. If you send a larger drawing, it will take more time and the telephone line will be used longer.

Along with the name of an attachment, such as a text or a picture, its size is always shown, expressed in MB or KB:

Attach: ▨ Desert Landscape.jpg (223 KB)

The size of a file is always indicated in KB or MB. These are units of measurements, just like pounds and ounces.

A **Kilobyte** is (about) one thousand bytes.
This means that: 20 Kilobytes is 20,000 bytes. The abbreviation of kilobyte is **KB**.

A **Megabyte** is (about) one thousand kilobytes.
This means that one Megabyte is (about) one million (one thousand times one thousand) bytes. The abbreviation of megabyte is **MB**.

How long does it take to send or receive something?
The speed at which something can be sent or received depends on a number or things, including the speed of your modem, the type of connection and how busy it is on the Internet. If for example, you are using dial-up networking to connect to the Internet, you can receive 6 KB per second with a regular modem. This translates into 360 KB or 0.36 MB per minute.

A message that consists of 16 KB will take about three seconds. The size of the picture attachment you used in this chapter, is 223 KB. It takes about 38 seconds to send or receive. An attachment that is 1.73 MB in size will take about three minutes. As you see, this is quite a long time. Your ISP may also have a limit on the amount of data you can receive in an e-mail. If the limit is exceeded the e-mail will not arrive. Try sending larger pictures, for example, in separate e-mails.

You can send different types of files with an e-mail message. You can even send sounds or video clips! But be careful: sound and video files are also usually quite large. It may take a very long time to send or receive files of this type. However, when you are using a broadband connection, for example a DSL line, this will not be a problem. This type of service offers high speed connection to the Internet.

A faster modem: internal or external?

Do you have an older computer and a dial-up Internet connection that requires you to connect manually? Are you dissatisfied with the speed of your internet connection? You might want to consider buying a faster modem.

The fastest modem available which uses the regular telephone line is a modem with a *speed* of *56K*. You can choose either an internal or an external modem:

Internal modem

External modem

An external modem has certain advantages:
- You can connect the modem easily. The computer does not have to be opened in order to install the modem, so you do not need a computer mechanic.
- An external modem has little lights that let you see what is happening on the telephone line. This is useful when the connection is not functioning properly.
- You can easily connect an external modem to a different computer.

But there are also disadvantages:
- An external modem is more expensive.
- The modem has more cables and often a separate power supply which has to be plugged into an outlet.
- You always have to turn the modem on.

If you want a really fast connection, you will have to switch to DSL or cable Internet. You need a special kind of modem for that. Your ISP can give you more information.

6.17 Tips

Tip

Security settings in Windows Mail
Windows Mail has various security settings. You can take a look at these settings:

Click Tools , Options...

You see the *Options* window:

Click the tab Security

On the *Security* tab, you see
check marks beside various
options:

These security settings
ensure that e-mail
attachments and images
cannot open automatically.

You have to give permission
each time before you open an
e-mail with an image or an
attachment.
Windows Mail notifies you
when that occurs.

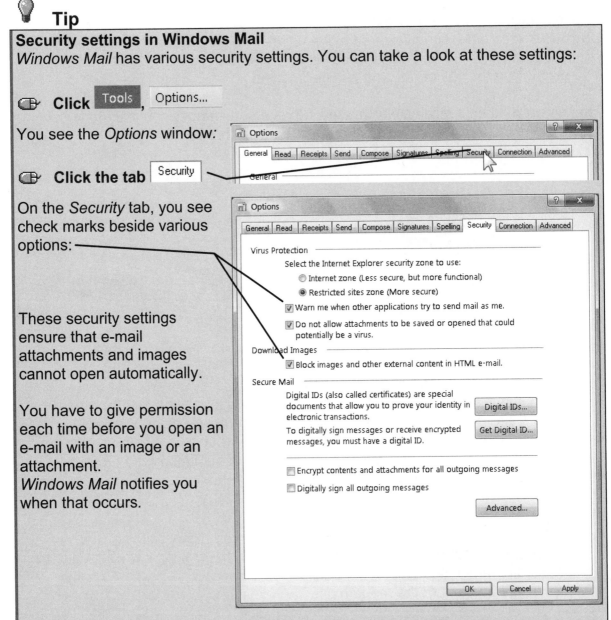

It is advisable to leave the security settings on this page just as they are. That keeps
you in control of any undesirable e-mails.

Check whether you trust the content or attachment on a per e-mail basis. If you have
any doubts, ask the sender for clarification about the e-mail, or delete it without
opening. Do not forget to empty the *Deleted Items* folder afterward.

Tip

Zipping and unzipping

When you send an attachment, you should consider the size of the file. Files containing only text are relatively small. Photos are much larger, and it takes longer to download them. Because this download time can be frustrating, programs have been developed that can shrink files. This technique is called *compressing* or *zipping*.

A compression program takes all the "extra air", so to speak, out of a file, making it smaller. This way, a photo (*bitmap*) with a size of 1400 KB (or 1.4 MB) can be reduced to 23 KB, a reduction of 98%! In order to be able to use the file again later, the reverse function must be applied. This is called *unzipping* or *extracting*.

Windows Vista offers a very easy way to zip files. Both *Windows Vista* and *Windows XP* users will be able to unzip a file that has been zipped that way.

You can try this with the website you saved earlier to the folder *Documents*. If you did not save the website, you can choose any other file:

☞ **Click** , Documents

☞ **Right-click the document**

A menu appears:

☞ **Click** Send To

☞ **Click** Compressed (zipped) Folder

The zipped folder appears in the list. You can recognise the zipped folder by the

zipper :

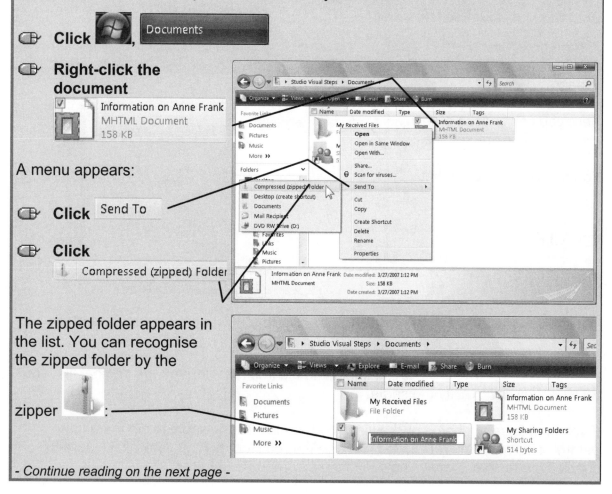

- Continue reading on the next page -

The original file had a size of 158 KB. Zipping decreased the size to 101 KB:

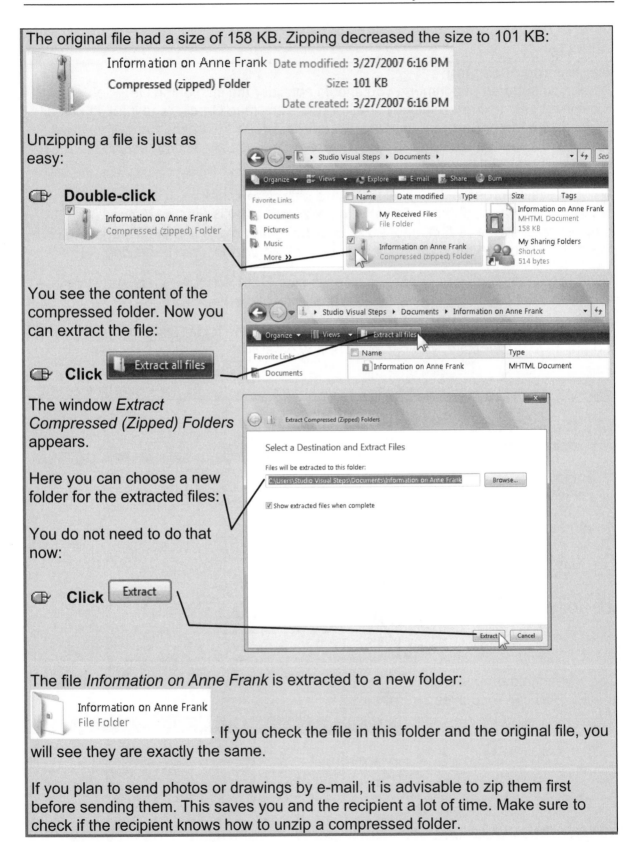

Unzipping a file is just as easy:

☞ **Double-click**

You see the content of the compressed folder. Now you can extract the file:

☞ **Click** Extract all files

The window *Extract Compressed (Zipped) Folders* appears.

Here you can choose a new folder for the extracted files:

You do not need to do that now:

☞ **Click** Extract

The file *Information on Anne Frank* is extracted to a new folder:

. If you check the file in this folder and the original file, you will see they are exactly the same.

If you plan to send photos or drawings by e-mail, it is advisable to zip them first before sending them. This saves you and the recipient a lot of time. Make sure to check if the recipient knows how to unzip a compressed folder.

Tip

Opening an attachment
When you choose *Open* in this window, the program to open the attachment in question is automatically opened.

Which program is opened depends on your computer's settings. Your computer may have a different program assigned to open a particular type of file.

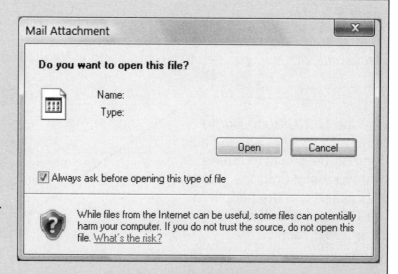

If the attachment is a text document, *MS Word* will automatically be opened. If you do not have *MS Word* on your computer, then *WordPad* will be opened.
If the attachment is a photo, *Windows Photo Gallery* will be opened. If another photo editing program has been installed on your computer, that program will be opened instead.
If the attachment is a computer program (a *.exe-file for example), then that program itself will be opened.

 Tip

How do I find an e-mail address?
The Internet is such a dynamic medium that there is no telephone book containing everyone who has an e-mail address. People also frequently change Internet Service Providers. When you switch to a new ISP, you usually get a new e-mail address. In addition, not everyone wants his or her private e-mail address to be published, to avoid unwanted e-mails, for example.

There are websites such as *Bigfoot Directories* and *Yahoo Search* that offer the possibility to search for e-mail addresses. Unfortunately, most *Bigfoot* and *Yahoo* search results come up empty. They only contain links to pages of commercial companies. These companies claim to have the information you want, but it is <u>not</u> free.

💡 Tip

CC and BCC
You can send an e-mail to multiple addresses in different ways. In the *Select Recipients* window, you see two more buttons beneath the To: -> button.

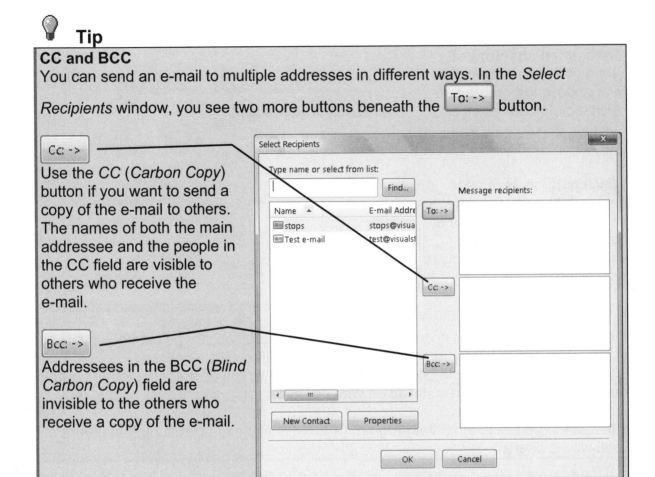

Use the CC (*Carbon Copy*) button if you want to send a copy of the e-mail to others. The names of both the main addressee and the people in the CC field are visible to others who receive the e-mail.

Addressees in the BCC (*Blind Carbon Copy*) field are invisible to the others who receive a copy of the e-mail.

Tip

Keyboard control

If you prefer, you can use the keyboard to operate *Windows Mail* rather than the mouse. The most important keys and their functions are listed below.

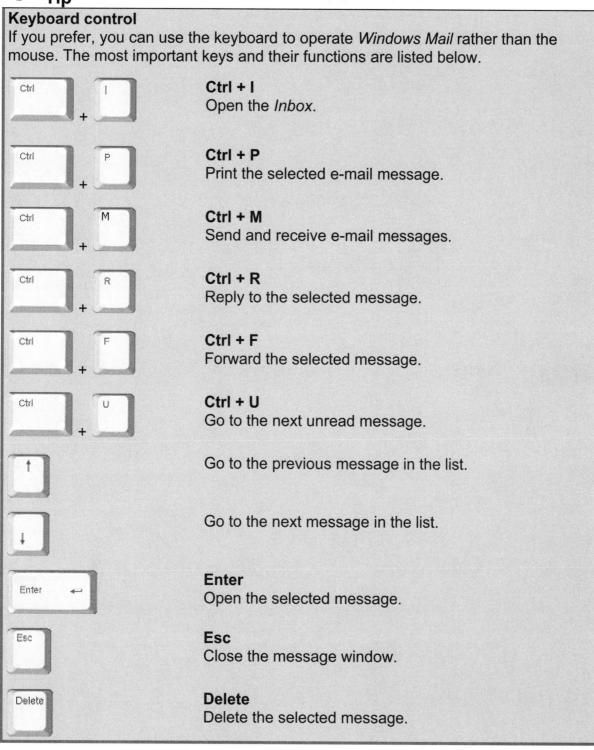

Ctrl + I
Open the *Inbox*.

Ctrl + P
Print the selected e-mail message.

Ctrl + M
Send and receive e-mail messages.

Ctrl + R
Reply to the selected message.

Ctrl + F
Forward the selected message.

Ctrl + U
Go to the next unread message.

Go to the previous message in the list.

Go to the next message in the list.

Enter
Open the selected message.

Esc
Close the message window.

Delete
Delete the selected message.

Notes

7. Special Functions in Windows Mail

Up to this point, you have created e-mails that consist only of text without any formatting. It is customary in the business world to send e-mails containing short texts without frills. For personal use however, it can be a lot of fun to send more interesting e-mails to your friends, children or grandchildren.

In fact, almost all the formatting you can use in a text-editing program can also be applied to an e-mail. You can choose different fonts and larger or smaller letters. An interesting background color or pattern is also possible. This is called *Rich Text*. *Windows Mail* also provides various kinds of stationery. A formatted e-mail message is actually a kind of webpage that is then sent as an e-mail. You can also use pictures and images in your e-mail messages.

It is also possible to quickly create an e-mail message using *Internet Explorer* to let someone know about an interesting website.

With *Windows Calendar*, the calendar application that comes with *Windows Vista*, you can easily keep track of your appointments. You can add an appointment and set a reminder to warn you that the appointment is approaching. You can also share your calendar with anyone in your *Contacts* folder by using e-mail to send and receive appointments and invitations.

In this chapter, you will learn how to:

- format an e-mail
- choose a different font and size
- change the background color
- use stationery
- use emoticons
- send e-mail using *Internet Explorer*
- use *Windows Mail* to keep track of your appointments
- invite someone else for an appointment by e-mail
- receive an invitation by e-mail
- set up reminders

7.1 Formatting E-mail

There are two kinds of e-mail:

- e-mail with unformatted text and no images, also called *plain text*
- e-mail with formatted text and images, also called *Rich Text* or *HTML*

You can format your e-mails. *Windows Mail* offers all the same options as a text-editing program like *WordPad* or *MS Word*. In fact, it has more options, for example: the use of stationery. First, create a plain new e-mail message:

☞ **Open *Windows Mail* ⌇⌇ 35**

In this chapter, *Windows Mail* does not need to connect to the Internet. Of course, you can check your e-mail if you would like.

👉 **Click** ▐ Create Mail

You see a toolbar with buttons for formatting:

This is called the *formatting bar*.
These buttons are still gray; that means you can not use them yet.

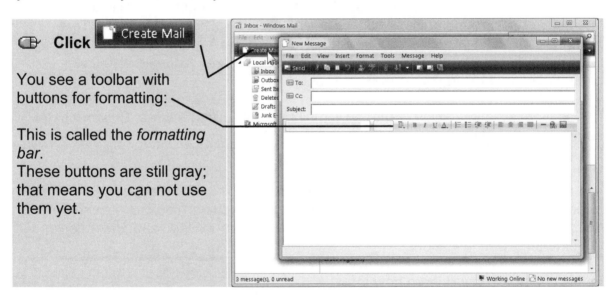

👉 **HELP! I do not see the formatting bar.**

If the formatting bar is not visible, then your *Windows Mail* has been set up differently:

👉 **Click** View

👉 **Click** Toolbars

👉 **Click** Formatting Bar

These buttons will not become active until you place the cursor in the main message area where you type the text of your e-mail:

 Click in the main message area

You see that all the buttons are now active:

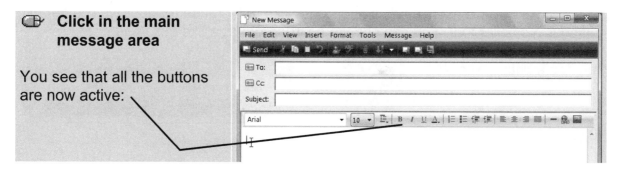

HELP! The buttons are still gray.

If the formatting bar is still gray, then your *Windows Mail* has been set up differently. You will need to choose another format for your e-mail message:

☞ **Click** Format

☞ **Click** Rich Text (HTML)

Most of the formatting you can do in *WordPad*, for example, is also available in *Windows Mail*. You can see your options on the formatting bar:

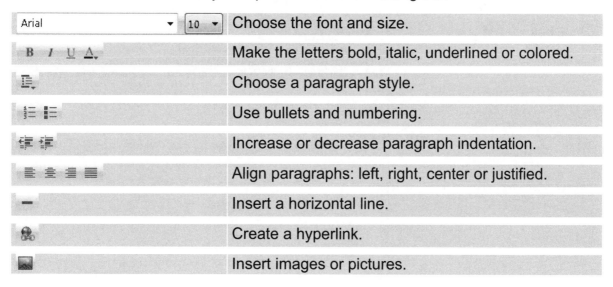

Arial ▾ 10 ▾	Choose the font and size.
B *I* U A̲	Make the letters bold, italic, underlined or colored.
▤	Choose a paragraph style.
⅓≣ ≣	Use bullets and numbering.
彊 彊	Increase or decrease paragraph indentation.
≣ ≣ ≣ ≣	Align paragraphs: left, right, center or justified.
—	Insert a horizontal line.
🔗	Create a hyperlink.
🖾	Insert images or pictures.

 Tip

Would you like to know more about text formatting and fonts?
Read the Visual Steps book *Windows Vista for Seniors*.
See **www.visualsteps.com/vista** for more information.

7.2 The Font Size

You can write your e-mails using a larger font size to increase readability. The default setting is a smaller font. You can choose a larger font size like this:

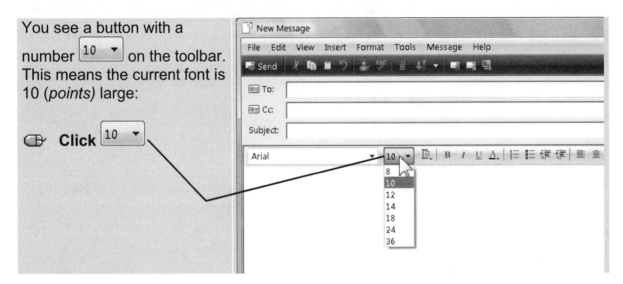

You see a button with a number [10 ▼] on the toolbar. This means the current font is 10 (*points*) large:

☞ **Click** [10 ▼]

Now you see a list of numbers. A low number means smaller letters; a large number larger letters:

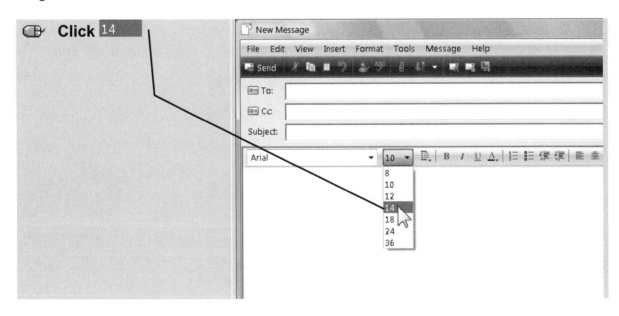

☞ **Click** 14

From now on, the text you type will be in a larger font.

Type:
This is a larger
font size, 14
points.

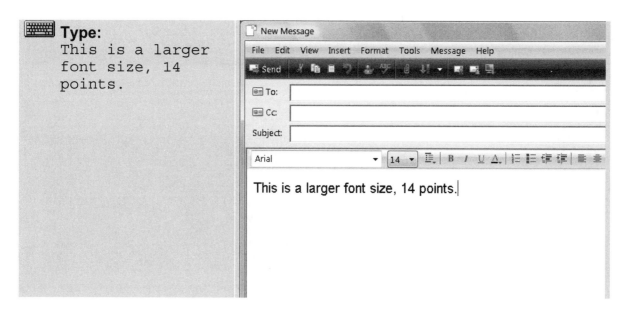

You see that the letters are larger.

7.3 The Background Color

You can also change the background color if you would like. For example, you can make it gray:

Click Format

Click Background

Click Color ▶

You see a list of colors from which you can choose:

Click Gray

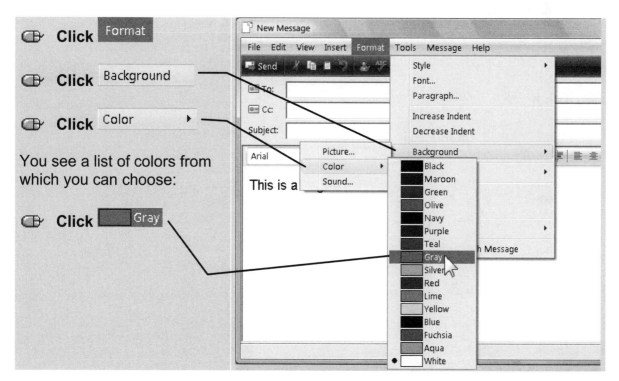

The background is now gray:

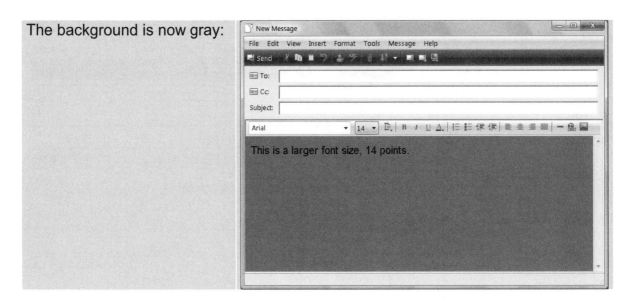

You can do all kinds of formatting this way. You can also draw a line or place an image into the e-mail text. Go ahead and experiment!

7.4 Stationery

Windows Mail also has ready-made stationery that you can use as a background. You can use it to give your e-mail message a whole new look. Here is how you choose stationery:

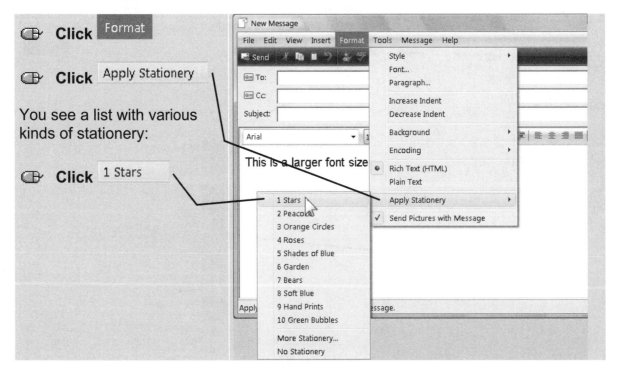

HELP! I do not have Stars.

It is possible that *Stars* is not on the list in your computer.
☞ **Choose a different stationery from the list**

You see a light background for your e-mail message:

The color of the letters has also changed:

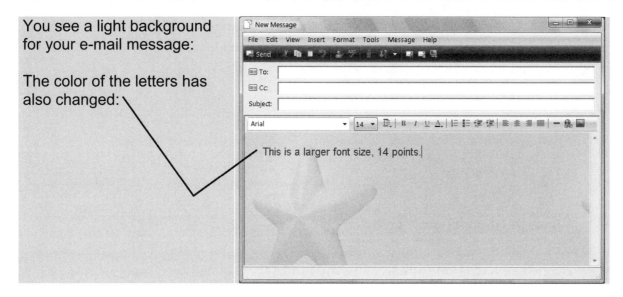

You can also remove the stationery:

👆 **Click** Format

👆 **Click** Apply Stationery

👆 **Click** No Stationery

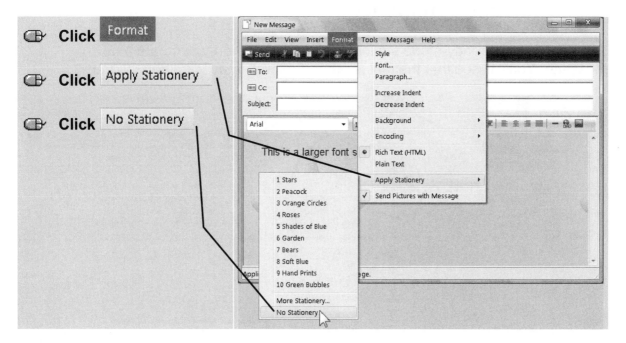

Now you see that the
stationery is gone:

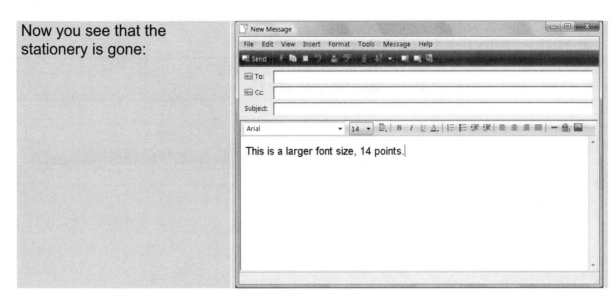

☞ **Close the message window** $\ell\ell^{32}$

☞ **Do not save the changes to the message** $\ell\ell^{55}$

7.5 Ready-made Stationery

You can also use ready-made stationery right away when you create a new
message. You will see that the font is altered as well to go with the stationery.

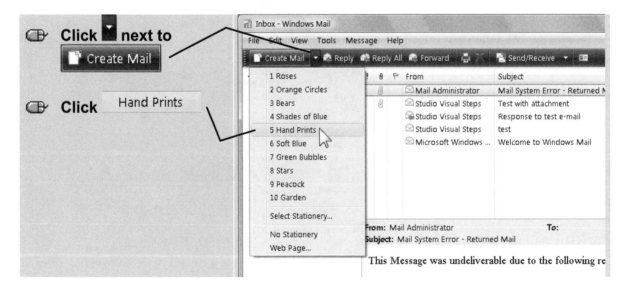

You see this "handy" stationery:

☞ **Increase the font size to 14** 🐾⁴⁷

Now you can add your own text:

☞ **Click in the main message area**

⌨ **Type:**
Can I give you a hand?

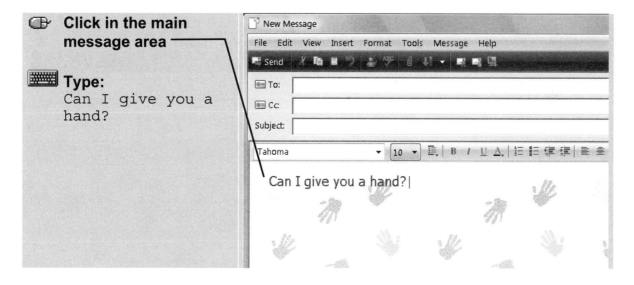

7.6 Emoticons

E-mail is primarily used to send short letters and messages. You usually type shorter sentences than you would in a regular letter. In order to make your intentions clear, you can use *emoticons*. Emoticon is a combination of the word emotion and icon. Emoticons show what you think of something, without using words. They are also known as *smileys*. The following emoticons are often used on the Internet:

:-) or :)	happy, smiling, joking	**;-)**	winking
:-(or :(	frowning, unhappy	**:-p**	sticking out your tongue
:-D	laughing	**:-c or :-<**	very unhappy
>:-<	angry	**:-x**	not saying anything
|-O	yawn	**{:-@**	angry
:-*	kiss	**:,-(**	crying
:-|	indifferent or ambivalent	**:-o**	surprised or concerned

If you lean your head to the left, you can see that these icons could be little faces. You can type these smileys using the letters and symbols on the keyboard.

Type: ; -)

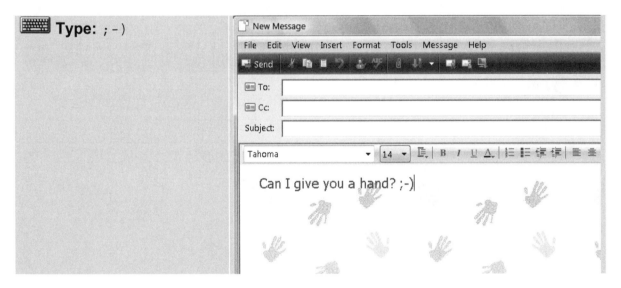

You can use these techniques to send an eye-catching e-mail to someone for special occasions like birthdays and holidays.

☞ **Close the message window** ℓℓ32

☞ **Do not save the changes to the message** ℓℓ55

Tip

Will they be able to see it?
You can easily send a formatted e-mail to anyone that has *Windows* and uses *Windows Mail* for their e-mail program.
If you are not sure whether the recipient uses this program, it is possible he or she will not be able to view your handsome e-mail.
You can send them a test e-mail first. They will let you know if they were able to read the message.

☞ **Close *Windows Mail*** 🐾43

7.7 E-mail Using Internet Explorer

The program *Internet Explorer* contains several functions that make it easy to send an e-mail when you are out on the World Wide Web. This can be useful if you have found an interesting website and want to send the web address to a friend. You can make use of this function as follows:

☞ **Open *Internet Explorer*** 🐾1

☞ **Open the *Internet for Seniors* practice website for this book** 🐾52

Now you see this page:

☞ **Click** File

☞ **Click** Send

You see two options for e-mail:

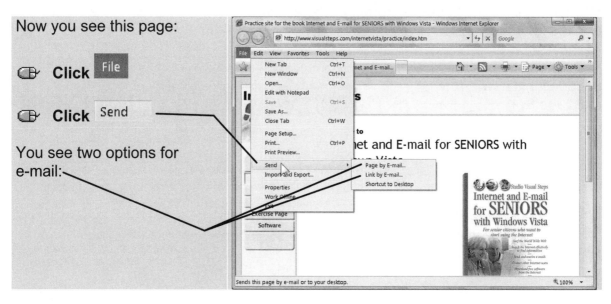

These two options are:

- send the page by e-mail
- send the web address (the link) by e-mail

You can send an *entire webpage* to someone by e-mail. It is more convenient, however, to send only the web address (the *link*). By clicking on the web address, the recipient of your e-mail can connect to the Internet and view the page in question. The great advantage of sending the link by e-mail is that the chance for error from typing the address (URL) is minimized. Try this:

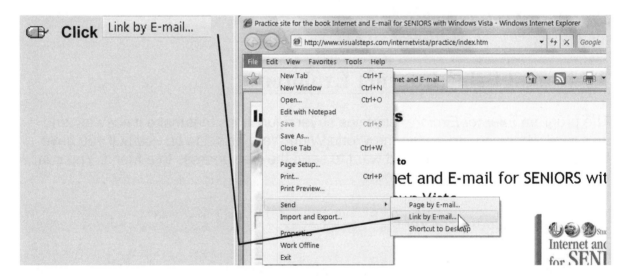

☞ **Click** Link by E-mail...

Windows Mail starts in the background and a new e-mail message is immediately created for you.

The subject has already been added in this new e-mail message:

The web address (the link) is already listed in the body of the message:

The recipient of this message just needs to click the link to view the webpage.

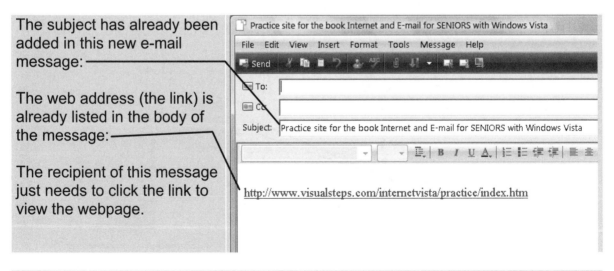

☞ **Close the message window** ⁄⁄32

7.8 An E-mail Address on a Website

Many websites list e-mail addresses you can use to contact a person, company or institution. Sometimes this is set up so that *Windows Mail* is started on your own computer with a new message. Give it a try:

👆 **Click** **Exercise Page**

There is a special link for creating an e-mail message:

👆 **Click** • Test e-mail

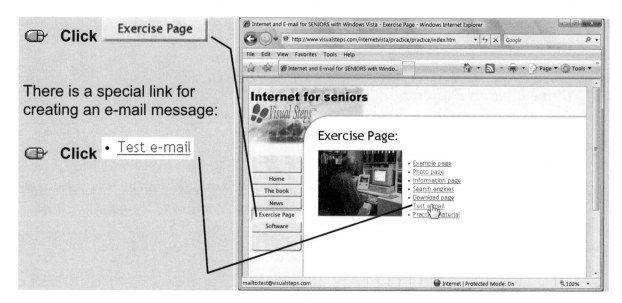

You will see a security warning, because a website is trying to open a program on your computer.

In this case it is safe to allow access:

👆 **Click** Allow

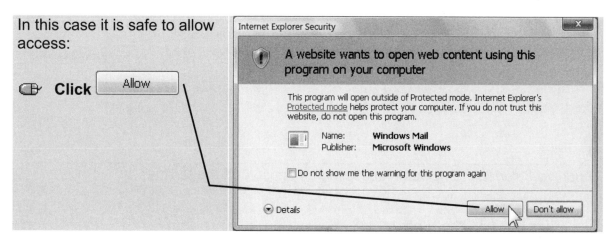

The standard program for e-mailing will be opened. In this case it is *Windows Mail*.

A new message is created.

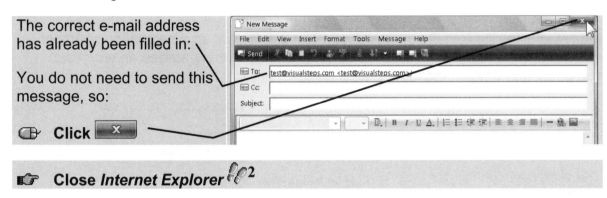

The correct e-mail address has already been filled in:

You do not need to send this message, so:

☞ **Click** ✖

👉 **Close** *Internet Explorer* 🦶²

7.9 Windows Calendar

Windows Calendar is a calendar application included in *Windows Vista*. The calendar can be accessed through *Windows Mail*. You can open *Windows Calendar* like this:

👉 **If necessary, open** *Windows Mail* 🦶³⁵

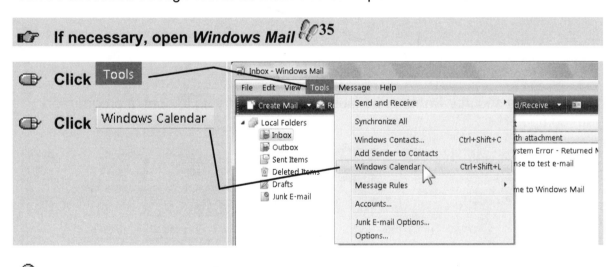

☞ **Click** Tools

☞ **Click** Windows Calendar

💡 **Tip**

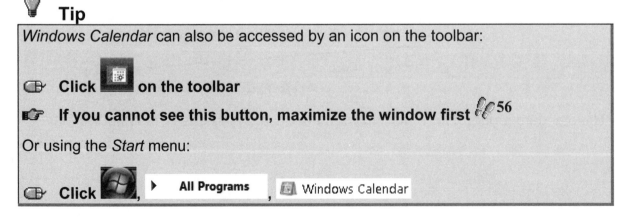

Windows Calendar can also be accessed by an icon on the toolbar:

☞ **Click** 📅 **on the toolbar**

👉 **If you cannot see this button, maximize the window first** 🦶⁵⁶

Or using the *Start* menu:

☞ **Click** ⊞ , ▶ **All Programs** , 📅 Windows Calendar

You see the *Windows Calendar* window:

The calendar shows the current day and time:

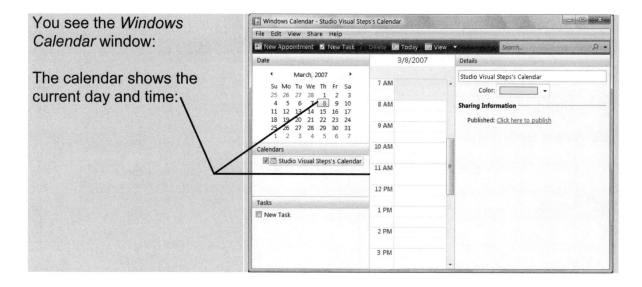

7.10 Adding a New Appointment

Just like your paper calendar, you can use *Windows Calendar* to keep track of your appointments. Give it a try:

Click

New Appointment

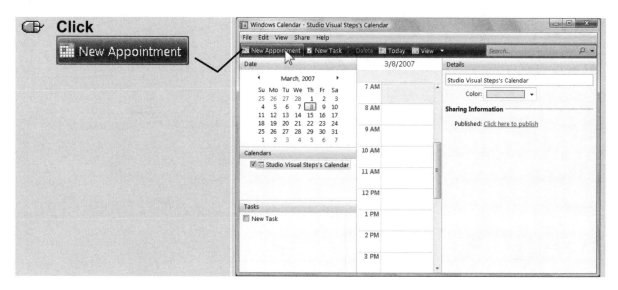

A new appointment appears in the current day and time:

You can type the title of this appointment right away:

Type: Meeting

Press Enter

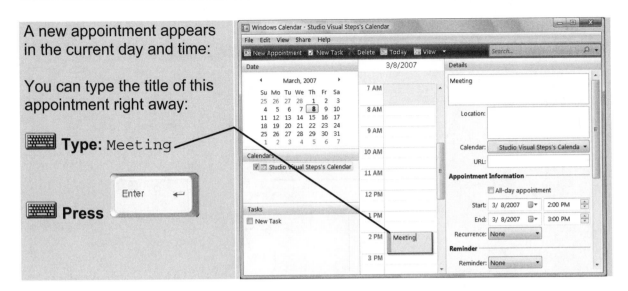

On the right hand side of the window, you can edit the details for the meeting. First enter the location of the meeting:

Click the text box next to Location:

Type: Office

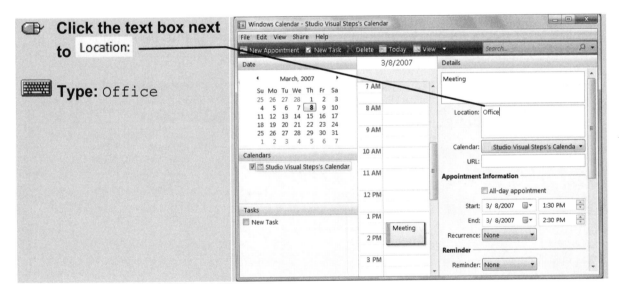

Below **Appointment Information** you can set more details for the meeting.

For an appointment that will last all day, check the box ☐ All-day appointment :

Otherwise you can enter the date and the start- and end-times here:

For a repeating appointment, set Recurrence: to weekly, monthly, etc.

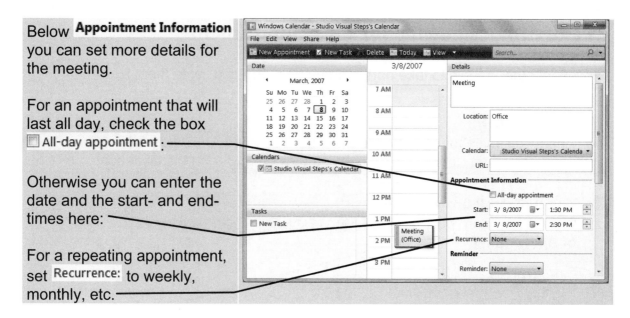

For this practice appointment, you do not need to change any of these items.

💡 Tip

Choosing a date and a time
In *Windows Mail* you can quickly set a date and a time for a new appointment like this:

👆 **Click on a date, for example the 23rd**

The date on display in *Windows Calendar* changes to the 23rd.

👆 **Double-click next to 1 AM**

A new appointment is created that will last from 1 AM until 2 AM:

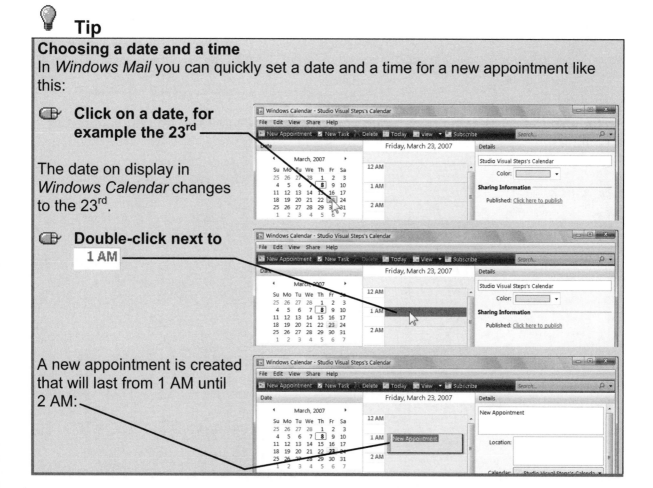

7.11 Inviting Someone for an Appointment

If you want other people to take part in a meeting, you can invite them by e-mail.

 Please note:

The people you invite for an appointment must use *Windows Calendar* or a comparable calendar application. Otherwise they cannot read the invitation.

☞ **Use the scroll box to view the bottom part of the window**

☞ **Click** Attendees:

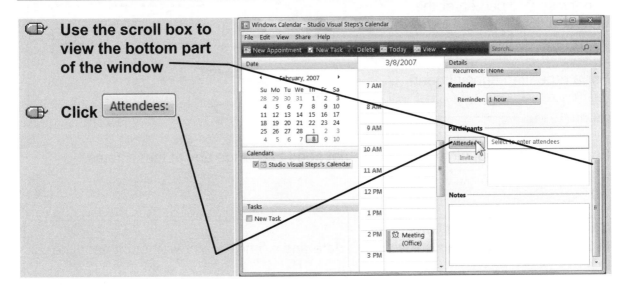

To be able to see what happens when you receive an invitation, first add yourself as a contact:

☞ **Click** New Contact

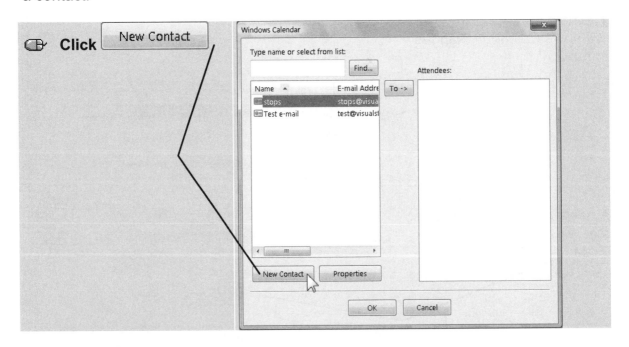

☞ **Enter your own name and e-mail address**

👆 **Click** OK

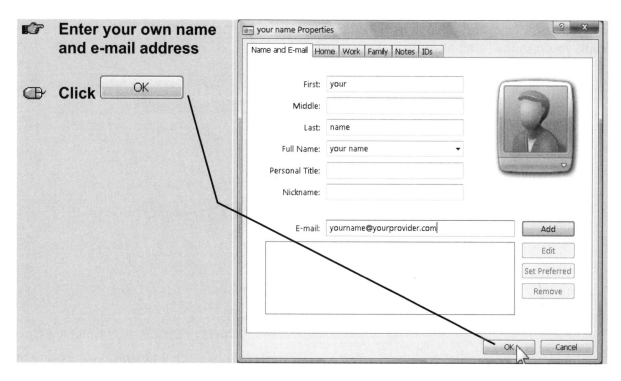

Your name is added tot the *Contacts* folder.

👆 **Click your name**

👆 **Click** To ->

Your name is added to the list of attendees:

👆 **Click** OK

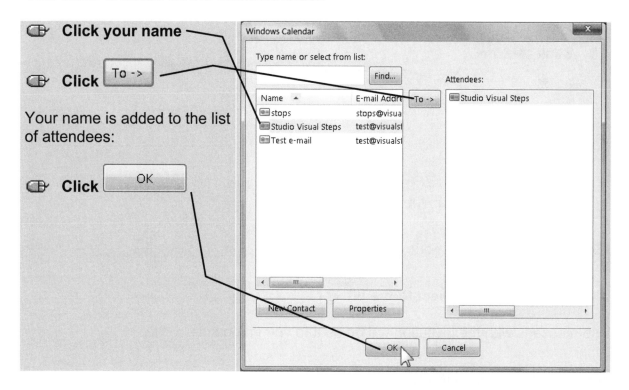

If necessary, you can always add more people to the attendees list. Then with one click you can invite all attendees for the meeting:

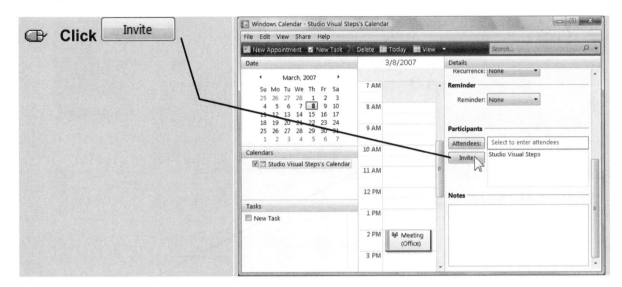

The standard program for e-mailing will be opened. In this case it is *Windows Mail*.

A new e-mail message is created:

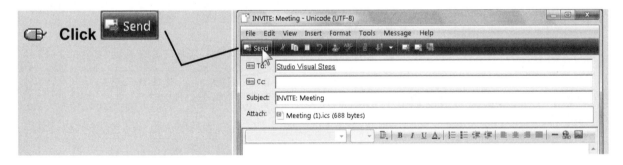

Your message is placed in the *Outbox.*

☞ **Send and receive your e-mail** 🐾 **39**

☞ **If necessary, connect to the Internet** 🐾 **3**

The message with the invitation will be sent to you immediately.

☞ **Check your mail in the *Inbox*** 🐾 **39**

7.12 Receiving an Invitation to an Appointment

The invitation has been received in your *Inbox*:

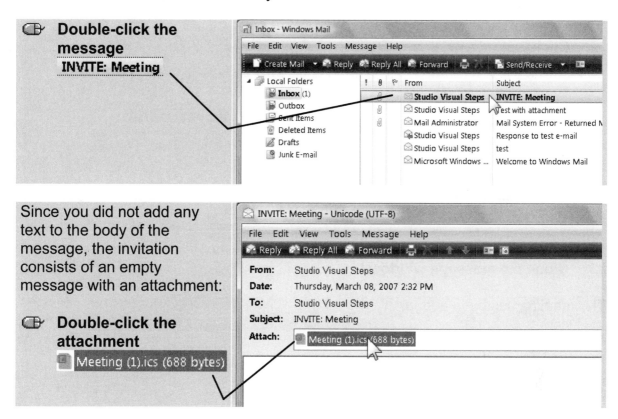

☞ **Double-click the message**
INVITE: Meeting

Since you did not add any text to the body of the message, the invitation consists of an empty message with an attachment:

☞ **Double-click the attachment**
Meeting (1).ics (688 bytes)

The attachment is an .ICS-file. This is the typical extension for an *iCalendar* file. *iCalendar* is a standard for calendar data exchange. This means you can import all appointments of that format into your own calendar.

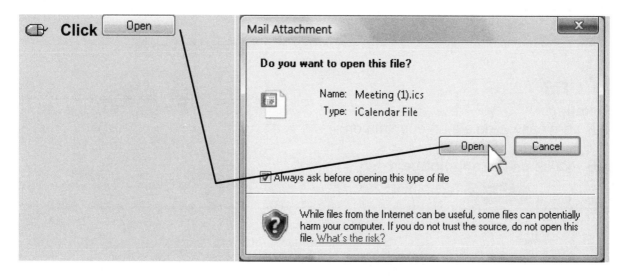

☞ **Click** Open

An appointment you receive can be merged with your own calendar, or created in a new calendar. Since the meeting is already in your own calendar, you create a new calendar. This way you can see the difference between the existing and the new appointment.

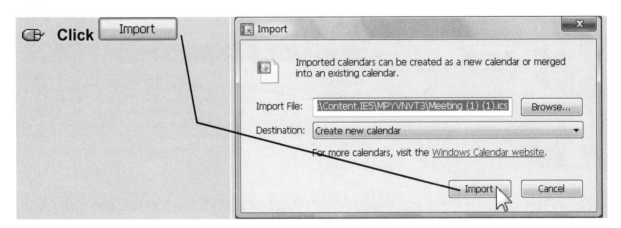

👉 **Close the message window** 〰️ 32

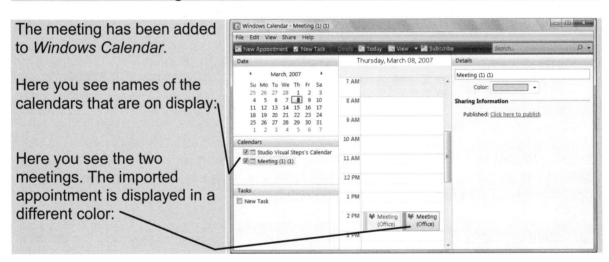

The meeting has been added to *Windows Calendar*.

Here you see names of the calendars that are on display:

Here you see the two meetings. The imported appointment is displayed in a different color:

💡 **Tip**

Deleting
It is very easy to delete an appointment:

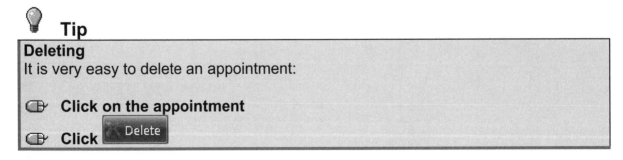

7.13 Setting and Receiving a Reminder

When you create an appointment, you can set a reminder to be warned before the meeting starts.

Click one of the appointments

Click None ▼ **next to** Reminder:

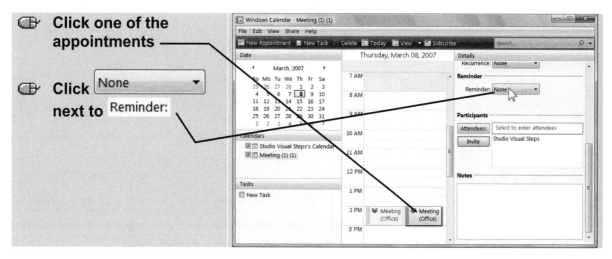

Now you can choose how long in advance you would like to be reminded of the meeting:

Click 15 minutes

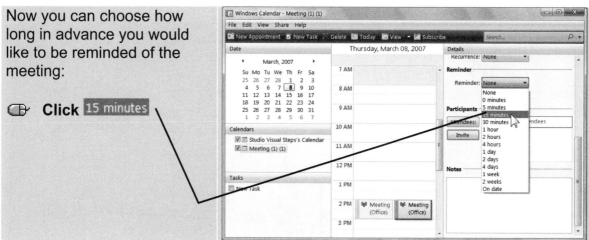

Since you did not set a specific time for the appointment, it was set at the current time of the moment you created it. If that is about 15 minutes ago, you will receive the reminder right away:

You see the window *1 Reminder*.

If you would like to receive another reminder for this appointment you can use the Snooze button:

Here you can set the time until the next reminder:

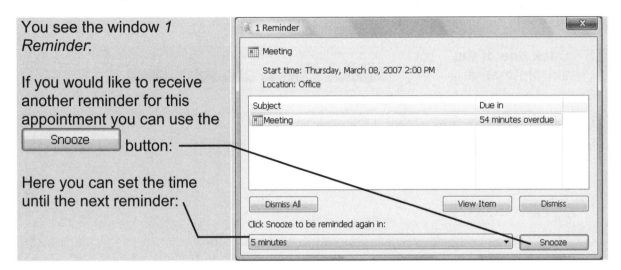

If you do not need another reminder, you can dismiss the reminder:

Click Dismiss

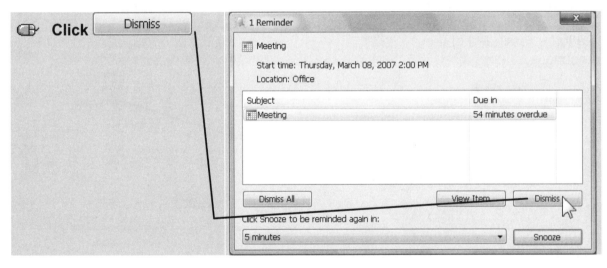

☞ **Close *Windows Calendar* 32**

☞ **Close *Windows Mail* 43**

You can practice what you have learned in this chapter by doing the following exercises.

7.14 Exercises

Have you forgotten how to do something? Use the number beside the footsteps to look it up in the appendix *How Do I Do That Again?*

Exercise: Creating a Formatted E-mail

In this exercise, you will practice creating a formatted e-mail.

✔ Open *Windows Mail.* ℓℓ³⁵

✔ Create a new e-mail message addressed to yourself. ℓℓ³⁶

✔ Choose a larger font size of 14 points. ℓℓ⁴⁷

✔ Type in the following message:
`Larger letters are easier to read.`

✔ Choose a ready-made stationery as background. ℓℓ⁴⁸

✔ Send this e-mail to the *Outbox.* ℓℓ³⁷

Exercise: Planning a Day Off

In this exercise, you will practice using *Windows Calendar.*

✔ Open *Windows Calendar.* ℓℓ⁴⁹

✔ Below Date , click on tomorrow.

✔ Create a new appointment. ℓℓ⁵⁰

✔ Type the following name for the appointment: `Day off`

✔ Set the appointment to last all day. ℓℓ⁶⁸

✔ Close *Windows Calendar* ℓℓ³² and *Windows Mail.* ℓℓ⁴³

7.15 Background Information

Glossary	
Rich Text	E-mail with formatted text and images, also called *HTML*.
Webmail	E-mail service that is offered through a website. If you have a webmail address, you can read your e-mail anywhere in the world, as long as Internet access is available.
Stationery	With *Windows Mail*, you can enhance the appearance of your e-mail messages using stationery that features custom backgrounds, fonts, and colors. A variety of stationery designs are included for you to choose from.
Emoticons	Sequences of keyboard characters that symbolize facial expressions. For example, :-) looks like a smiling face when you look at it sideways.
HTML	A language used to create documents for the web. The term HTML is also used for an e-mail with formatted text and images, also called *Rich Text*.
.ICS	The typical extension for an *iCalendar* file. An *iCalendar* file is a standard file format that makes it possible to share and transfer calendar entries.
Font	A font is a collection of numbers, symbols, and characters. A font describes a certain typeface, along with other qualities, such as size and spacing.
Formatting bar	The toolbar that you can use to format the text of your e-mail message.
Windows Calendar	Calendar application that comes with *Windows Vista*. It can be accessed directly, or via *Windows Mail*. Supports the *iCalendar* file format and has the ability to publish and subscribe to web-based calendars.

Source: Windows Help and Support

E-mail abroad
Almost everywhere in the world, you can find public places with access to the Internet. There are Internet cafés where you can access the World Wide Web for a fee. Many libraries have Internet enabled computers, and more and more hotels are offering similar services.

For sending and receiving e-mails while you are away from home, it is useful to have an e-mail address you can access via the World Wide Web. This is called *webmail*. The most well known webmail services are *Windows Live Mail*, *Hotmail*, *G-Mail* (from *Google*) and *Yahoo! Mail*.

If you have a webmail address, you can read your e-mail anywhere in the world.

Internet abroad
If you will be traveling abroad for a long time and want to have Internet access while you are away, you will need to arrange for local access. It would be very costly to have your computer connect through your dial-up number in the United States. There are several options.

- Ask your ISP if it has dial-up numbers in the countries where you will be traveling. This is called *roaming*. Many American ISPs have foreign dial-up numbers. If your *Internet Service Provider* does not have options for a local dial-up connection where you will be traveling, you can explore other options.

- You can consider using an ISP with a worldwide presence. For example, *Compuserve* is a worldwide organization with local dial-up numbers around the world. If you have a subscription in the US, you will also have access abroad.

- Another possibility is a temporary subscription with a free ISP abroad, such as *FreeSurf* in France, *Wanadoo* in the Netherlands, or *LiveDoor* in Japan. You can keep your regular Internet subscription and have your mail forwarded to your new free e-mail address in the other country. One disadvantage is that the instructions and installation software will probably be in a foreign language.

E-mail services from ISPs
Many ISPs offer various kinds of services for processing your e-mail.

- **Webmail**
  Many *Internet Service Providers* offer the option of using *webmail.* You can view and send your e-mail from your regular account on your ISP's website by navigating to their *Webmail* option. You do this using *Internet Explorer.* You will need your account information: username and password on hand. In this way, you have access to your e-mail on any computer with internet access.

- **Forwarding your e-mails**
  Every incoming e-mail is sent through (forwarded) to an e-mail address you specify. For example, you can have your e-mails forwarded to your *Hotmail* address if you have one.

- **Automatic reply**
  Every incoming e-mail is automatically answered with a message you have written beforehand. This is useful if you are on vacation, to let people know that you are away and will not be able to reply immediately to an e-mail. This service is also called *Vacation Service.* But be careful, by using this option you will also reply to every spam e-mail you receive. This confirms to the company sending the spam that your e-mail address is in use, which will lead to even more spam.

- **A second e-mail address**
  Many ISPs give you the opportunity to request multiple e-mail addresses, for example, for additional family members. It can also be useful to have multiple e-mail addresses if you want to keep your e-mails separated; for example, your private correspondence and the e-mail you receive as secretary for a club. You can read how to set up multiple e-mail addresses (accounts) in *Windows Mail* in Appendix B.

- **Changing your e-mail address**
  You can usually change your e-mail address if it works better for you. You may need to do that if you use multiple e-mail addresses to help prevent confusion.

- **Changing your password**
  Your ISP probably gave you your own password for your e-mail account. In most cases you did not choose this password yourself. It can be useful, however, to choose a password you can easily remember.

- **Links to other communication media**
  Some ISPs provide a service for sending e-mail to cellular phones, for example.

- **Spam filter**
  Some ISPs can filter out unwelcome commercial e-mails for you.

You can read which services are available on your ISP's subscriber service website.

Newsgroups

There is a special kind of e-mail called *newsgroups*, or *discussion groups*. These are comparable to bulletin boards where people place messages and others react to them. There are thousands of newsgroups covering nearly every subject imaginable. If you have subscribed to one of these newsgroups, you can read the messages and responses to them in *Windows Mail*. You can participate in the discussion by posting a message of your own if you so desire.

In order to set up *Windows Mail* to read newsgroups, you must first have the name of a *news server.* You can get this from your *Internet Service Provider*. Then you can download all available newsgroups from that server.

That is an enormous list containing thousands of groups:

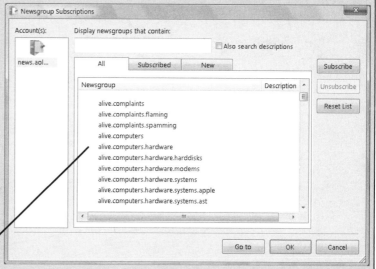

You can then subscribe to one or more of these newsgroups. "Subscribe" is actually a confusing word, because your name and so forth are not recorded. The only thing that happens is that all the messages in the newsgroup you have chosen are downloaded.

When you open the newsgroups in *Windows Mail,* you can *synchronize* the messages. That means that your list is updated with the current list of messages on the news server.

The content and quality of each newsgroup differs tremendously from one subject to the next, and a word of warning is in order. In some newsgroups, the "dark side" of the Internet emerges: the most extreme subjects are "discussed" by strangers, and it often becomes clear that someone is hiding behind anonymity. On the Internet, you can never be certain of someone's identity.

7.16 Tips

 Tip

A photo as background
You can use a photo or illustration as a background for your e-mail.
In the *New Message* window:

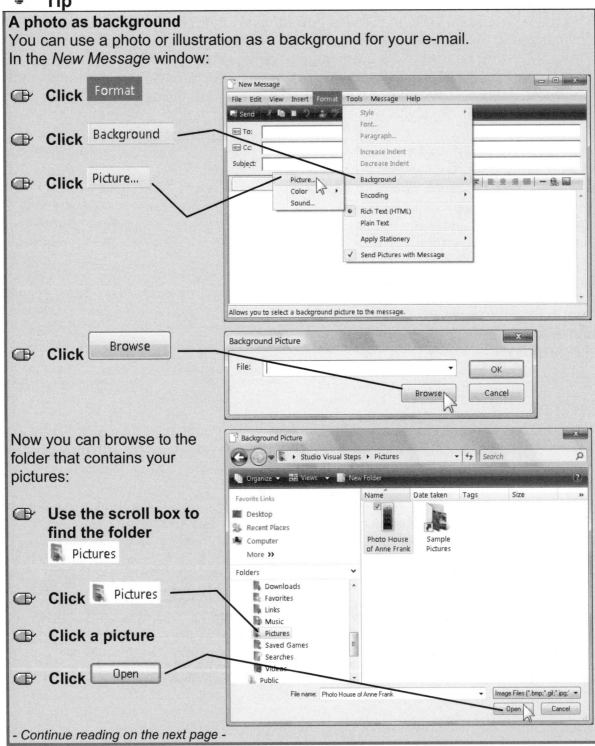

☞ **Click** Format

☞ **Click** Background

☞ **Click** Picture...

☞ **Click** Browse

Now you can browse to the folder that contains your pictures:

☞ **Use the scroll box to find the folder** Pictures

☞ **Click** Pictures

☞ **Click a picture**

☞ **Click** Open

- Continue reading on the next page -

Click OK

The picture has been added as a background for your e-mail:

💡 Tip

Unusual fonts

Try to use only well-known fonts such as *Times New Roman* and *Arial* in your e-mails. Not everyone has the same fonts installed on his or her computer. Some drawing programs, for example, will install the most beautiful fonts, but that does not mean the recipient of your e-mail has the same font on his computer. In that case, your handsome e-mail will be shown in a default font.

Tip

How to access your Contacts folder directly

You have used your *Contacts* folder as an address book for *Windows Mail*. But you do not need to open *Windows Mail* to access your contacts. You can find the folder *Contacts* in your *Personal* folder. This is a folder containing your most frequently used folders (such as *Documents, Pictures, Music, Favorites, Contacts*).

Your *Personal* folder is labeled with the name you use to log on to your computer and is located at the top of the *Start* menu.

☞ **Click**

☞ **Click your *Personal* folder**

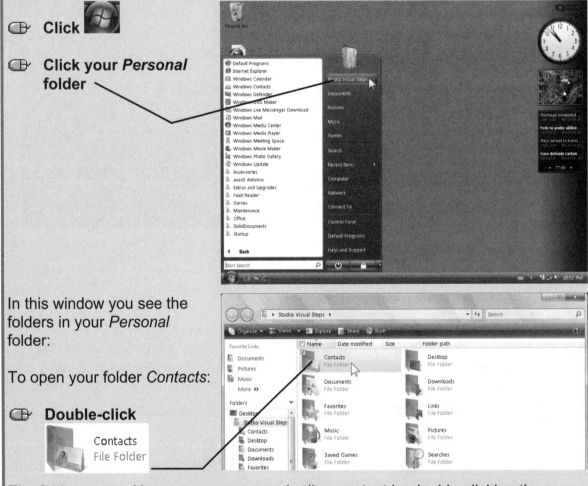

In this window you see the folders in your *Personal* folder:

To open your folder *Contacts*:

☞ **Double-click**

The folder opens. Now you can open and edit a contact by double-clicking the

picture next to a contact.

You can use the button ▣ New Contact to add a new contact. Alternatively, you can right-click in the white area of the window where you see the pictures of your

contacts. Choose New and ▣ Contact from the menus that appear.

8. Downloading Files

There is a vast amount of information on the Internet that you can copy onto your own computer. This copying is called *downloading*. The opposite of *downloading* is *uploading* (sending files from your computer to the Internet).

You can download just about anything: computer programs, music, video films and more. After you have downloaded something, you usually save it to your computer's hard drive so that you can use it again later.

For computer programs, the second step after downloading is usually installing the program onto your computer. Installation makes the program ready for use so that you can work with it. For example, the program gets added to the *Start* menu so you can start it easily.

There is a separate webpage for this chapter on the *Internet for Seniors* website. Here you will find different kinds of files to practice downloading. In addition, we have included a small computer program, the *Alarm clock*, to demonstrate how you install a program that you have downloaded. Once you know how to do this, a wealth of (free) computer programs lies waiting for you on the Internet. Not only programs that are enjoyable or useful for you, but also for your grandchildren, for example.

The Internet is also becoming an increasingly important medium for computer and software manufacturers. You can often download the latest versions of software from the Internet, and it is frequently the best way to replace faulty software with the most recent improved version. In short, downloading is becoming more and more important in the maintenance of your computer.

In this chapter, you will learn how to:

- download the *Alarm clock*
- install the program
- remove the installation program from the folder *Downloads*

8.1 The Practice Website

There is a practice page for this chapter on the *Internet for Seniors* website. To work through this chapter, you will first connect to the Internet and then open this web page.

☞ **Start *Internet Explorer*** 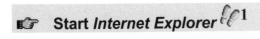¹

☞ **Connect to the Internet if necessary** 👣³

☞ **Open the *Internet for Seniors* website** 👣52

There is a page for practicing downloading on the website. Take a look at this page:

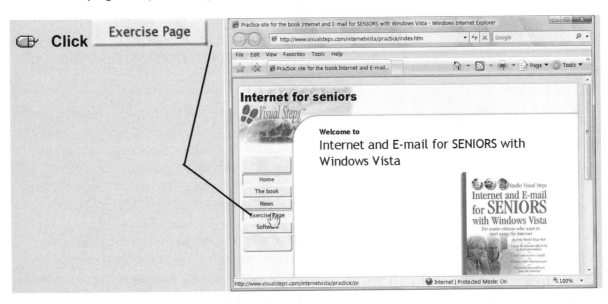

Click Exercise Page

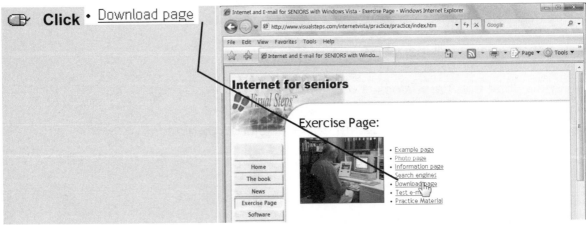

Click • Download page

8.2 Downloading the Alarm Clock

In order to practice downloading software, there is a small program on the website called the *Alarm clock*. You will see how to download this program and then install it.

You see a page with different kinds of files:

Among them is the *Alarm clock* program. You can start downloading it by clicking on the name:

☞ **Click** <u>Alarm clock</u>

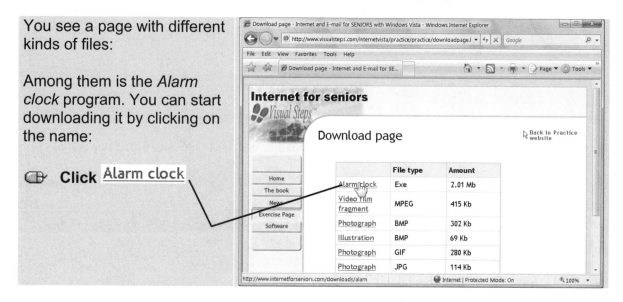

A window appears where you can choose between two options:

You can choose to:

○ *run* the file.
  In this case, the installation program is immediately started;
○ *save* the file.
  Then the file will be saved to your computer first. Afterwards, you have to start the installation program yourself.

In this case, it is a good idea to save the file first:

🖰 **Click** [Save]

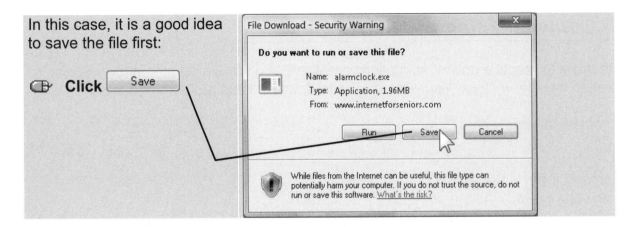

A window appears in which you can specify where you want to save the file:

By default, a downloaded file will be saved in the folder
▶ Downloads in your *Personal* folder:

The file already has a name, alarmclock:

🖰 **Click** [Save]

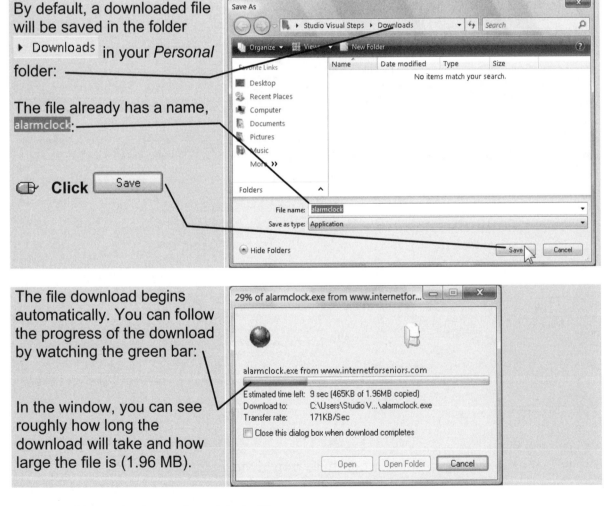

The file download begins automatically. You can follow the progress of the download by watching the green bar:

In the window, you can see roughly how long the download will take and how large the file is (1.96 MB).

Has the entire file been downloaded?

🖰 **Click** [Close]

Now you can close *Internet Explorer* and disconnect from the Internet.

☞ **Close *Internet Explorer*** 2

☞ **Disconnect from the Internet if necessary** 5

The *Alarm clock* program has been downloaded and is stored on your computer's hard drive. Now you can install the program on your computer.

💡 **Tip**

Downloading? Always save to the same folder.
It is a good idea to save the files you have downloaded in the same folder, for example in ▸ Downloads . It makes it easier to find your files later on.

8.3 Installing the Program

Most computer programs contain several parts. In order for the program to work properly, all these parts have to be correctly installed on your computer. The different parts are then copied to the right place on your hard drive and the program name is added to the *Start* menu in *Windows*. All this work is done by the installation program. This is also how the *Alarm clock* installation works.

You saved the installation program to the folder *Downloads* in your *Personal* folder. First you open that folder:

👉 **Click**

👉 **Click the folder with your name**

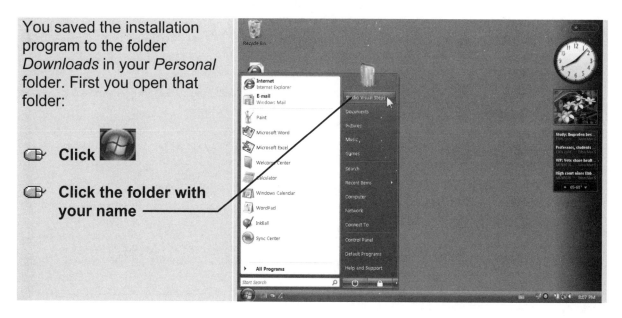

You see the folder with the
contents of your *Personal*
folder:

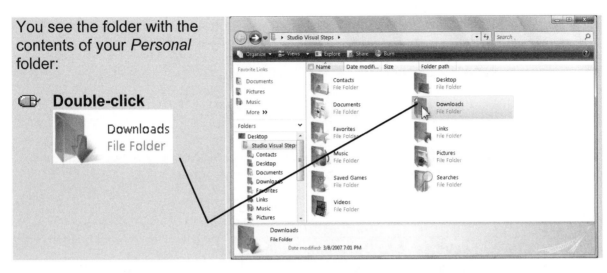

☞ **Double-click**

The file 🕰 alarmclock has
been stored in this folder.

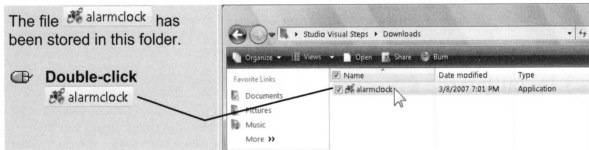

☞ **Double-click**
🕰 alarmclock

First you see a security warning. *Windows Vista* wants to verify that you really want
to run the installation program:

☞ **Click** [Run]

Your screen goes dark and you see this window with a warning:

In this case you can allow the program to continue the installation:

☞ **Click**

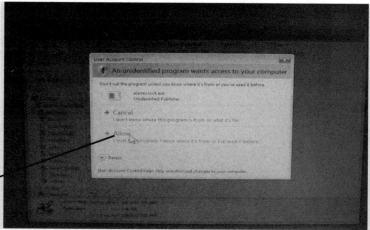

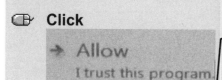

Various windows will appear one after another as the installation is being set up:

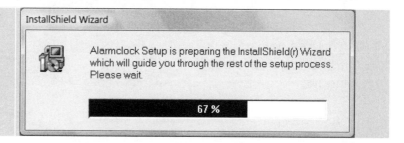

Then you see this window:

☞ **Click** _____

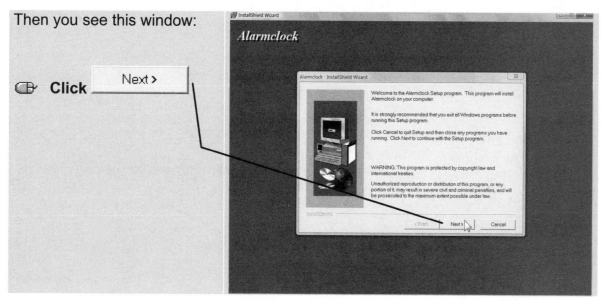

This program uses the word *setup*. This means the same thing as *installation*. You will see four more windows in a row, all of which can be left unchanged. This means you can keep going to the next window:

☞ **Click in the next four windows on** _____ Next >

Finally, you see this last window:

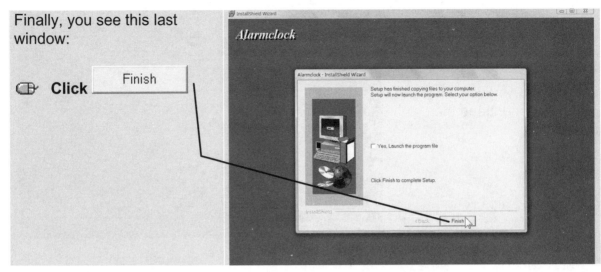

➥ **Click** [Finish]

When you see a window with the *Alarm clock* icon, close that window:

➥ **Click** [X]

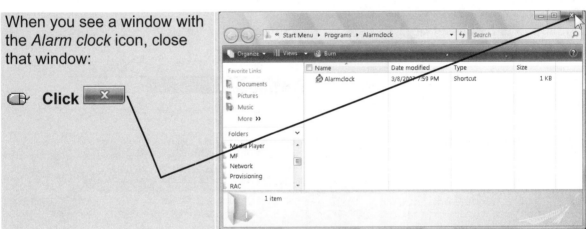

You see the *Downloads* folder window again:

You can close this window as well:

➥ **Click** [X]

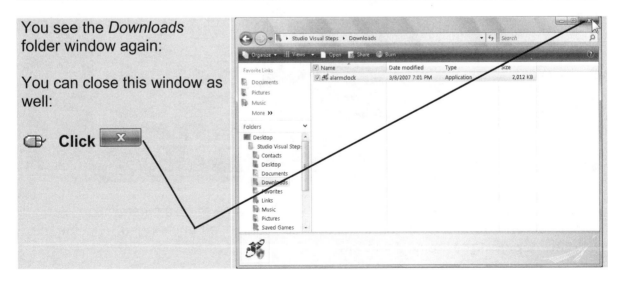

Most installation programs work more or less the same way as the *Alarm clock*. You have seen how this kind of installation works. Now you can start the *Alarm clock* program.

 Please note:

You do not need the installation program anymore. A little further in the book, you will read how you can remove the installation program.

8.4 Starting the Alarm Clock

You use the *Start* button to start a new program:

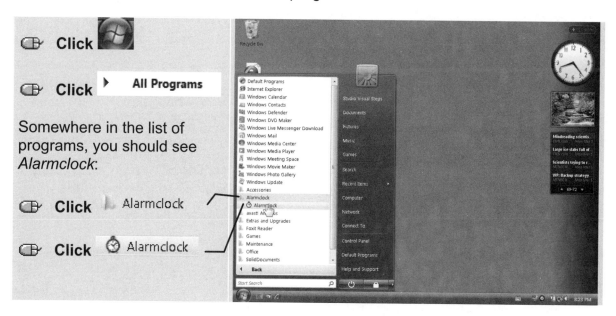

Click

Click ▶ **All Programs**

Somewhere in the list of programs, you should see *Alarmclock*:

Click Alarmclock

Click 🕐 Alarmclock

The program starts.

You see this little window:

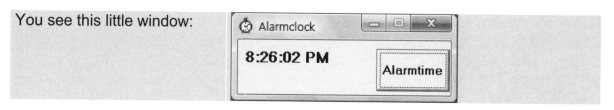

Tip

How does the alarm clock work?

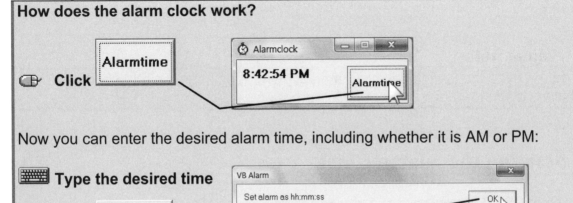

Now you can enter the desired alarm time, including whether it is AM or PM:

The alarm time has now been set. You can minimize the window to the taskbar. As soon as the time you set is reached, a small pop-up window appears and you hear a sound.

The *Alarm clock* comes in handy when you need to be reminded of an appointment, or for example, when you want to keep track of how long you are working at the computer. This way you can prevent RSI from developing in your hands and wrists.

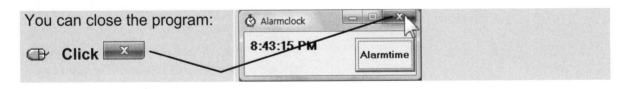

8.5 Deleting the Installation Program

Now that the *Alarm clock* works, you can remove the installation program. You can delete it as follows:

☞ **Open the folder *Downloads*** $\ell\ell^{61}$

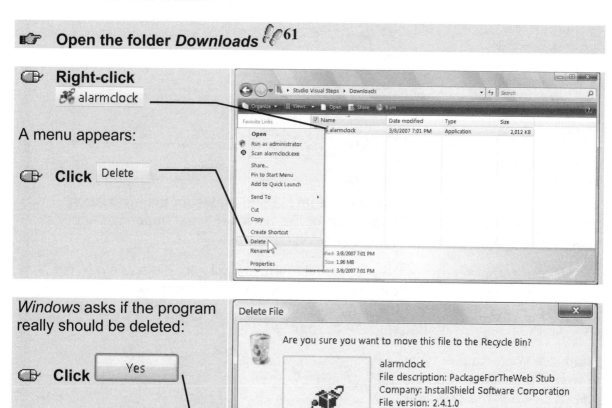

⊕ **Right-click**
      🐞 alarmclock

A menu appears:

⊕ **Click** Delete

Windows asks if the program
really should be deleted:

⊕ **Click** Yes

The installation program is removed.

☞ **Close the folder *Downloads*** $\ell\ell^{32}$

8.6 Open or Save?

When you download a file, you will usually be asked if you want to *run* it or *save* it on the hard drive. Then you see this window:

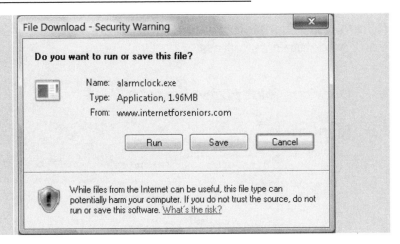

You have seen how you can save a program file and then start the installation process. If you download a different type of file, however, what happens depends upon the kind of file and your computer's settings.

- If your computer recognizes the file type, the file will sometimes be opened right away, and you will not be able to choose between *run* and *save*.
- Depending on the programs available on your computer, the appropriate program may be started and the file opened.

There are various other types of files to practice with on the *Internet for Seniors Download page*:

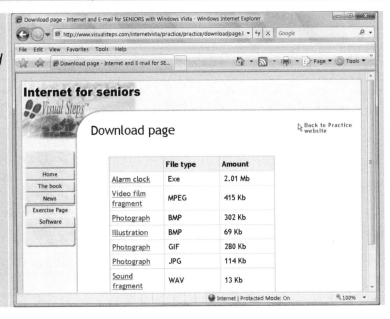

These are photos and music in different file formats. Some of these files will open on the web page itself, others require another program to be opened.
In the following exercises, you can download these files and see what happens with them on your computer.

8.7 Exercises

Have you forgotten how to do something? Use the number beside the footsteps to look it up in the appendix *How Do I Do That Again?*

Exercise: Downloading

In this exercise, you will practice downloading files.

✔ Start *Internet Explorer.* 𝕱𝕱¹

✔ Connect to the Internet if necessary. 𝕱𝕱³

✔ Open the *Internet for Seniors* practice website. 𝕱𝕱⁵²

✔ Click   Exercise Page .

✔ Click • Download page .

✔ Open a video clip (MPEG). 𝕱𝕱⁵¹

✔ Open a photo (JPG). 𝕱𝕱⁵¹

✔ Open a photo (GIF). 𝕱𝕱⁵¹

✔ Open a music file (MIDI). 𝕱𝕱⁵¹

✔ Close *Internet Explorer.* 𝕱𝕱²

✔ Disconnect from the Internet if necessary. 𝕱𝕱⁵

8.8 Background Information

Glossary	
AVI	Filename extension for compressed video files. The acronym stands for *Audio Video Interleave.*
BMP	*BMP* was developed by Microsoft and is the native graphics format for *Windows* users. The files are usually not compressed and can be quite large. Also known as *bitmap.*
Cable Internet	Cable Internet access is a broadband connection that uses the same wiring as cable TV. To use cable, you need an account with a cable *Internet Service Provider* in your area. The ISP usually provides any necessary equipment, and often sends a technician to set it up for you.
CDA	Filename extension for a small (44 bytes) file generated by *Microsoft Windows* for each track on an audio CD. Tells where on the disc the track starts and stops.
Download	Copying a file from one computer to another using a modem or network. For example, copying software from a website.
Installation	In order for a program to work properly, all parts have to be correctly installed on your computer. This means that the different parts are copied to the right place on your hard drive and the program name is added to the *Start* menu in *Windows.* All this work is done by the installation program. How you add a program depends on where the installation files for the program are located. Typically, programs are installed from a CD or DVD, from the Internet, or from a network.
JPG, JPEG	Filename extension for compressed image files such as photographs, in the format developed by the *Joint Photographers Experts Group.*
EXE	Filename extension for an executable file, a program that can be installed or run on your computer.
MPG, MPEG	Filename extension for compressed video files, in the format developed by the *Moving Pictures Experts Group.*

- Continue reading on the next page -

MP3	Filename extension for compressed audio files, in the *MPEG Audio Layer 3* format. MP3 is the most popular way for compressing audio files and exchanging them on the Internet.
Setup	Installation.
WAV	Filename extension for uncompressed audio files, the acronym stands for *Waveform Audio Format.* The system sounds on your computers are also stored in this format.
WMA	Filename extension for compressed audio files in the *Windows Media Audio* format.

Source: Windows Help and Support

Types of software
Various types of software are available on the Internet:

Freeware
This software may be freely used and copied. It is sometimes also called *Public Domain* software.

Shareware
The program may be used free of charge for a period of time so you can try it out. If you would like to keep using it after the trial period, you must pay.

Cardware
Similar to shareware, but the maker wants you to recognize that this is his or her intellectual property. The user is expected to send a postcard indicating that he or she is using the program. Also called postcardware.

Demos
Demos are free software in which some functions have been disabled. The functions that still work give a good idea of the software's capabilities.
Sometimes the demo works fully, but only for a limited time.

Updates
These are additions, patches or improvements to existing software. They are often provided free of charge to people who have a license for the original program.

Cookies
Cookies are small text files that websites put on your computer to store information about you. This information can be requested by websites in order to determine various things, such as your settings or user name for that website. Using cookies, you only have to enter that information once. Cookies can be misused, however. Information about your browsing behavior may be made available to marketing companies.

Plug-ins
A *plug-in* is an accessory program which can be installed as an extra in *Internet Explorer*. Plug-ins are often required for viewing video clips and animations or listening to music. You usually download them free of charge from the Internet. The following programs are required in order to open specific file types:

- *Macromedia Flash Player:* for viewing and interactive use of animations on websites.
- *RealPlayer:* for playing sound and music; among other things, this program makes it possible to follow radio broadcasts over the Internet.
- *MP3-Player:* plays highly-compressed music files at near-CD quality.
- *Adobe Reader:* reads PDF documents; many manuals and brochures on the Internet are distributed in this file format.

Windows Media Player
You can play music and video without plug-ins, too: *Media Player* is installed when you install *Windows*.

This program can play various file types:
- WMA, MP3, WAV: music and sound
- CDA: CD Audio Track
- WMV, MPEG, AVI: video files

Windows Live Messenger

You can use *Windows Live Messenger* to stay in touch with friends, colleagues and family.

The principle is simple. When you are connected to the Internet, the *Live Messenger* window shows which one of your contacts is online. Your contacts can also see if you are online or not.

You can start up an online conversation with a contact by typing and sending instant messages (IM). This is also called *chatting*.
It is also possible to start a conversation using a microphone and by using a webcam you can have a *face-to-face* experience.

You can download the *Messenger* program free of charge at http://get.live.com/messenger/overview.

The cable modem

A cable company offers Internet access by using the same cables which are used for TV broadcasts to transmit both upstream and downstream data from the Internet.

The cable TV outlet

An external cable modem

- *Continue reading on the next page -*

The way in which your computer connects differs greatly from one cable provider to the next. Sometimes a mechanic will install an *internal cable modem* into your computer. Alternatively, an *external modem* might be placed between your computer and the cable outlet. The modem is then connected to your computer with another cable.

The ISDN Modem

ISDN has a number of advantages over the regular telephone line. First, its speed is greater than that of the regular telephone network. This is particularly evident when you are surfing the Internet. Another advantage is that you have two telephone lines. This means that you can use the telephone and the Internet at the same time.
If you choose ISDN, you will need to buy an ISDN modem in order to benefit from the increased speed. There are external and internal ISDN modems. They look just like regular modems, with a slightly different telephone jack. An internal modem is sometimes called an *ISDN card*.

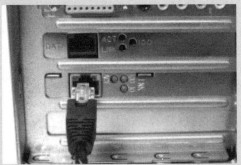
An ISDN card in the computer

An external ISDN modem

DSL

The most recent development is DSL. With DSL, the telephone line coming into your home is split. Your telephone connects to one jack, and your computer connects to the other through a modem. The big advantage of DSL is that, just as with a cable connection, you are connected to the Internet twenty-four hours a day. The DSL connection is very fast and you can call on the telephone and use the Internet all at the same time.

8.9 Tips

 Tip

Updating Windows Vista
Updating means replacing your system files with the very latest versions. The *Windows Update* program scans your computer, creates a list of files that can be updated, and then installs the files. These files are automatically downloaded from the *Microsoft* website. Here is how you start *Windows Update*:

👉 **Click**

👉 **Click** ▶ **All Programs**

👉 **Click** 🖼 Windows Update

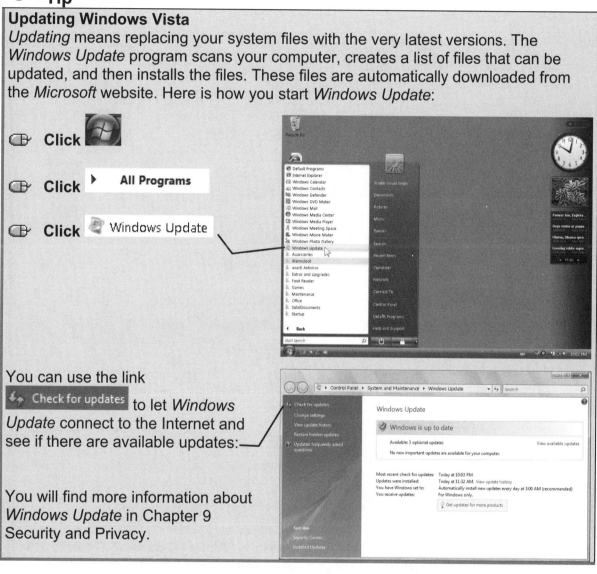

You can use the link

 Check for updates to let *Windows Update* connect to the Internet and see if there are available updates:———

You will find more information about *Windows Update* in Chapter 9 Security and Privacy.

 Tip

Where can I find programs?
There are websites with huge software libraries.
On the *Internet for Seniors* website, you will find a special software page with up-to-date information on locations where you can find interesting programs.

Tip

Uninstalling a program

You can uninstall a program from your computer if you no longer use it or if you want to free up space on your hard drive. This is the safest way to uninstall a program:

In the group :

You see a list of programs that have been installed on your computer:

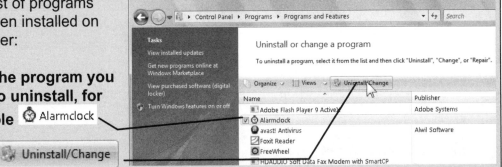

First, your screen goes dark: *Windows Vista* wants your permission to continue the operation. To grant permission you click the *Continue* button.

As a safety measure, you must confirm again that you want to remove the program. You do that by clicking the *Yes* button.

Finally, the *Uninstall Shield* window appears. You see the various components of the program being removed. When you see the message "Uninstall successfully completed", the program has been removed from your computer.

9. Security and Privacy

In previous chapters, you have acquired a lot of experience with the Internet. This chapter describes the settings and programs you can use to make using the Internet both easier and safer. For example, you will read how you can let *Internet Explorer* connect or disconnect from the Internet automatically. To ensure your privacy, this chapter also describes how you can delete your browsing history.

Security is essential for computers that are regularly connected to the Internet. A good security system reduces the risk of viruses or other harmful software on your computer.

An infected computer can be very frustrating: not only for you, but also for others. If your computer is infected with harmful software, it could in turn infect other computers. This could happen when you send an e-mail or an instant message, but also when sharing a file on a CD, DVD or USB stick. As a computer owner you are therefore responsible for making sure your computer is protected by a *firewall* and regularly scanned for the presence of viruses and other harmful software.

Windows Vista offers a helpful security tool: *Windows Security Center*. In this *Security Center* you can check the security settings for *Windows Vista* on your computer and adjust them if necessary.

At the end of this chapter you can read more about two programs. The first one is *Windows Defender*. *Windows Defender* is the antispyware program that comes packaged with *Windows Vista*. This program is however not enough to protect you against computer viruses and other malicious software (*malware*).

To be protected against all types of malware, you need to install an antivirus program. *Windows Live OneCare* is one of the many antivirus programs on the market. *OneCare* provides not only antivirus protection, but also a firewall and antispyware protection. In this chapter you read how you can download and install the free 90-day trial version of *OneCare*.

In the first part of this chapter, you will find information about some specific problems and frequently asked questions:

Browsing security and privacy
- Should I connect automatically to the Internet?
- Should I save my password?
- How do I adjust the security settings in *Internet Explorer*?
- How do I adjust the privacy settings in *Internet Explorer*?
- How do I delete my web browsing history?
- How do I change the number of days webpages are stored in *History*?
- How do I disconnect automatically from the Internet?

Phishing and junk mail
- What is meant by phishing and phishing e-mails?
- How does the *Phishing Filter* in *Internet Explorer* work?
- How does the *Junk Mail Filter* in *Windows Mail* work?

In the second part, you will learn more about the specific safety features *of Internet Explorer* and *Windows Vista*. Furthermore, you will see how you can download, install and use the free 90-day trial version of *Windows Live OneCare, Microsoft's* complete computer security solution.

More safety features in *Internet Explorer*
- Pop-up blocker
- Parental controls
- Managing add-ons

Windows Security Center
- *Windows Firewall*
- *Windows Update*
- Malware protection:
  - Using *Windows Defender*
  - Downloading *Windows Live OneCare*
  - Installing *Windows Live OneCare*
  - Using *Windows Live OneCare*

9.1 Browsing Security and Privacy

You can adjust a number of settings related to browsing the Internet. Some of these settings will make using the Internet easier, others will increase your privacy:

- choose whether or not you connect to the Internet automatically
- choose whether or not your password is saved
- adjust the security settings in *Internet Explorer*
- adjust the privacy settings in *Internet Explorer*
- delete your webpage history
- change the number of days the webpages you visited are kept in *History*
- choose whether or not you disconnect from the Internet automatically

To find out how to do these things, you first start *Internet Explorer*:

Do you have an external modem?
☞ **Turn on the modem**

☞ **Open *Internet Explorer*** ℓℓ¹

After it starts, you see this *Dial-up Connection* window:

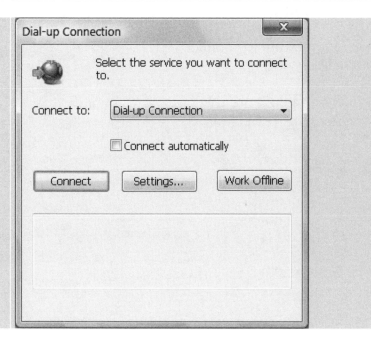

9.2 Connecting Automatically

Whether or not to connect automatically is a matter of personal preference.

Connect Automatically
Naturally, it is convenient to let the computer connect automatically; that way you do not always have to click the *Connect* button every time. If you have a permanent connection to the Internet, for example over the cable or another network, this is certainly the preferred setting.

Do not Connect Automatically
In some cases, it is useful to have the choice whether or not to connect.
Some programs will try to make a connection to the Internet without asking. This setting prevents that from happening, which avoids undesirable and unexpected telephone costs (to e.g. 900 numbers) and keeps your telephone line free for calls.

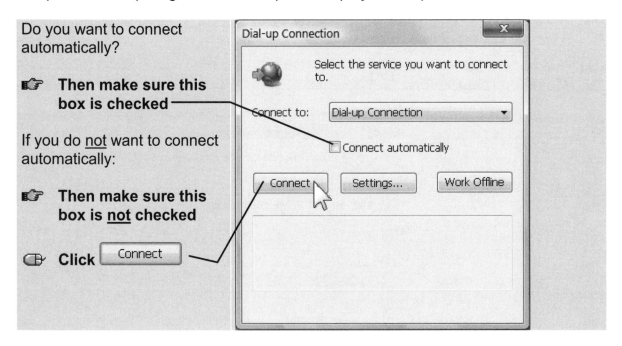

Do you want to connect automatically?

☞ **Then make sure this box is checked**

If you do <u>not</u> want to connect automatically:

☞ **Then make sure this box is <u>not</u> checked**

☞ **Click** Connect

9.3 Saving Your Password

Whether you should save your password or not depends a great deal on how accessible your computer is to others. If you are the only user and no one else has access to your computer, the situation is very different than when the same computer can be used by others.

Do not save
If you choose not to save your password, you will have to type it in yourself every time. This is recommended when you want to be certain that no one else can use your Internet connection.

Save for me only
If you are the only person who uses your computer and you are reasonably certain no one else can use it, you can choose the convenience of allowing your password be saved.

Save for anyone who uses this computer
This way, everybody who has a user account on this computer, can use the dial-up connection that you have set up. For security reasons, this option is only available when you set up a dial-up connection for the first time.

Do you want your password to be saved?

⌨ **Type your password**

☞ **Make sure this box is checked**

By default, the password will be saved for you only.

If you do **not** want your password to be saved:

☞ **Make sure the box is not checked**

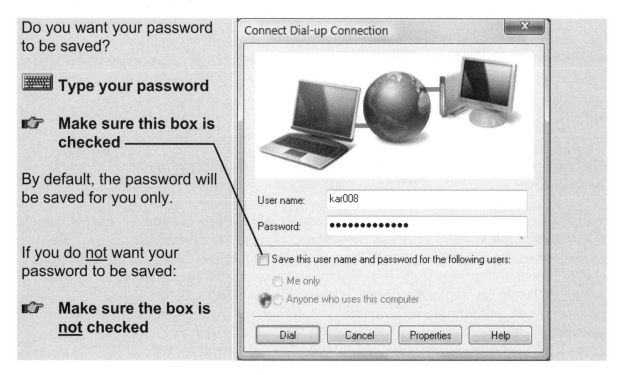

To store these settings for your connection, you need to connect to the Internet:

 Click Dial

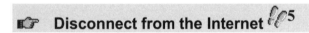

Connect Dial-up Connection   ✕

User name: kar008

Password: ●●●●●●●●●●●●●●

☑ Save this user name and password for the following users:

◉ Me only

◯ Anyone who uses this computer

[Dial]   [Cancel]   [Properties]   [Help]

Wait until the connection has been completed. Then you can disconnect again:

☞ **Disconnect from the Internet** &%⁵

💡 **Tip**

Changing your password
The password you type into the *Dial-up Connection* window is the password your *Internet Service Provider* (ISP) gave you.

You can not just change your password on your own. If you do, you will not be able to connect to the Internet anymore. In order to change your password you will need to go to the service page of your ISP's website. Login to the customer area with your current account information (user name and password). In the customer area you will find a link to an "e-mail manager". More information about changing your password can be found there. Your ISP will encourage you to change your password on a regular basis.
Once you have received confirmation of the new password from your ISP, you can type it into the dial-up window and save it.

Choosing a password

Your password is an identification word known only to you and your ISP. By entering the password, you let your ISP's computer know that you really are who you say you are. You will need a password if you want to send or receive electronic mail, or enter the World Wide Web.

A password is only intended for use by people who have the right to access. That is why you should keep your password a secret. If you want to write it down somewhere just to be safe, do it somewhere that makes sense to you, so you can find it again.

Choosing a password is a painstaking task. Make sure in any case that your password:
- meets your ISP's requirements
- is not an existing word
- does not consist of letters that are next to each other on the keyboard

Because many people have trouble coming up with a good password and then remembering it, it is often suggested that you create your password from the first letters of an existing sentence. How about: Mccnbc ("My computer can not be cracked")? Last but not least, it is a good idea to change your password regularly.

9.4 Security Settings in Internet Explorer

In *Internet Explorer* you can select a security level for Internet access. This way you can determine how *Internet Explorer* interacts with various types of websites. You can find the security settings on a tab in the window *Internet Options*.

☞ **Open *Internet Explorer***^{1}

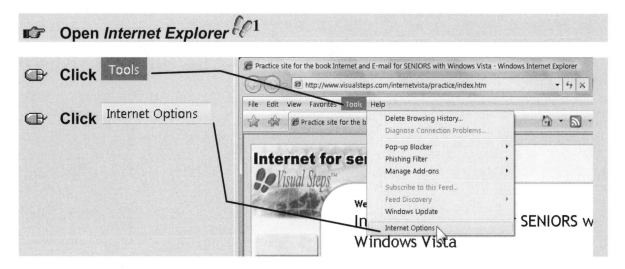

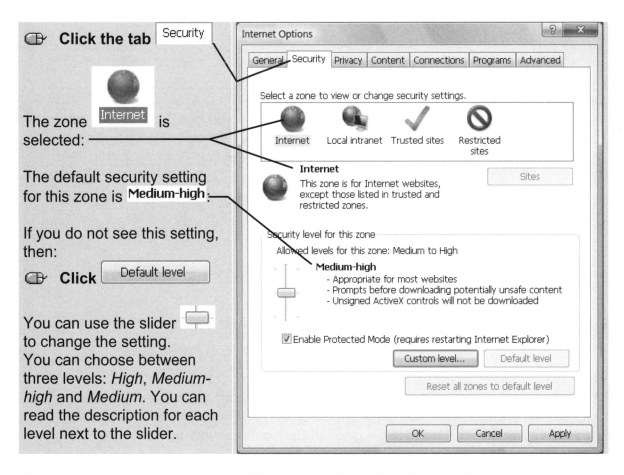

☞ **Click the tab** Security

The zone Internet is selected:

The default security setting for this zone is Medium-high:

If you do not see this setting, then:

☞ **Click** Default level

You can use the slider to change the setting. You can choose between three levels: *High*, *Medium-high* and *Medium*. You can read the description for each level next to the slider.

If necessary, you can choose a different security setting for specific websites you trust and do not trust. Take a look at the *Trusted sites* zone:

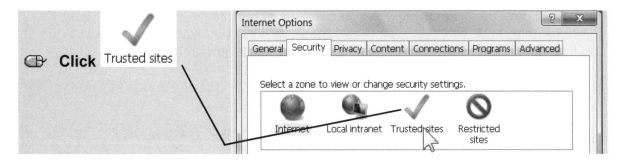

☞ **Click** Trusted sites

You see that the default security level for this zone is **Medium**.

You can use the slider to change the setting.
You can choose between five levels: *High*, *Medium-high*, *Medium*, *Medium-low* and *Low*.

The setting *Low* is exclusively intended for websites you fully trust.

To add a website to the *Trusted sites* zone manually:

☞ **Click** Sites

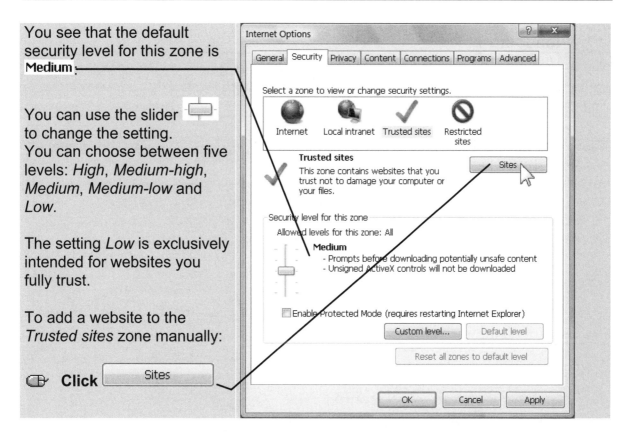

Internet Explorer assumes that you want to add the website that is currently displayed to the *Trusted sites*. To add a new website, for example your bank's online website:

☞ **Double-click the text box below**
   Add this website to the zone:

⌨ **Type the address**
   https://www.bank ofamerica.com

☞ **Click** Add

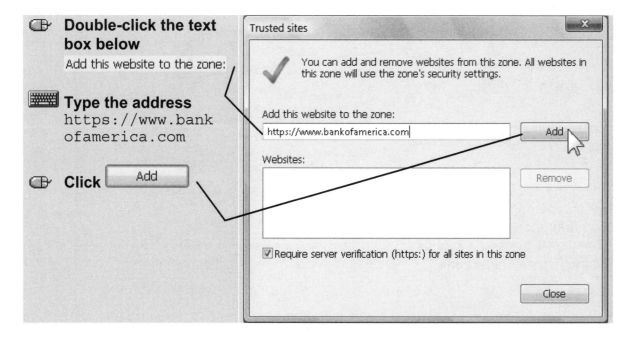

Please note:

The default setting ☑ Require server verification (https:) for all sites in this zone means that sites you add to the *Trusted sites* zone must have the **https://** prefix.
This prefix assures a secure, encrypted connection.

There may already be some trusted websites in the list on your computer.

To remove one of these websites:

☞ **Click**
https://www.bankofamerica.com

☞ **Click** Remove

You can close this window:

☞ **Click** Close

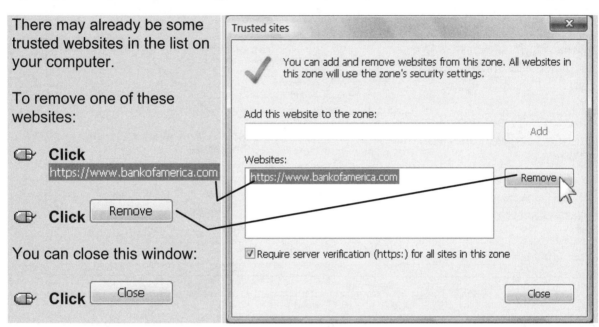

You see the *Internet Options* window again.

☞ **Click** Restricted sites

The default security level for this zone is **High** :

Using the Sites button you can add specific web addresses to this zone. That works the same way as for the *Trusted sites* zone.

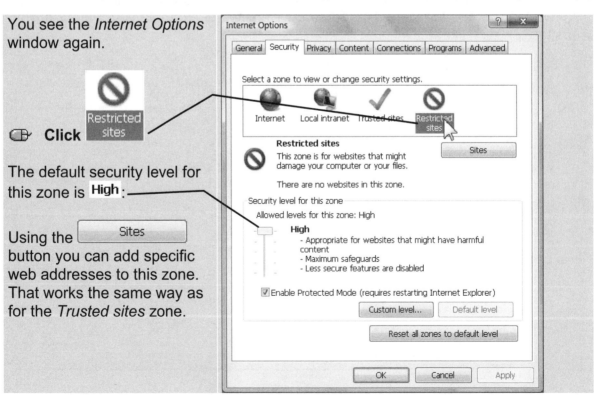

9.5 Privacy Settings in Internet Explorer

In *Internet Explorer*, you can also specify how *cookies* should be handled. Cookies are small text files that are placed on your hard drive while you surf the Internet. These little files contain information about data you have entered. If you look at flight details on an airline's website for example, the site may create a cookie containing the dates and cities you entered. The text files cannot be executed on your computer, and their maximum size is quite small.

 Please note:

Cookies are not dangerous. A website has access only to the information you provide yourself. After a cookie has been stored on your computer, only the website that created the cookie can access it.

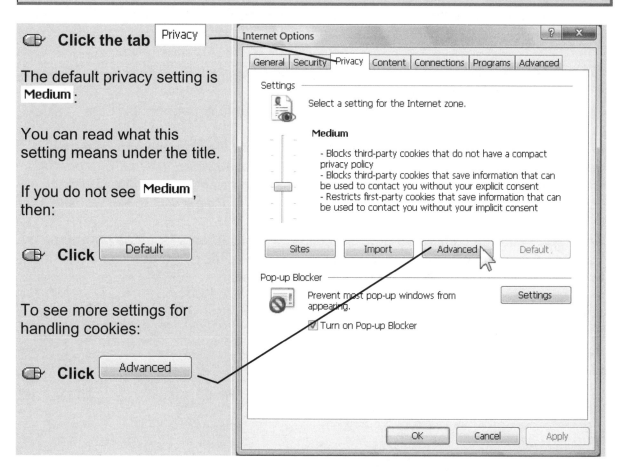

☞ **Click the tab** `Privacy`

The default privacy setting is `Medium`:

You can read what this setting means under the title.

If you do not see `Medium`, then:

☞ **Click** `Default`

To see more settings for handling cookies:

☞ **Click** `Advanced`

You see the window
Advanced Privacy Settings.
By default, cookies are
handled automatically.

You can change this:

☞ **Check the box**

☑ Override automatic cookie handling

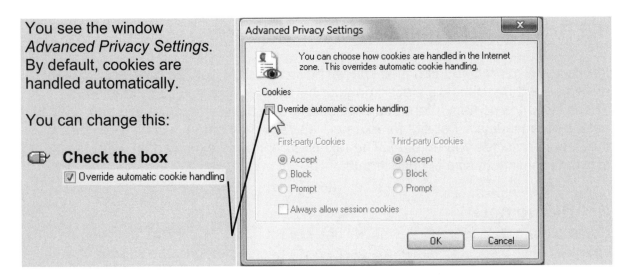

Now you can take a better look at the options. You can specify what you want to do
with first-party and third-party cookies separately:

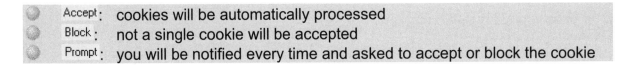

Accept : cookies will be automatically processed
Block : not a single cookie will be accepted
Prompt : you will be notified every time and asked to accept or block the cookie

First-party cookies come from the website that you are viewing and can be either
permanent or *temporary*. A temporary cookie is removed when *Internet Explorer* is
closed. A permanent cookie is stored on your hard drive and stays there. Then the
cookie can be read by the website that created it on your next visit to the website.

Third-party cookies come from other websites' advertisements (such as pop-up or
banner ads) on the website that you are viewing. Websites might use these cookies
to track your browsing behavior for marketing purposes.

In this example the automatic
cookie handling will not be
overridden. You can choose a
different setting of course.

☞ **Uncheck the box**

☑ Override automatic cookie handling

☞ **Click** [Cancel]

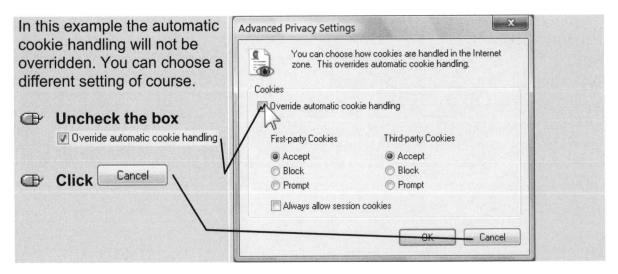

Please note:

You may prefer to block all cookies. Keep in mind that if you do, you run the risk of viewing websites which can not function properly. Of course you can experiment with different settings; it is very easy to return to the default setting.

 Tip

Always allow session cookies
Some websites use cookies while you are visiting the site, but remove them afterward. These are called *session cookies*. Session cookies are also called *temporary cookies*, because they are removed after *Internet Explorer* is closed.

Session cookies are used for online banking, for example. If you have specified that all cookies should be blocked, including session cookies, you will not be able to login to that website anymore. You will see a warning message from the website.

For this reason, always select the option ☑ Always allow session cookies when you make other changes:

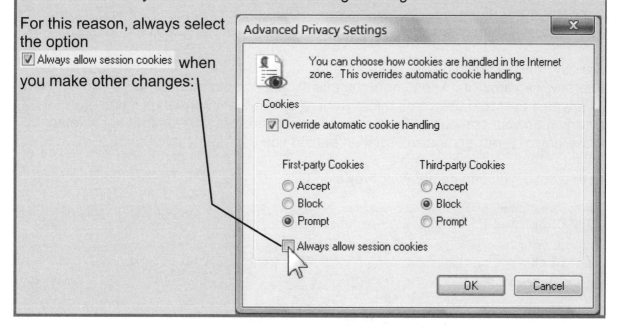

You can easily remove the stored cookies from your hard drive. You can read how to do this in the next section.

Did you make any changes in the security and privacy settings?

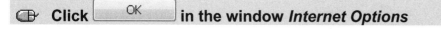 **Click** OK **in the window *Internet Options***

If you did not make changes:

Close the window *Internet Options* 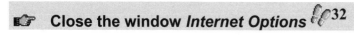32

9.6 Deleting Your Browsing History

As you browse the web, *Internet Explorer* stores information about the websites you visit and information that you are frequently asked to provide (for example, your name and address). The browsing history consists of various items:

Temporary Internet Files : webpages are stored in a temporary Internet files folder the first time you view them in your web browser. This speeds up the display of pages you frequently visit or have already seen, because *Internet Explorer* can open them from your hard disk instead of from the Internet.

Cookies : small text files that websites put on your computer to store information about you and your preferences.

History : a list of all the websites you have visited.

Form data : information that you have entered into forms on websites or the address bar (like your name, address, and website addresses).

Passwords : every time you type a password on a webpage, *Internet Explorer* asks if it should be saved. These saved passwords can also be deleted.

Usually, it is helpful to have this information stored on your computer because it can improve web browsing speed or automatically provide information so you do not need to retype it over and over. You might want to delete that information if you are cleaning up your computer. If you are using a public computer and do not want to leave any of your personal information behind you can delete everything too.

In that case, you can delete your browsing history:

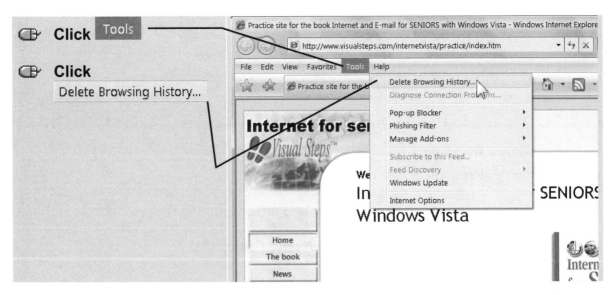

In this window, you can choose which part of your browsing history you want to delete.

For example: do you want to delete the history of websites you have visited?

☞ **Click**

Delete history...

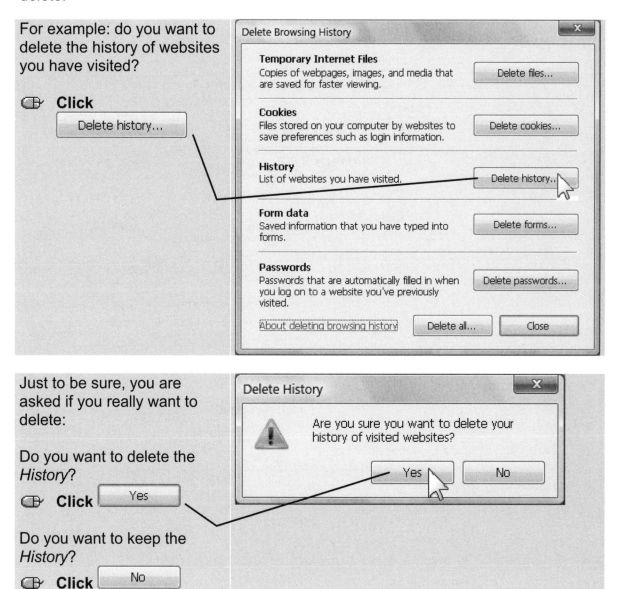

Just to be sure, you are asked if you really want to delete:

Do you want to delete the *History*?

☞ **Click** Yes

Do you want to keep the *History*?

☞ **Click** No

It is also possible to delete all saved information at once:

☞ **Click** Delete all...

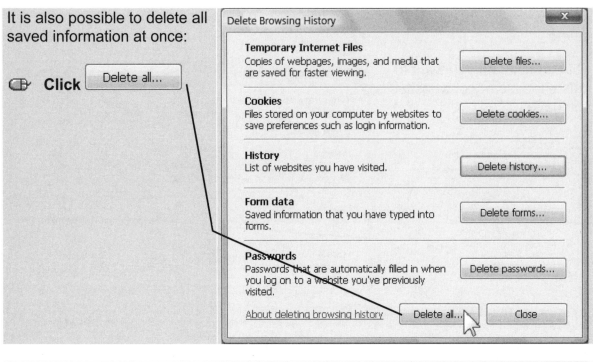

Again, you are asked if you really want to delete:

Do you want to delete the *History*?

☞ **Click** Yes

Do you want to keep it?

☞ **Click** No

☞ **If necessary, close the window *Delete Browsing History*** 👣³²

9.7 Changing the Number of Days to Save Webpages

In the window *Internet Options* there are other settings you can adjust. You can select the number of days that webpages should be saved in the *History* setting.

☞ **Open the window *Internet Options* ℓℓ60**

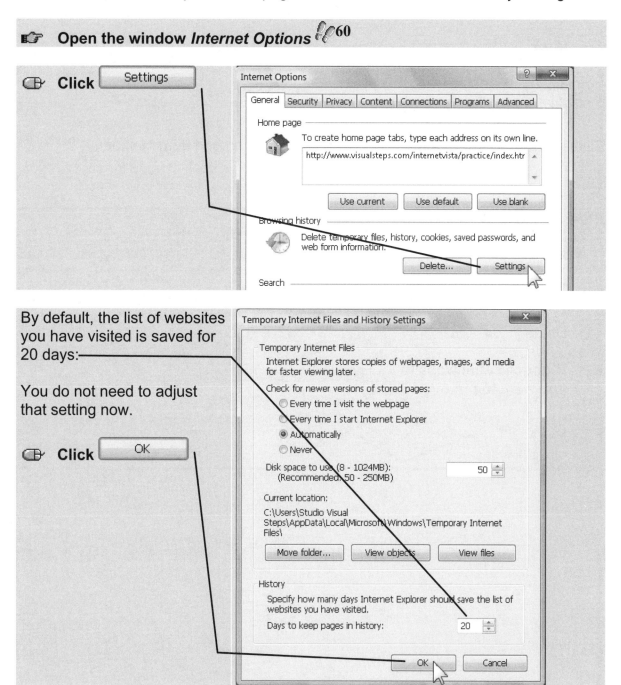

Click | Settings |

By default, the list of websites you have visited is saved for 20 days:

You do not need to adjust that setting now.

Click | OK |

☞ **Close the window *Internet Options* ℓℓ32**

Once you have cleared your *History*, the folder will be empty. You can check this yourself:

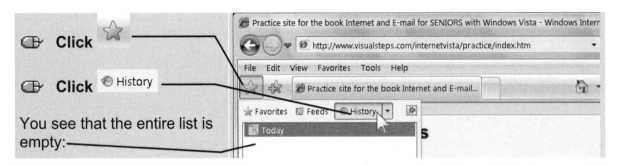

All the websites you have recently visited have been erased from memory.

Tip

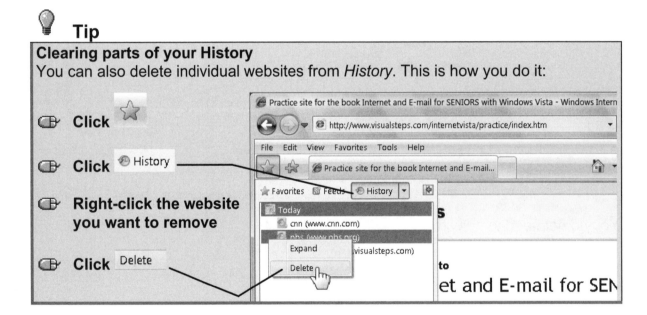

9.8 Disconnecting Automatically

It is useful to have *Internet Explorer* disconnect automatically when you close it, or when you have not used it for a while.

Especially if you connect over the telephone, this can prevent tying up your phone line unnecessarily and missing incoming calls. If you have a DSL or cable connection, you can just read through this section.

☞ **Open the window *Internet Options*** **60**

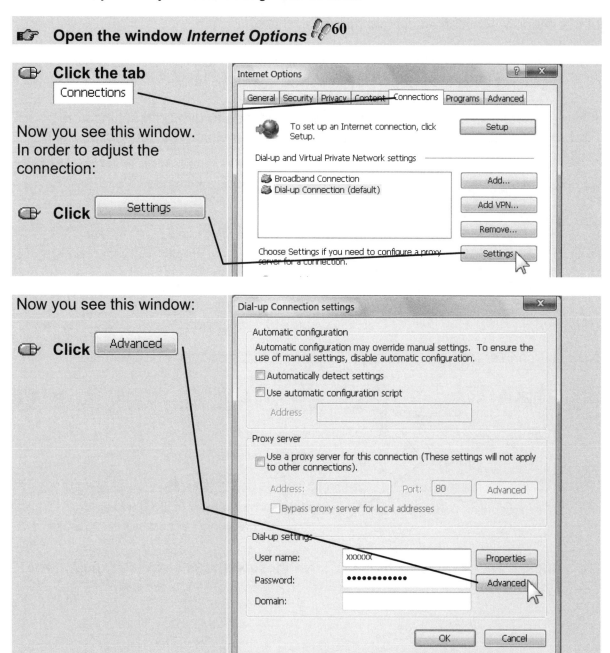

☞ **Click the tab**
    Connections

Now you see this window.
In order to adjust the
connection:

☞ **Click** Settings

Now you see this window:

☞ **Click** Advanced

A small window opens:

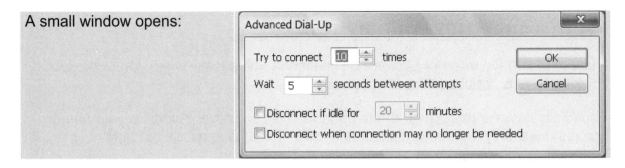

In this window, you can adjust two things:

- Disconnect automatically if you have not used the connection for a while.
- Disconnect automatically when you close *Internet Explorer*.

If you connect over the telephone line, it is a good idea to turn both settings on. First, choose the time period allotted for idle time after which the connection will be broken:

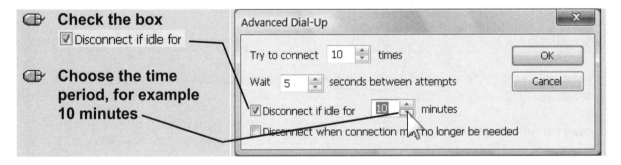

☞ **Check the box**
☑ Disconnect if idle for

☞ **Choose the time period, for example 10 minutes**

Now you can set *Internet Explorer* to disconnect automatically when you stop:

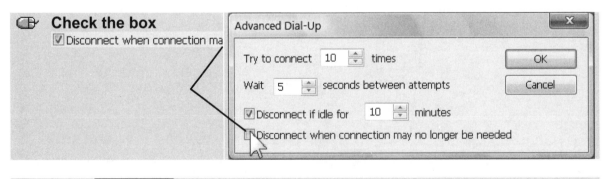

☞ **Check the box**
☑ Disconnect when connection ma

☞ **Click** [OK] **three times to save these settings and leave the *Internet Options* window**

9.9 Phishing

The Internet is used more and more these days: for online banking, shopping, ordering your favorite pizza, purchasing airline tickets, selling your old furniture, studying a new subject, etc. Almost anything it seems can be done on the Internet. Along with these useful, pleasant, even rewarding activities however, have come some rather unsavory practices. Criminals have found their way to the Internet. One of the latest scams is known as *phishing*.

What is phishing?
Online phishing (pronounced like the word *fishing*) is a way to trick computer users into revealing personal or financial information through a fraudulent e-mail message or an innocent looking website. Phishing is in fact "fishing" for information.

A common online phishing scam starts with a fake e-mail message that looks like an official notice from a well-known trusted source. This can be your bank, your credit card company, or an online shop or auction site you have dealt with before. The same message is sent randomly to thousands of e-mail addresses. In the e-mail message, recipients are linked to a website where they are asked to provide personal information, such as their account number or password.

These e-mails and the websites they link to look so official that many people think they are real. Unsuspecting people may comply and enter their credit card number or password. The information is sent directly to the criminal who sent the e-mails and made the fake website.

Once the criminal has gathered the information, he or she can use it to buy things, open new credit cards in your name or otherwise assume your identity.

Windows Vista provides protection against phishing in both *Internet Explorer* and *Windows Mail*.

9.10 The Phishing Filter in Internet Explorer

In *Internet Explorer*, the *Phishing Filter* helps detect phishing websites. The *Phishing Filter* uses three methods to help protect you from phishing scams:

- it compares the addresses of websites you visit against a list of sites reported to *Microsoft* as legitimate. This list is stored on your computer.
- it analyzes the sites you visit to see if they have the characteristics common to a phishing website.
- you can also submit a website address to *Microsoft* to be checked against a frequently updated list of reported phishing websites.

If the site you are visiting is on the list of reported phishing websites, *Internet Explorer* will display a warning webpage and a notification on the address bar. From the warning web page, you can continue or close the page. If the website contains characteristics common to a phishing site but is not on the list, *Internet Explorer* will only notify you in the address bar that it might possibly be a phishing website.

You can find the various options for the *Phishing Filter* here:

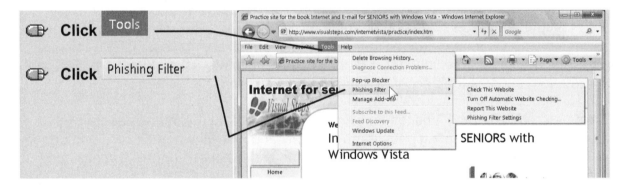

☞ **Click** `Tools`

☞ **Click** `Phishing Filter`

○   `Check This Website` : if you do not trust a website you visit, you can use this option to manually check the website against the updated *Microsoft* list.

○   `Turn Off Automatic Website Checking...` : if you choose this option, the websites you visit will no longer be checked. This is not recommended.

○   `Report This Website` : if a website is not flagged as a suspicious website or a phishing website and you have reason to believe it is a fraudulent site, you can report the website to *Microsoft*.

○   `Phishing Filter Settings` : you can follow this link to turn the *Phishing Filter* off. Again, this is not recommended.

☞ **Close** *Internet Explorer* $\ell\ell^2$

9.11 The Junk Mail Filter in Windows Mail

In *Windows Mail*, the *Junk Mail Filter* prevents phishing e-mails and other junk mail from entering your *Inbox.* These messages are moved to the folder *Junk E-mail.*

☞ **Open** *Windows Mail* 🖱️**35**

When a message is suspected to be phishing or junk e-mail, it is moved to the *Junk E-mail* folder and you see a message like this one:

🖱️ **Click** [Close]

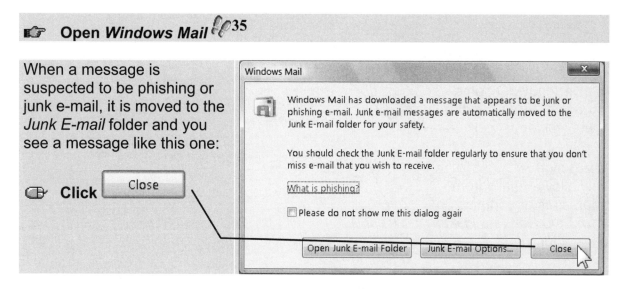

A suspected phishing e-mail will be shown in the *Junk E-mail* folder with a pink message bar to warn you:

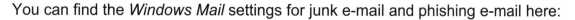
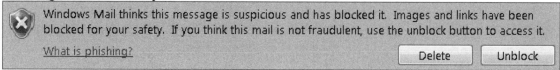

The message header will be shown in red letters with this sign: ⊗

You can find the *Windows Mail* settings for junk e-mail and phishing e-mail here:

🖱️ **Click** Tools

🖱️ **Click** Junk E-mail Options...

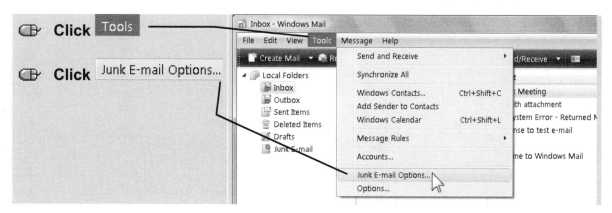

By default, the level of junk e-mail protection is set to `Low:`, which means only the most obvious junk e-mail is moved to the *Junk E-mail* folder.

You could set a higher level of protection, but this might inadvertently put some "innocent" e-mails in the *Junk E-mail* folder as well:———

The option `Safe List Only:` will only allow e-mails from addresses or domains on your *Safe Senders List* to enter your *Inbox*:———

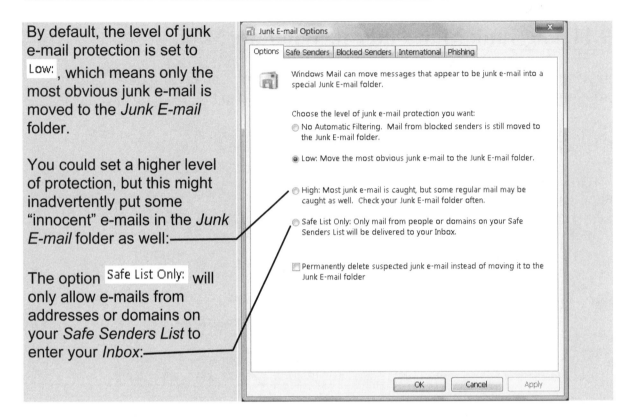

It is very easy to add e-mail addresses or domains to your *Safe Senders List*:

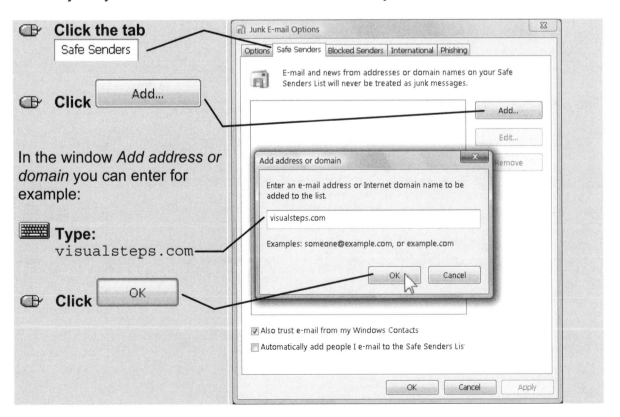

👆 **Click the tab**
　　Safe Senders

👆 **Click** Add...

In the window *Add address or domain* you can enter for example:

⌨ **Type:**
　　visualsteps.com

👆 **Click** OK

The domain has been added to your *Safe Senders List*. Using the tab | Blocked Senders | you can also add people or domains to your *Blocked Senders List*. E-mails from these senders will be moved to the *Junk E-mail* folder automatically.

At the bottom of the | Safe Senders | tab, you can specify which groups of e-mails you want to trust as well. Addresses from people in your *Contacts* folder and from people you have already e-mailed can safely be added:

 Check the box
☑ Also trust e-mail from my Wind

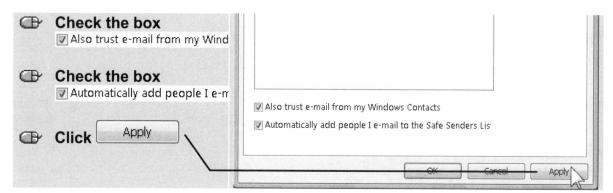

 Check the box
☑ Automatically add people I e-m

☞ **Click** | Apply |

 Tip

The *Junk Mail Filter* will not always see the difference between a junk or phishing e-mail and an innocent e-mail. That is why you should check your *Junk E-mail* folder from time to time. Use the button | 🅟 Not Junk | to move a selected message to the *Inbox*.

💡 **Tip**

Blocking international e-mails
In the tab | International | you can specify languages or domains to be added to the *Blocked Senders List*.

If you receive e-mails in a foreign language that you do not want to see anymore, you can use the button | Blocked Encoding List... | to choose that language.

You can use the button | Blocked Top-Level Domain List... | to block all e-mail messages from addresses that end with a specific top-level domain code. For example, all addresses that end with .mx or .ru.

On the last tab, | Phishing |, you can adjust the settings for phishing e-mails.

☞ **Click the tab** | Phishing |

The option ☑ Protect my Inbox should always be checked, for maximum protection against phishing:——————

The option ☑ Move phishing E-mail makes sure all e-mails with potential phishing links are moved to the *Junk E-mail* folder:——

☞ **Make sure both options are checked**

☞ **Click** [OK]

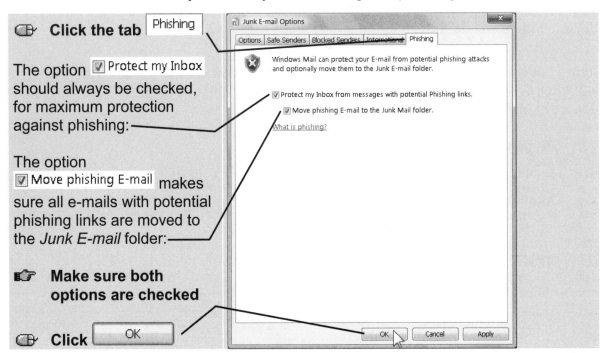

Tip

What else can I do to protect myself?
In addition to applying the measures described previously:

- Never give out personal or financial information in an e-mail, instant message, or pop-up window. Your bank will never e-mail you to ask you for your passwords or PIN numbers! Call the company or the organization if you have any doubts about the origin of the e-mail. Even messages from friends and family can be faked, so check with the sender to be sure they actually sent the message.
- Do not click links in e-mail and instant messages from strangers or any link that looks suspicious. Visit websites by typing the known address into the *Internet Explorer* address bar.
- Check if the website uses secure encoding: a secure website begins with the prefix https:// in the web address.
- Only use websites that provide privacy statements or information about how they use your personal information.
- Regularly check your bank- and credit card statements.
- Report suspected abuse of your personal information to the authorities.

At **www.antiphishing.org** you can find more information about phishing and known phishing scams.

☞ **Close** *Windows Mail* ℓℓ43

9.12 Pop-up Blocker

Pop-ups are very annoying for Internet users. A pop-up is a small web browser window that appears on top of the website you are viewing. Pop-up windows often open as soon as you visit a website and are usually created by advertisers.

Pop-up Blocker is a feature in *Internet Explorer* that lets you limit or block most pop-ups. When *Pop-up Blocker* is turned on and a pop-up is detected, the information bar displays this message: 🗐 Pop-up blocked. To see this pop-up or additional options click here...

☞ **Open *Internet Explorer*** 📖¹

☞ **If necessary, connect to the Internet** 📖³

☞ **Open the website** www.cnn.com 📖⁴

This website tries to show a pop-up window and you see this message on the information bar: 🗐 Pop-up blocked. To see this pop-up or additional options click here...

Click the information bar

Click Settings

Click More Settings...

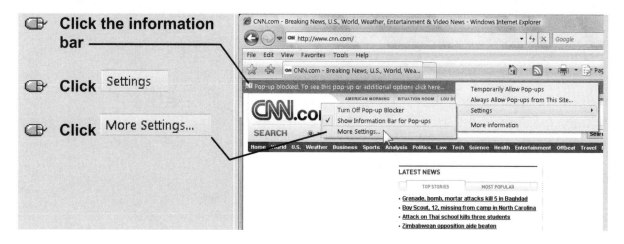

You can choose the level of blocking you prefer, from blocking all pop-up windows to allowing the pop-ups that you want to see.

By default, the filter level is set to Medium:. This means most automatic pop-ups will be blocked.

☞ **Click**
Medium: Block most automatic pop-ups

You see the other two filter levels: High: Block all pop-ups and Low: Allow pop-ups from secure sites.

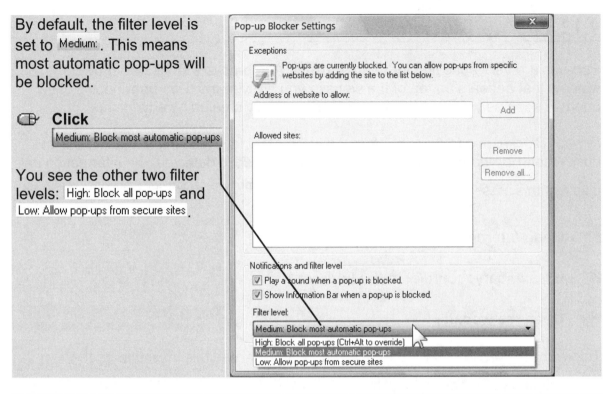

If there are pop-ups from specific sites that you would like to allow, you can type the address here:

Use the button Add to add the address to the list of allowed sites:

You do not need to adjust these settings. You can close this window:

☞ **Click** Close

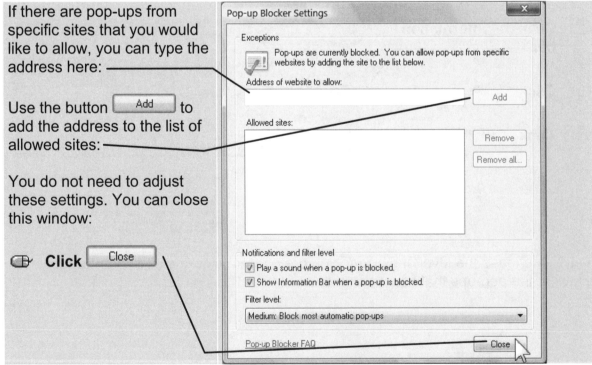

☞ **If necessary, disconnect from the Internet** ℓ℘5

9.13 Parental Controls

You can use *Parental Controls* to help manage how your (grand)children use the computer. For example, you can set limits on your (grand)children's access to the Internet, the hours that they can log on to the computer, and which games they can play and programs they can run.

When *Parental Controls* blocks access to a webpage or game, a notification is displayed that the webpage or program has been blocked. Your (grand)child can click a link in the notification to request permission for access to that webpage or program. You can allow access by entering your account information.

You can reach the *Parental Controls* settings through the *Control Panel*:

➯ **Click** ⊞ , Control Panel

⇨ **Please note:**

Each (grand)child that you want to set up *Parental Controls* for must have his or her own user account. *Parental Controls* can only be applied to standard user accounts.

You cannot set *Parental Controls* for a domain-joined group of machines.

To set up *Parental Controls* for your (grand)child, you will need an administrator user account yourself. Your administrator user account and any other administrator accounts must be password protected. Otherwise the child could bypass the *Parental Controls* through another user account.

To add an extra user account or to protect an account with a password, use the option 🛡 Add or remove user accounts in the *Control Panel*.

➯ **Click**
🛡 Set up parental controls for any us│

As soon as you click
🛡 Set up parental controls for any user ,
your screen goes dark and
Windows asks your
permission to continue. Click
on the *Continue* button if you
want to apply this setting.

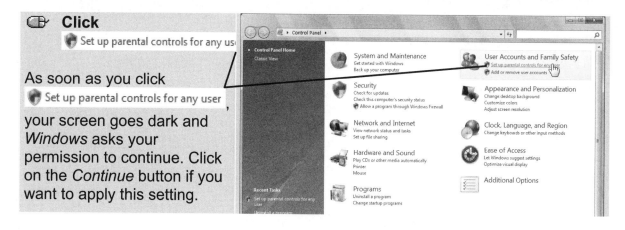

In this example, the *Parental Controls* need to be set up for the account called Mary.

Both user accounts are already password-protected and both accounts are administrator accounts.

☞ **Click the account** ——

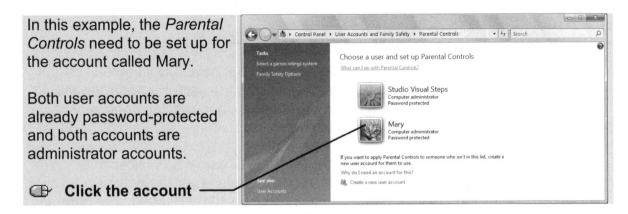

First, the account Mary must be changed to a standard user account.

☞ **Click** [Yes]

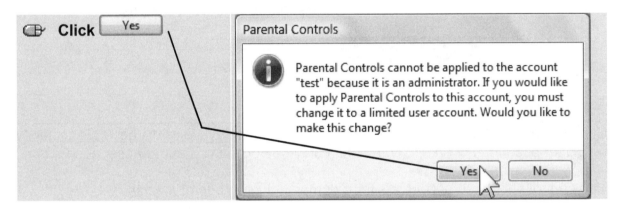

Now you can set up how Mary will be allowed to use the computer. First you activate the *Parental Controls* for this account.

☞ **Check the option**
   ◉ On, enforce current settings

By default, the option
Activity Reporting: is ◉ On,. This means that information will be gathered on Mary's use of the computer.

You can use the link
View activity reports to see the information: ——

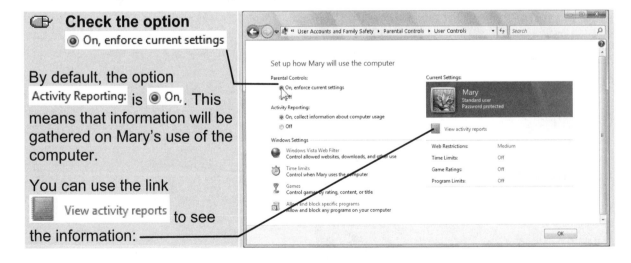

The *Parental Controls* can be set for four specific fields:

Windows Vista Web Filter: here you can restrict the websites that (grand)children visit, check an age rating, indicate whether you want to allow file downloads, and set up which content you want the content filters to block and allow. You can also block or allow specific websites.

Time limits: you can set time limits to control when (grand)children are allowed to log on to the computer. Time limits prevent children from logging on during specified hours. You can set different logon hours for every day of the week. If they are logged on when their allowed time ends, they will be automatically logged off.

Games: here you can prevent your (grand)children from playing games you do not want them to play. You can for example choose an age rating level, choose the types of content you want to block, and decide whether you want to allow or block specific games.

Allow and block specific programs: prevent (grand)children from running programs that you do not want them to run.

You do not need to adjust these settings now. Instead, you go back to the *Control Panel*:

 **Click** 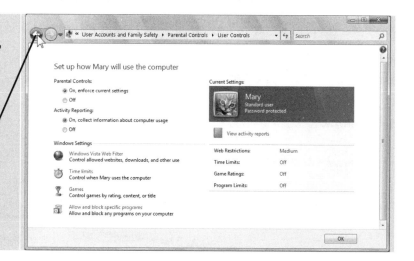 **twice**

9.14 Managing Add-ons in Internet Explorer

Add-ons
An *Add-on* is a program that adds extra functionality to a web browser like *Internet Explorer*. Examples of add-ons include extra toolbars, animated mouse pointers, and programs that block pop-up windows. Add-ons are also known as *ActiveX controls*, *plug-ins*, *browser extensions*, or *Browser Helper Objects*.

On the Internet, many add-ons are available. For most of them, you have to give permission before they are downloaded to your computer. Some add-ons, however, are downloaded without your knowledge. This could happen if the add-on is part of a program you have installed. Some add-ons are installed with *Windows Vista*.

An add-on can be used most of the time without any problem. Sometimes the add-on can cause *Internet Explorer* to close unexpectedly. This could happen if the add-on was poorly designed or was made for another version of *Internet Explorer*.

You are going to take a look at the add-ons that are already on your computer.

☞ **If necessary, open *Internet Explorer*** 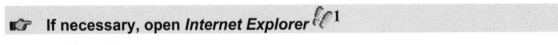1

👆 **Click** Tools

👆 **Click** Manage Add-ons

👆 **Click**
Enable or Disable Add-ons...

In the *Manage Add-ons* window you can see which add-ons are currently loaded in *Internet Explorer:*

The list you see in this example may be different from the list you see on your screen.

For each add-on, the name, publisher and status are displayed:

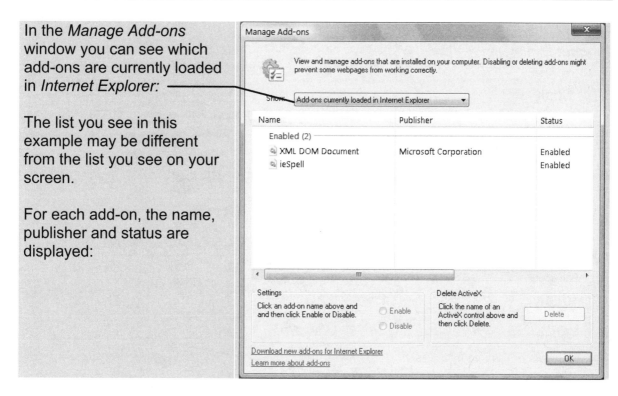

If you do not trust or do not want to use an add-on, you can disable it:

🖰 **Click the add-on you want to disable**

🖰 **Click the option**
⊙ Disable

To close the window and apply the change you have made:

🖰 **Click** ⟦ OK ⟧

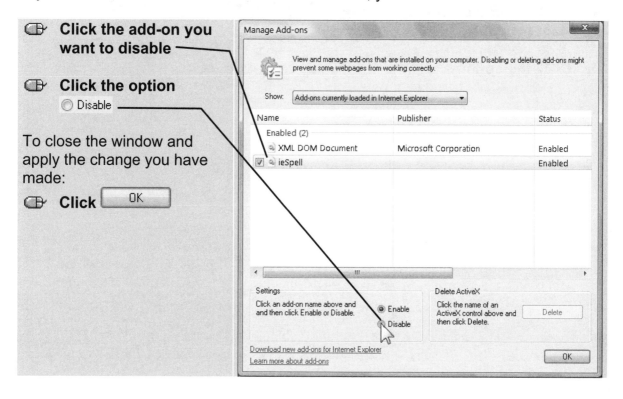

You are encouraged to restart
Internet Explorer:

👉 **Click** OK

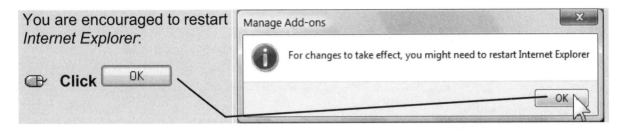

👉 **Close** *Internet Explorer* 🐾² **and open the program again** 🐾¹

If you want to start using the add-on again, you can enable it:

👉 **Click** Tools

👉 **Click** Manage Add-ons

👉 **Click**
Enable or Disable Add-ons...

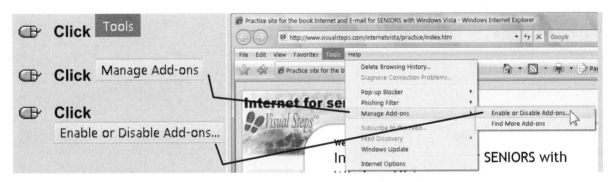

👉 **Click the add-on you
want to enable**

👉 **Click the option**
⊙ Enable

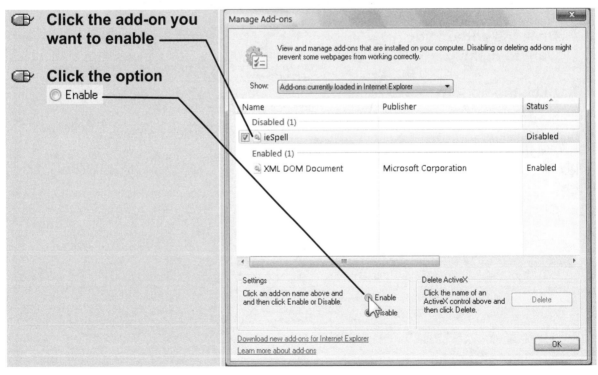

The next time you start *Internet Explorer*, this change will take effect. Before you close this window, take a look at all the add-ons on your computer that *Internet Explorer* can use:

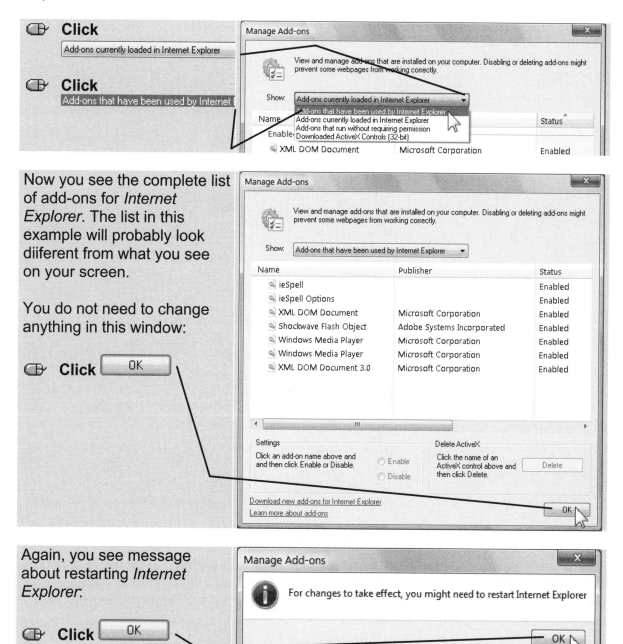

Click

Add-ons currently loaded in Internet Explorer

Click

Add-ons that have been used by Internet

Now you see the complete list of add-ons for *Internet Explorer*. The list in this example will probably look diiferent from what you see on your screen.

You do not need to change anything in this window:

Click OK

Again, you see message about restarting *Internet Explorer*.

Click OK

☞ **Close *Internet Explorer*** ²

☞ **If necessary, disconnect from the Internet** 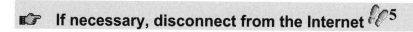⁵

9.15 Windows Security Center

Windows Vista contains a *Security Center* that checks your computer's security settings and keeps tracks of updates to *Windows Vista*. This is how you open the *Security Center*:

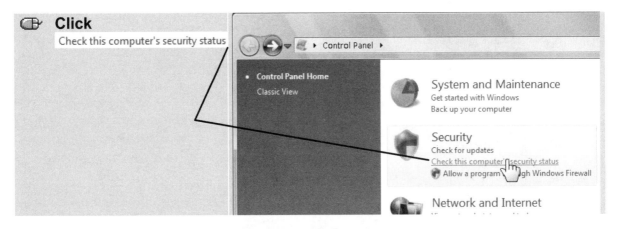

This window displays the status of the four main security essentials:

- *Firewall*
- *Automatic updating*
- *Malware protection*
- *Other security settings*

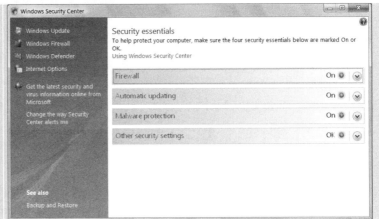

In this example, each area has the status On ⊙.
This is the most ideal situation, but the settings may be different on your computer. Perhaps you are using antivirus software or a firewall that *Windows* does not recognise. In that case, you will have to monitor that program directly to keep your computer secure; it cannot be checked by *Windows*.

In this case, you will see the status Off ⊙.

9.16 Windows Firewall

Firewall

A *firewall* is software or hardware that checks information coming from the Internet or a network, and then either blocks it or allows it to pass through to your computer, depending on your firewall settings.

The word *firewall* sounds safer than it actually is: a firewall **does not** protect you against computer viruses. If your e-mail program is allowed access to the internet through your firewall, you can still receive an e-mail with an attachment that contains a virus.

🖰 **Click** 🛡 **Windows Firewall**

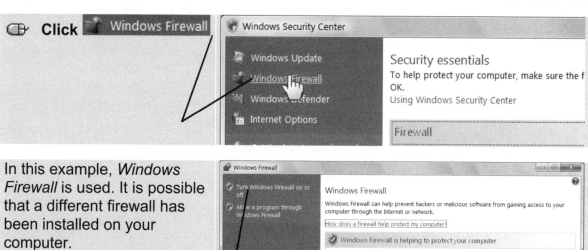

In this example, *Windows Firewall* is used. It is possible that a different firewall has been installed on your computer.

If you install a different firewall, *Windows Firewall* must be turned off using the **Turn Windows Firewall on or off** link:
Otherwise the two firewalls might interfere with one another.

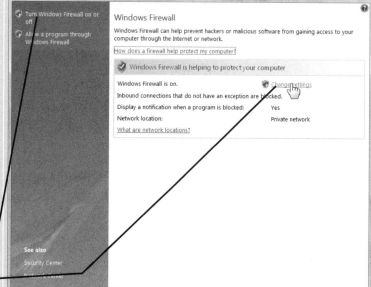

🖰 **Click** 🛡 Change settings

Your screen goes dark, *Windows* needs your permission to continue.

🖰 **Click the *Continue* button**

After clicking the *Continue* button, you see the window *Windows Firewall Settings*.

You see that *Windows Firewall* is on:

You can check the option ☐ **Block all incoming connections** when you connect to a less secure network such as a public network at an airport:

When this option is not checked, programs on the *Exceptions* tab are allowed access to your computer.

👆 **Click the tab** Exceptions

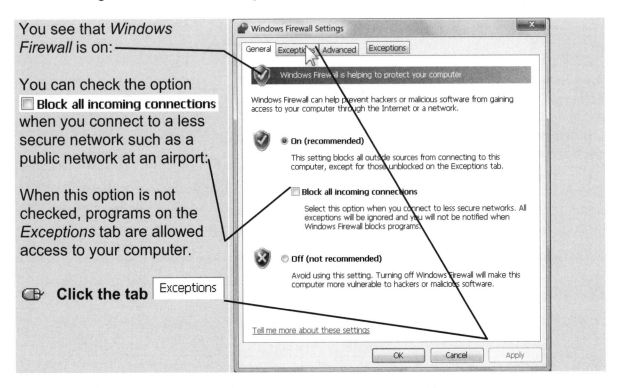

If you are using a program that has to receive data from the Internet or a network, the firewall will ask if you want to allow the connection. For each allowed connection, an exception is added to this list:

You can use the button Add program... to add exceptions directly:

You do not have to change these settings now:

👆 **Click** Cancel

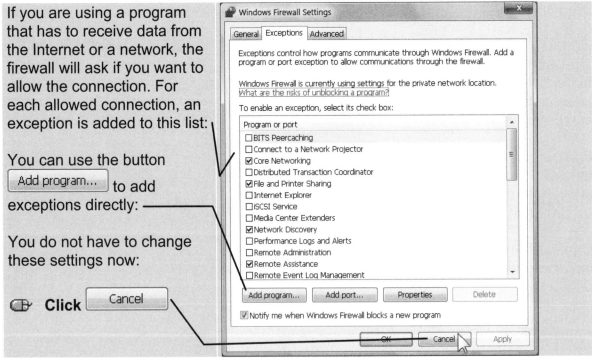

👉 **Close the window** *Windows Firewall* 📖 32

Please note:

A firewall **cannot** search for or disable computer viruses if they enter your computer or when they are already present on your computer. The check for computer viruses must be done by an antivirus program.

A firewall **cannot** prevent receipt of unwanted or unsolicited e-mail in your *Inbox*.

A firewall **cannot** prevent you from opening suspicious attachments received with an e-mail.

 Tip

Allowing exceptions in Windows Firewall

When you are using a program that has to receive data from the internet or a network, the firewall will ask if you want to allow the connection. For each allowed connection, an exception is added to this list. Exceptions can also be added directly.

Whenever you make an exception for a program to communicate through the *Windows Firewall*, your computer becomes a bit more vulnerable. With each exception, a hole is made in the firewall and the protection level goes down. Unknown intruders often use software that scans the Internet looking for computers with unprotected Internet connections. If you have a lot of exceptions and open ports, your computer could fall victim to these intruders.

In order to enjoy your computer some exceptions may be necessary. In practice you will give permission to a program so it can contact the Internet. For example, when you are playing a multiplayer game on the Internet, you can add the game as an exception. The firewall will then allow the game information to reach your computer.

You can limit the security risks by paying attention to the following points when you are making exceptions:

- Never allow an exception that is not absolutely necessary.
- Never allow an exception for a program that you do not recognize.
- Remove an exception when you no longer need it.

9.17 Windows Update

Automatic updating
A very important part of the *Windows Security Center* is *Windows Update.* This is a system that checks if you are using the most recent version of *Windows Vista.* *Windows Vista* is constantly being modified, expanded and made more secure. The additions and fixes for known security leaks and any (programming) errors are dispersed by *Microsoft* in the form of software *updates.*

 Please note:

Microsoft **never** sends software updates by e-mail. Anyone who receives an e-mail claiming to contain *Microsoft* software or a *Windows* update is strongly advised **not** to open the attachment and immediately delete the e-mail.

If you want to make sure your version of *Windows Vista* stays up to date, you should make sure *Automatic Updating* is turned on.

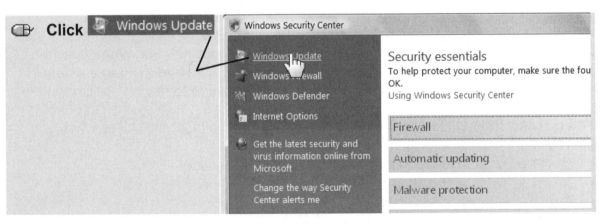

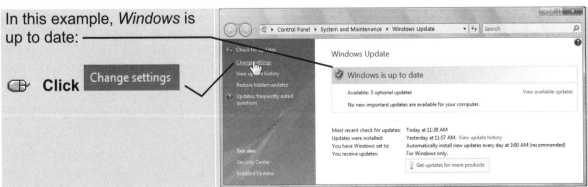

You see the current settings on your computer: ———

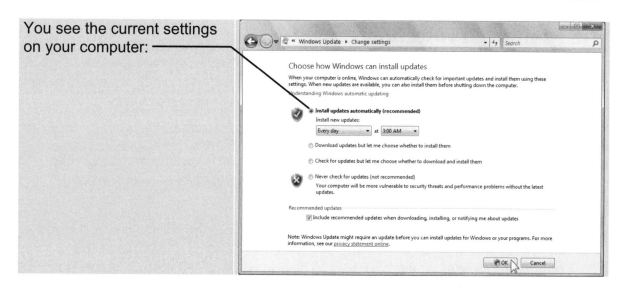

In this example, *Automatic Updates* is set to check for new updates and install these daily at 3:00 AM. If the computer is not on at that time, the check takes place when the computer starts up. The updates are then automatically downloaded and installed. *Windows* places a notification about this at the bottom of the screen, but in most cases you can just keep on working. For critical updates, it may be necessary to restart the computer.

It is a good idea to select the ⊙ **Install updates automatically (recommended)** setting. You can change the time to a moment that is most convenient for you.

☞ **Adjust your settings if necessary**

☞ **Click** [🌐 OK]

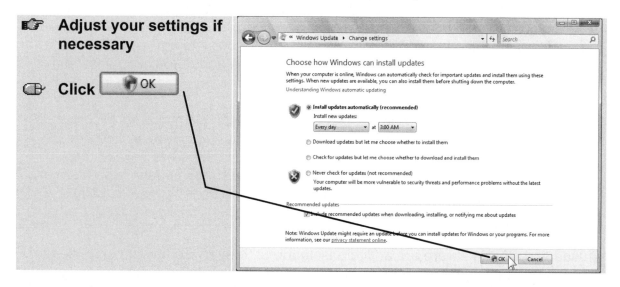

Your screen goes dark, *Windows* needs your permission to continue. You can use the *Continue* button to give permission.

☞ **If necessary, close the *Windows Update* window** ✐*32*

9.18 Malware Protection

Malware
Malware is short for "malicious software", software that is designed to deliberately harm your computer. Viruses, worms, spyware and Trojan horses are forms of malicious software.

- A **virus** is a program that attempts to spread from computer to computer and either cause damage (by erasing or corrupting data) or annoy users (by printing messages or altering what is displayed on the screen). Viruses can damage software, hardware and files. Not all viruses are equally destructive though.

- A **worm** is a self-replicating program. A typical worm sends out copies of itself to everyone in your *Contacts* folder, then does the same thing on the recipients' computers. This creates a domino effect of busy network traffic that slows down corporate networks and could possibly bring down the whole Internet. A worm does not infect or corrupt files, but it can dig itself into the system, allowing someone else to operate the computer remotely.

- **Spyware** is software that can display advertisements (such as pop-up ads), collect information about you, or change settings on your computer, generally without obtaining your consent. *Windows Defender*, the antispyware program that comes packaged with *Windows Vista*, offers good protection against this kind of malware.

- A **Trojan horse** is a program that contains or installs a malicious program. The term is derived from the classical myth of the Trojan horse. The Trojan horse seemed to be a gift, but turned out to be hiding Greek soldiers that conquered the city of Troy. Today's Trojan horses may appear to be harmless useful or interesting programs to an unsuspecting user, but are actually harmful when executed.

Viruses and other malware are an increasing threat to every computer connected to the Internet. The source of infection may be an attachment to an e-mail message or a file downloaded from the Internet. You can also become infected by exchanging USB sticks, CDs or other storage media.

The *Malware protection* component of *Windows Security Center* indicates whether an up-to-date antivirus program is installed on your computer.

👉 **Click**

　　Malware protection

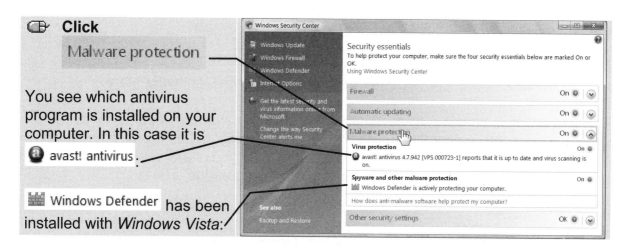

You see which antivirus program is installed on your computer. In this case it is

🅐 avast! antivirus .

🔳 Windows Defender has been installed with *Windows Vista*.

Windows recognizes the 🅐 avast! antivirus program and can therefore display the On 🔵 status in the *Security Center*. When the antivirus program has been turned off or removed, or was not installed in the first place, you will see this status:

From time to time, an extra warning will be shown in the form of a text balloon at the bottom of your screen:

> 🛡 Check your antivirus software status ✕
> avast! antivirus 4.7.942 [VPS 000723-2] is turned off.
> Click this notification to fix the problem.

This status will also be shown if you have installed an antivirus program that is not recognized by *Windows Security Center*. There are excellent antivirus programs on the market for which that will be the case.

If you have installed an antivirus program that is not recognized:

👉 **Click**

　　Show me my available options.

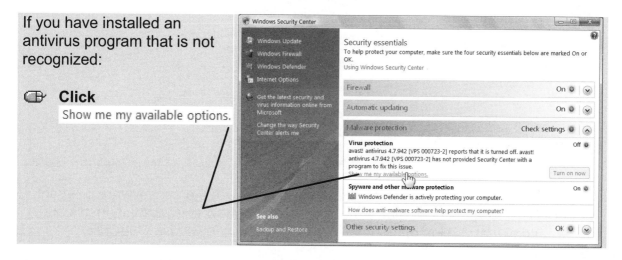

Windows Security Center gives you three options:
- go online and get a different antivirus program;
- monitor your antivirus program yourself;
- do not let *Windows Security Center* monitor your antivirus software state.

This last option is absolutely **not** recommended. Your computer is seriously at risk if you do not use antivirus software. Without proper protection, you are also a risk for the people you communicate with online or the people you share your files with using an USB stick. A virus on your computer could easily spread to them!

If you have installed an antivirus program that is not recognized:

☞ **Click**
    🛡 I have an antivirus program

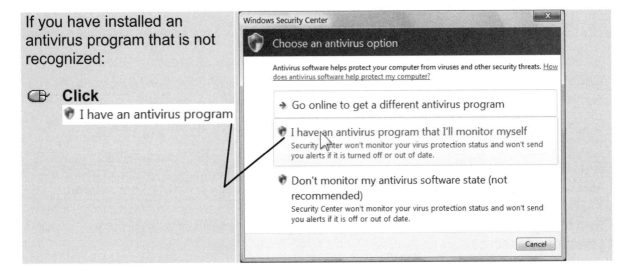

Your screen goes dark and *Windows* asks your permission to continue. Use the *Continue* button to leave the darkened screen.

You see the status
Not monitored 🔘 for the virus protection component of the *Malware protection*:

If you want to go back to the monitored state use the
button 🛡 Monitor now .

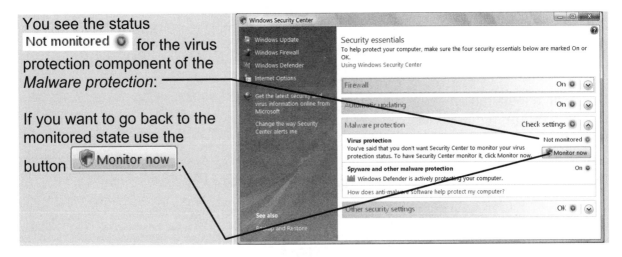

In the next section, you can read about the functionality of the antispyware program *Windows Defender*. In the section after that, you learn how to download, install and use the 90-day trial version of the antivirus program *Windows Live OneCare*.

9.19 Windows Defender

Spyware
You can find all kinds of interesting and useful things on the Internet. Most Internet users will occasionally take advantage of one or more of the many free programs available. However, many people do not realize that some of these applications can contain components that gather information about users.

For example, you might download a handy little program for keeping track of your household budget that secretly monitors your surfing behavior. Information about your visits to stores is silently sent to the software's creators. They can then pester you with advertisements and annoying pop-ups about certain products. Programs that monitor your computer activities in this way are called *spyware*.

It is even more frustrating when a website silently downloads a program to your hard drive that changes system files or settings on your computer, or captures your keystrokes and sends them to the program's creator. And then there is the infamous hijacking software, which repeatedly takes over your selected home page and/or silently selects a different, more expensive dial-up connection. If you are using a regular dial-up Internet connection, this *autodialer* can make your telephone bill skyrocket.

Windows Defender is a program from *Microsoft* that is packaged with *Windows Vista*. You can use it to find and remove known spyware from your PC. Its continuous protection allows you to use the Internet safely. The program checks for more than fifty different ways in which spyware can be installed on your PC.

 Please note:

Windows Defender is not enough to protect your computer against viruses!

There is no antivirus program packaged with *Windows Vista*. This means you have to purchase and install one yourself. If you do not, your computer will not be adequately protected against viruses and other threats. In the section **9.23 Downloading and Installing Windows Live OneCare** you learn more about protecting your computer against viruses.

You can open *Windows Defender* from the *Security Center*:

The *Windows Defender* start screen appears.

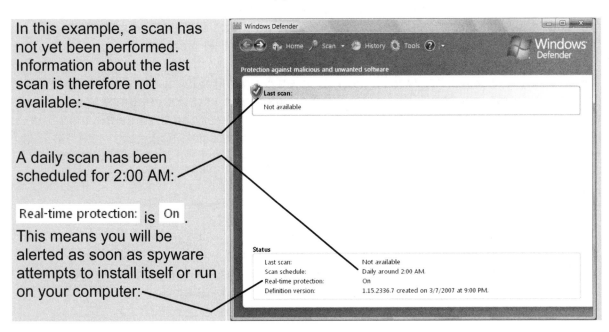

Before you perform a scan manually, it is a good idea to check if there are any updates for the spyware definitions *Windows Defender* uses.

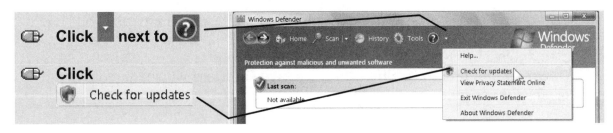

Your screen goes dark and *Windows* asks your permission to continue. Since you started this action, you can give permission by clicking the *Continue* button.

These balloons show what *Windows Defender* is doing:

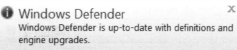

9.20 Scanning Your Computer with Windows Defender

In *Windows Defender*, you can choose between three scan types:

Quick Scan : only scans the locations where spyware is often found.
Full Scan : scans all files and folders on your computer.
Custom Scan... : only scans the folders you specify.

In this example the full scan is chosen:

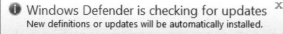

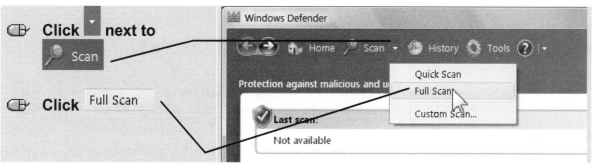

Click ⬇ **next to** Scan

Click Full Scan

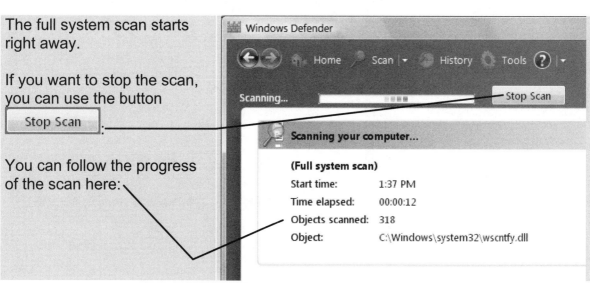

The full system scan starts right away.

If you want to stop the scan, you can use the button Stop Scan :

You can follow the progress of the scan here:

The scan can take from 15 minutes up to half an hour, depending on the speed of your computer and the number of files. When the scan is completed, you can view the scan results.

If nothing was found, you see this window:

You see that no unwanted or harmful software has been detected: ————————

If you see this window you do not need to do anything. Just read through the next part of this section to see what happens when something *is* found.

If something is found on your computer, the window will look like this:

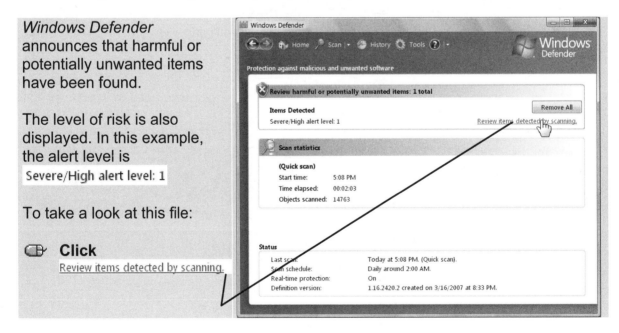

Windows Defender announces that harmful or potentially unwanted items have been found.

The level of risk is also displayed. In this example, the alert level is

Severe/High alert level: 1

To take a look at this file:

👆 **Click**

Review items detected by scanning.

In this example, *Windows Defender* found one item. You see detailed information about this item here:

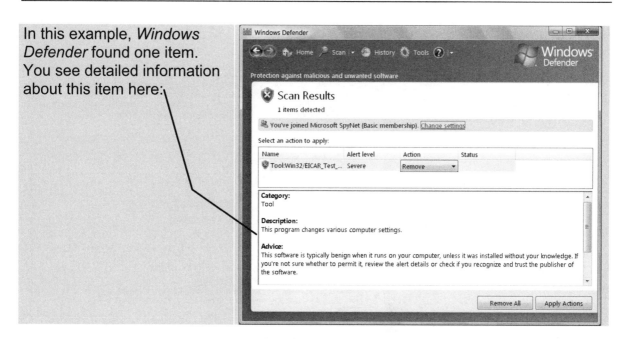

The information describes the item and shows you *Microsoft's* advice on the best course of action to take. If you scroll down, you see where the item was found on your hard drive. There may also be a link to a *Microsoft* webpage where you can read more about this item.

9.21 Remove, Ignore, Quarantine or Allow Items

When potentially harmful software has been found, you can choose what you want to do with it. These are your options:

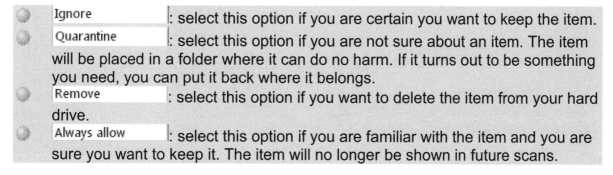

If anything was found on your computer, you can decide what you want to do with the items. If you are not sure, check the detailed information for a link to more information on the *Microsoft* website. If there is no link, you can also search the Internet.

In this example, the item will be placed in quarantine:

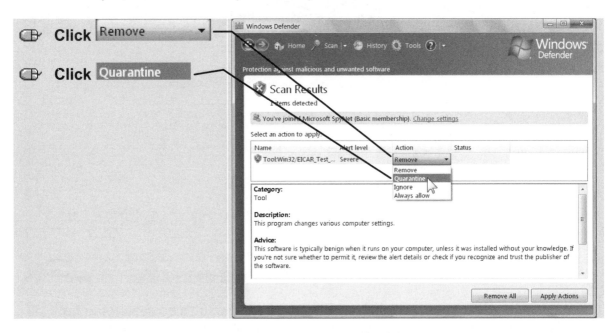

Of course, you can select one of the other actions by your own computer. If more than one item was found on your computer, you can select a different action for each separate item.

☞ **Review the item(s) found on your computer and select the desired action(s)**

You can carry out the selected action(s) as follows:

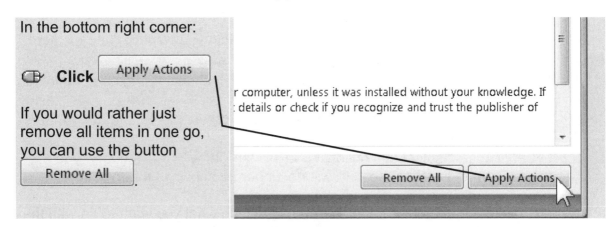

Windows Defender has applied the selected actions. The status has changed to:

Name	Alert level	Action	Status
Tool:Win32/EICAR_Test_...	Severe	Quarantine	Succeeded

Tip

Restoring or removing a quarantined item

You can restore a quarantined item. You may discover that you actually need it for something else to function for example. Or you can remove the item if you are sure you no longer need it. You can perform both actions in the same window:

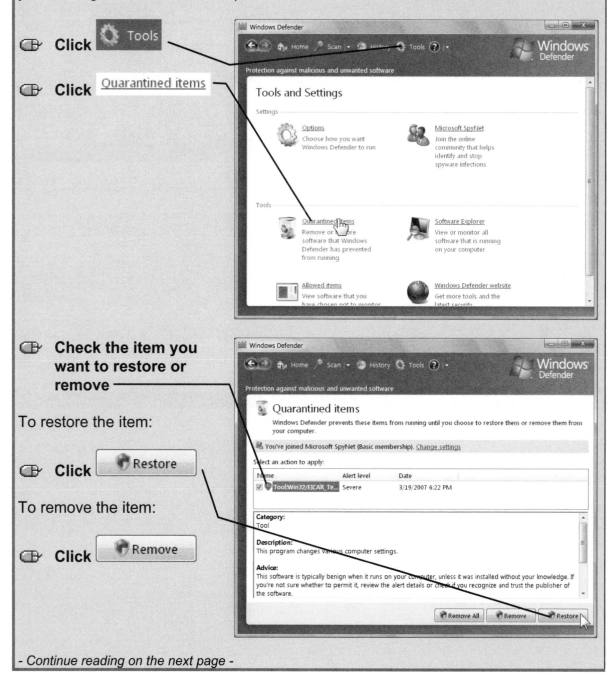

☞ **Click** Tools

☞ **Click** Quarantined items

☞ **Check the item you want to restore or remove**

To restore the item:

☞ **Click** Restore

To remove the item:

☞ **Click** Remove

- Continue reading on the next page -

When you choose to restore an item, *Windows Defender* asks if you are sure you want to do that. If you are sure:

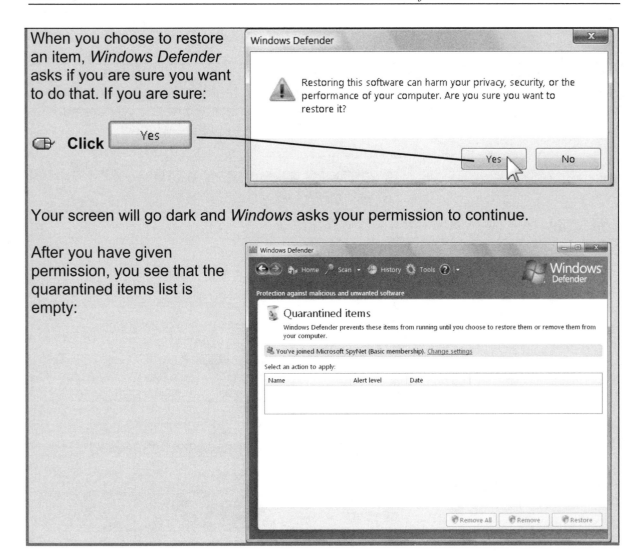

👆 **Click** ⬚Yes⬚

Your screen will go dark and *Windows* asks your permission to continue.

After you have given permission, you see that the quarantined items list is empty:

Tip

Microsoft SpyNet Community

By default, you become a member of the *Microsoft SpyNet Community* when you use *Windows Defender*. This notification is displayed:

👤 You've joined Microsoft SpyNet (Basic membership).

This means that *Windows Defender* automatically sends information to *Microsoft* about spyware, potentially unwanted software, and software or changes by software that have not yet been analyzed for risks. The actions that you take when unwanted software is found are also reported to *Microsoft*.

To change or cancel your membership:

Click 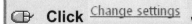 Change settings

In this window you can read more about *Microsoft SpyNet*. You can choose between three options:

Join with a basic membership
Join with an advanced membership
I don't want to join Microsoft SpyNet

☞ **Read the descriptions and select an option**

Click 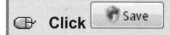 Save

If you do not want to make any changes:

Click  Cancel

9.22 Changing Settings in Windows Defender

You can change the *Windows Defender* settings to suit your preferences. You do that in the *Tools* window:

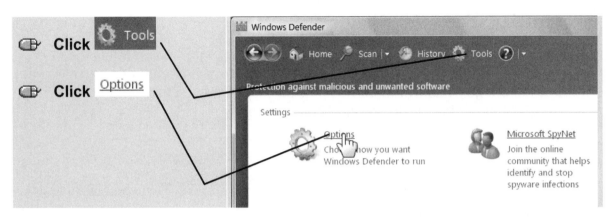

Click Tools

Click Options

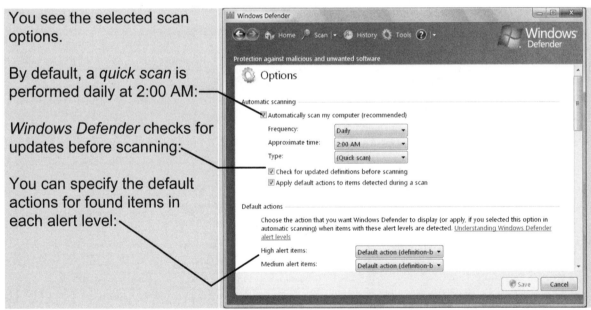

You see the selected scan options.

By default, a *quick scan* is performed daily at 2:00 AM:

Windows Defender checks for updates before scanning:

You can specify the default actions for found items in each alert level:

You may want to pick a different time for the daily *quick scan*. But it is not really necessary: if your computer is not on at 2:00 AM, the scan will be done when you turn your computer on.

More options are shown at the bottom of the window.

☞ **Drag the scroll box down a little**

Now you see the settings under the header *Real-time protection options*:

Real-time protection means that *Windows Defender* continuously monitors all activity while you use the Internet. Any attempt to download spyware to your computer will be blocked.

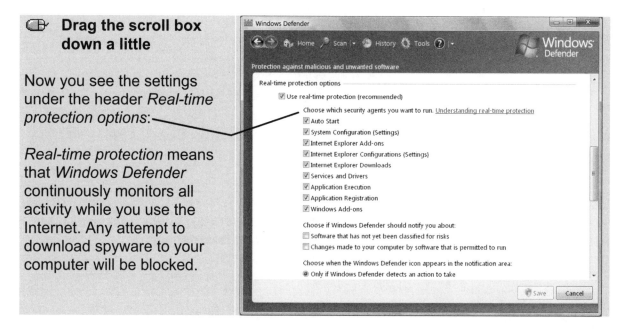

When an attempt to download spyware is blocked, you will see a message about the attempt. Then you can decide whether you want to allow the download. It is a good idea to leave these *Real-time protection options* unchanged.

☞ **Drag the scroll box all the way down**

You see the *Advanced options* and the *Administrator options*:

You do not need to make any changes here.

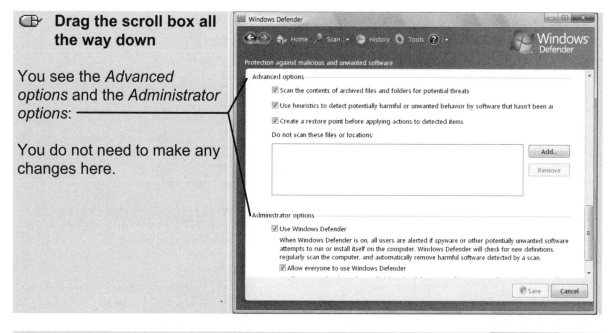

☞ **If desired, change the settings on your computer and click**

You have learned about several options for the program. Now you can close *Windows Defender*:

☞ **Click**

👉 **Close the windows of *Windows Security Center* and *Control Panel*** $\mathscr{C}$32

💡 **Tip**

Software Explorer
You can use the *Software Explorer* in *Windows Defender* to see which programs are active on your computer. If you suspect that something is wrong with your PC, it is useful to see if any unwanted programs have been started.

☞ **Click** Tools, Software Explorer

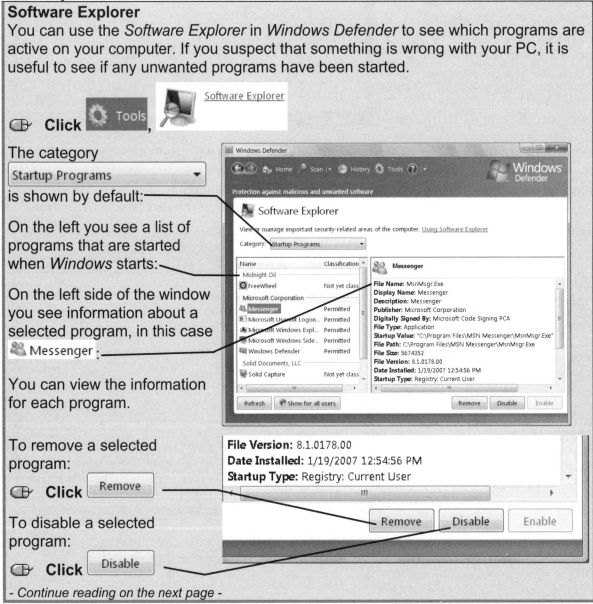

The category

Startup Programs ▼

is shown by default:

On the left you see a list of programs that are started when *Windows* starts:

On the left side of the window you see information about a selected program, in this case Messenger :

You can view the information for each program.

To remove a selected program:

☞ **Click** Remove

To disable a selected program:

☞ **Click** Disable

- Continue reading on the next page -

In addition to the *Startup Programs*, you can also view the *Currently Running Programs.*

☞ **Click**
Currently Running Programs

You see the list of active programs:

If you want to end one of these programs, click the
[Task Manager] button:

☞ **If necessary, click the tab** [Applications]

In this window, you can end the selected program by clicking the [End Task] button:

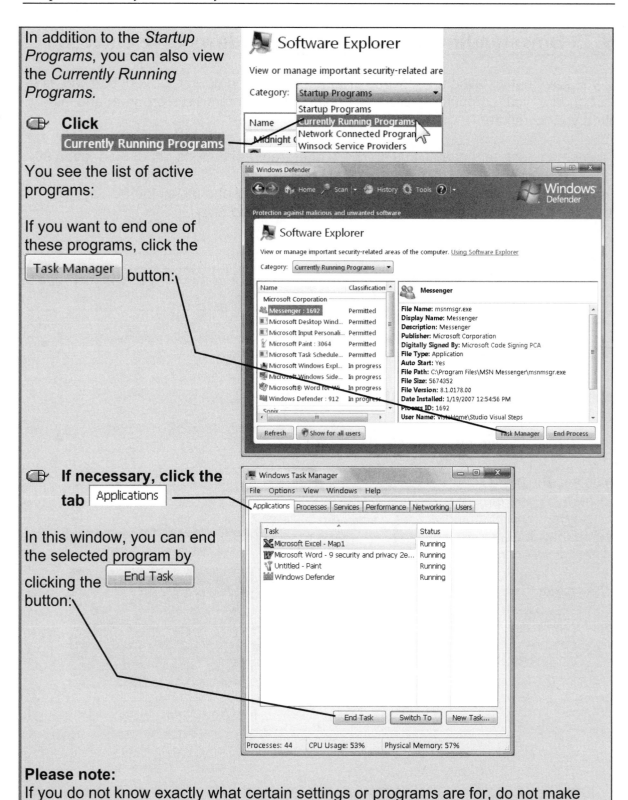

Please note:
If you do not know exactly what certain settings or programs are for, do not make any changes. In that case, you should ask for help from a more experienced computer user or consult your hardware supplier.

9.23 Downloading and Installing Windows Live OneCare

If you have not installed an antivirus program on your computer, or your software is out of date, your computer is at risk. You should buy an antivirus program and install it on your computer.

Many manufacturers of antivirus software offer free trial periods of 30, 60 or even 90 days. That way you can try before you buy and decide which antivirus program suits you best. In this section you can read how to download and install the 90-day free trial version of the antivirus program *Windows Live OneCare*.

 Please note:

If you already have a working antivirus program on your computer you can just read through this section.

☞ **Open** *Internet Explorer* 𝒞𝒞¹

☞ **If necessary, connect to the Internet** 𝒞𝒞³

☞ **Go to the website** onecare.live.com 𝒞𝒞⁴

You see the homepage of *Windows Live OneCare.* Since the Internet changes constantly, it may look different on your screen.

☞ **Click**

Download the 90-day free trial

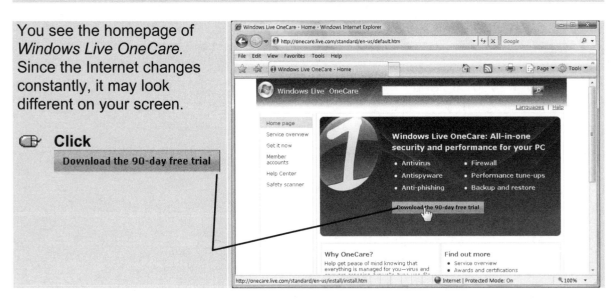

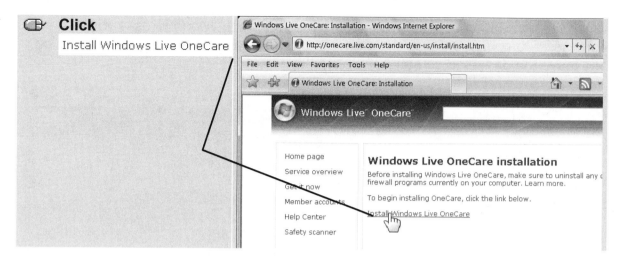

You can install the file right away:

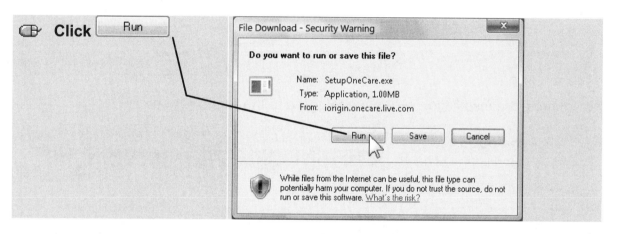

The installation file is downloaded. You see the progress in this window:

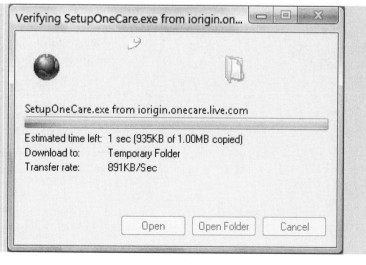

When the installation begins, your screen goes dark and *Windows* asks your permission to continue. Since you want the program to be installed, give permission and leave the darkened screen.

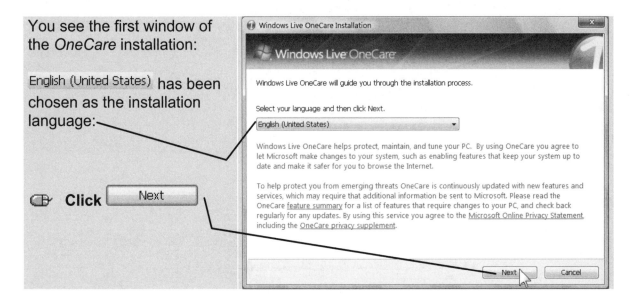

To continue the installation, you have to agree to the terms of use:

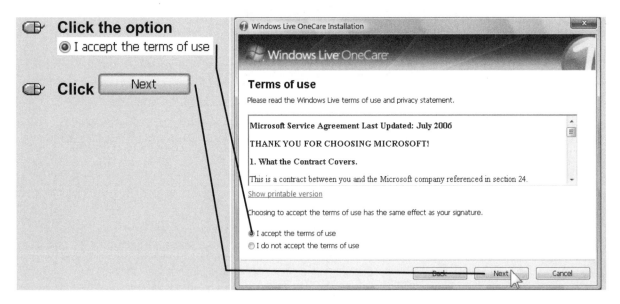

You can follow the progress of the download and the installation in this window:

Please note:
If you are using a dial-up connection, the download and installation may take as long as 30 to 60 minutes.

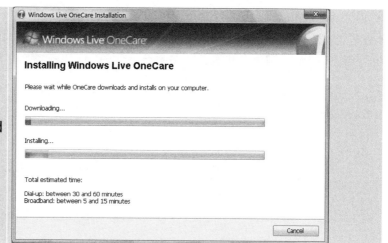

During the installation, *Windows Defender* is turned off because it is replaced by *Windows Live OneCare*.

☞ **Click** [Close]

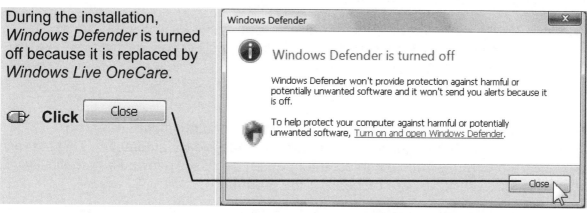

To complete the installation you must restart your computer:

☞ **Close** *Internet Explorer*

☞ **Click** [Finish]

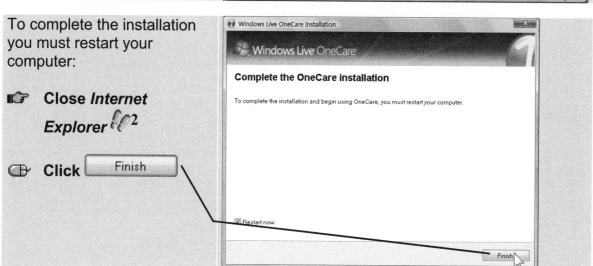

After restarting your computer, *Windows Live OneCare* will be opened automatically.

You see a window that
explains the 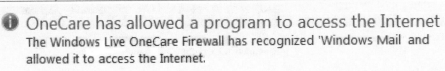 icon in the
system area of the taskbar:

After you have read the
information:

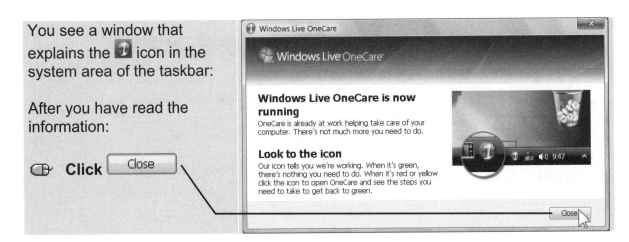

At the bottom of the screen you see this message balloon:

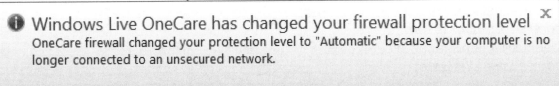

Windows Live OneCare has a built-in firewall that has automatically replaced
Windows Firewall. The protection level has been changed to "automatic". This means
that when a program wants to contact the Internet, access is allowed automatically
when *Windows Live OneCare* recognizes the program.

For example, when you check your e-mail in *Windows Mail,* you will see this

ⓘ OneCare has allowed a program to access the Internet X
The Windows Live OneCare Firewall has recognized 'Windows Mail' and
allowed it to access the Internet.

message:

The program has also replaced *Windows Defender* for spyware protection. When you
open the *Windows Security Center*, you can see the current protection levels:

☞ **Open *Windows Security Center*** ℓℓ**69**

Click *Firewall*

You see that *Windows Live OneCare Firewall* is on.

Click

Malware protection

Windows Live OneCare provides both virus and spyware protection:

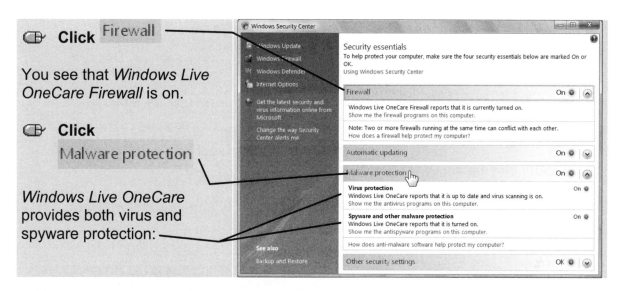

Windows Live OneCare is a complete solution for your Internet safety. The program will not only protect your computer against viruses, but will also provide a firewall and antispyware protection. Both *Windows Firewall* and *Windows Defender* are replaced by *Windows Live OneCare*.

☞ **Close** *Windows Security Center* 32

Now you see the main window of *Windows Live OneCare*:

In the top part of the window you see the current status:

Here you see the three components of the program:

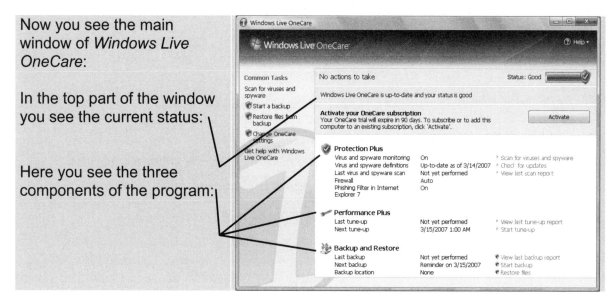

These are the three components of *Windows Live OneCare*:

⊘ **Protection Plus**: this component provides virus, spyware and phishing protection and manages a two-way firewall.

⚲ **Performance Plus**: you can use this tool to perform maintenance tasks to keep your computer running smoothly.

⚙ **Backup and Restore**: this component helps protect your files in case of accidental deletion or hardware failure.

To make sure your computer has not been infected by a virus or other malware, you can let *Protection Plus* perform a scan of your computer:

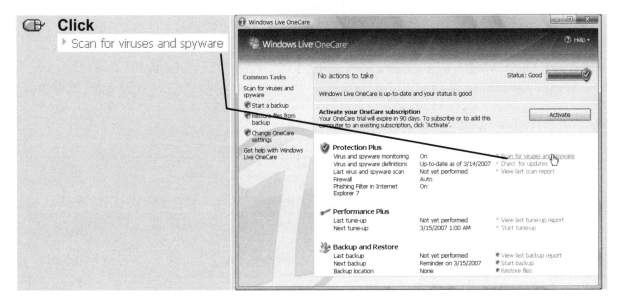

☞ **Click**

▸ Scan for viruses and spyware

You can choose between three scan types:

● **Quick Scan**: only scans the locations where malware is often found.

● **Complete Scan**: scans all files and folders on your computer.

● **Custom Scan**: only scans the folders you specify.

9.24 Scanning Your Computer

To get an idea of what a scan looks like, you can perform a quick scan.

Click Quick Scan

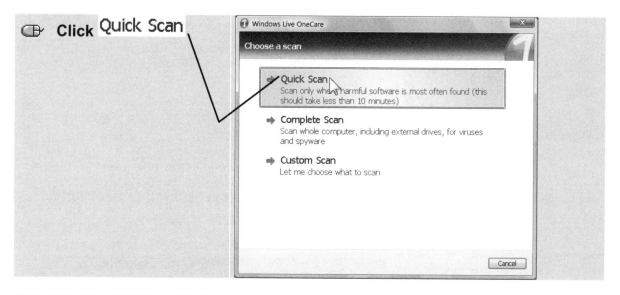

During the scan you see this window:

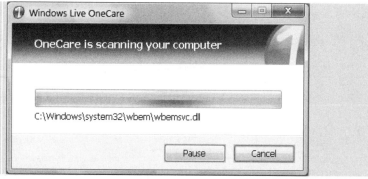

When the scan has finished, you will see a scan report.

In this example, no suspicious files were found:

Click Close

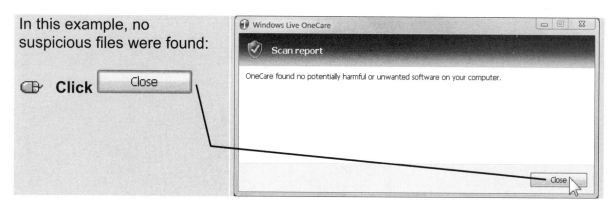

☞ **If there were no suspicious files on your computer you can just read through the rest of this section**

If a harmful program has been found, you see this message:

You can take a look at the details:

👆 **Click** <u>View details</u>

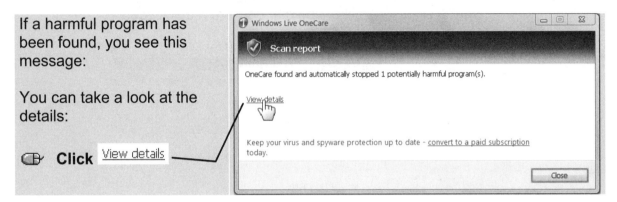

OneCare takes automatic action against potentially harmful software rated high or severe.

In this example, the suspicious program has been removed immediately:

👆 **Click** Close

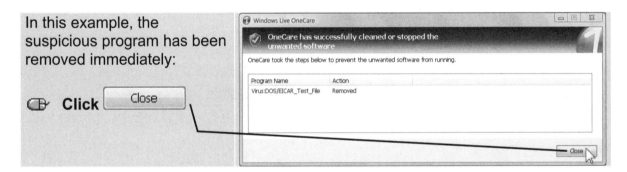

You can close this scan report.

👆 **Click** Close

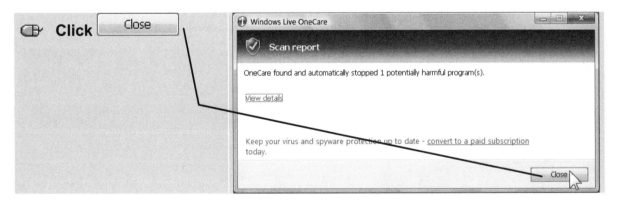

Tip

> **Help! A virus!**
> If you do not open questionable e-mail attachments or use suspicious programs, the chance is fairly small that any form of malware will end up on your computer. But sooner or later your antivirus program may find a suspicious file.
>
> Your antivirus program will then warn you and possibly take action automatically. It will identify the infected file, give the name of the virus and it will tell you what action has been taken.
>
> With low risk items, the program will ask you what you want to do with the item:
>
> - **Repair the file:** if a file on the computer is infected, the program tries to repair the file by removing the virus. If it is a standalone virus like a Trojan horse or a worm, it will be removed.
> - **Place the file in quarantine:** the infected file or virus is not removed but placed in a separate folder where it can do no damage.
> - **Remove the file:** the infected file or virus is deleted from the computer. This means the data in the file will be lost if you do not have a backup copy. Usually, this is only done when there is no other way to solve the problem.

9.25 Changing the OneCare Settings

Instead of starting a scan manually, you can also set a time during the day for the scan to be performed automatically.

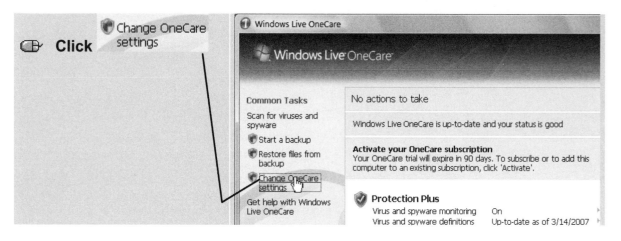

Your screen goes dark and the program needs your permission to continue. After you have given permission the window *Windows Live OneCare Settings* is opened:

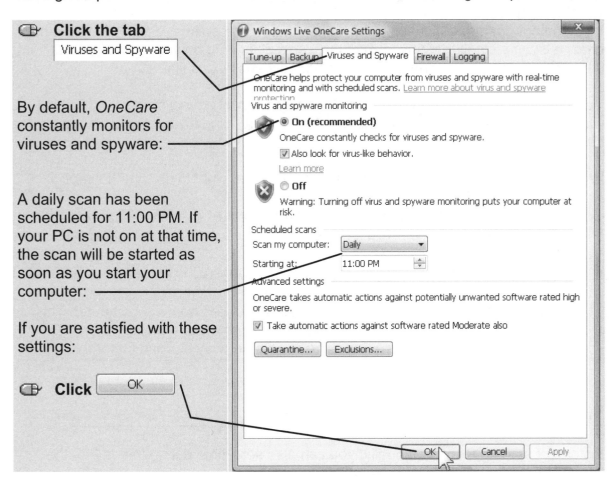

☞ **Click the tab**

Viruses and Spyware

By default, *OneCare* constantly monitors for viruses and spyware:

A daily scan has been scheduled for 11:00 PM. If your PC is not on at that time, the scan will be started as soon as you start your computer:

If you are satisfied with these settings:

☞ **Click** OK

☞ **Close *Windows Live OneCare*** ℓℓ³²

Tip

Update your antivirus program
New viruses and other malware are constantly being developed. To stay on top of all these threats, it is important to keep your program updated with the latest virus and spyware definitions.

Every antivirus program has an option, text link or a button to contact the manufacturer's website to search for updates.

In *Windows Live OneCare* you can check for updates like this:

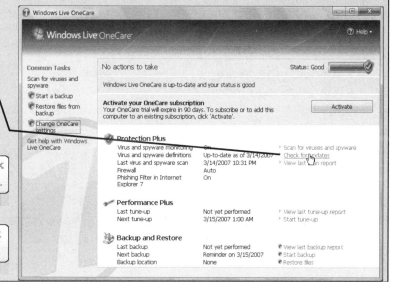

Click ▶ Check for updates

The progress is shown in these message balloons:

ⓘ Windows Live OneCare Updates ✕
Windows Live OneCare is checking for updates.

ⓘ Windows Live OneCare Updates ✕
Windows Live OneCare is up to date.

 Tip

After the 90-day trial
Windows Live OneCare can be used for free for 90 days. Every couple of days you will see a reminder that you need to activate your subscription before the trial expires.

To continue the trial:

Click ➡ Not yet

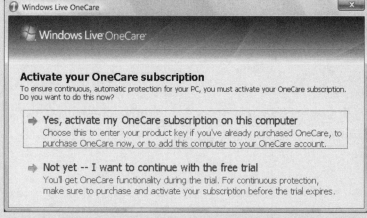

If you want to buy *OneCare* online, or enter a product key after purchasing:

Click ➡ Yes, activate my OneCare subscription on this computer

Tip

Tune-up

By default, *Tune-up* is started automatically every 4 weeks.

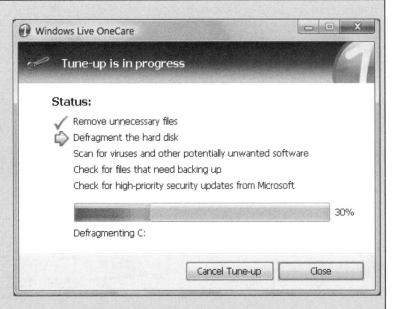

The following tasks will be performed:

- remove unnecessary files, like installation files and temporary files (see below)
- defragment the hard disk, so that files and folders can be accessed more efficiently
- scan for malware
- check for updates from *Microsoft* that have not been installed yet

Also, a check is performed to see which files have not yet been backed up. If *Tune-up* finds files that are new or have changed since your last backup, they will appear in the *Actions to take* list in the *OneCare* main window.

If the *Tune-up* starts at an inconvenient moment:

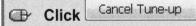 **Click** `Cancel Tune-up`

If you want to change the day, time or interval for the scheduled tune-up, you can access the settings from the *OneCare* main window:

Click `Change OneCare settings` **, then click the tab** `Tune-up`

By default, *OneCare* does not remove the unnecessary files automatically. To change that, check the option 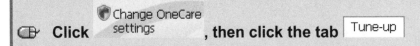 ☑ Remove unnecessary files from my computer during Tune-up .

9.26 Test Your Knowledge

You have reached the end of this Visual Steps Book. You have learned a lot about *Internet Explorer* and *Windows Mail*. Now you can test your knowledge with our free online quizzes. Visual Steps offers a series of multiple choice quizzes over a range of different topics created specifically for seniors.

A special certificate is available to all individuals who can successfully answer the questions. If a sufficient score is achieved you will be able to receive your Computer Certificate by e-mail. This service is free for all participants.

The online quizzes are available at the website **www.ccforseniors.com**

☞ **Open *Internet Explorer*** 🦶¹

☞ **If necessary, connect to the Internet** 🦶³

☞ **Open the website www.ccforseniors.com** 🦶⁴

You will see this website:

Click on one of the tests listed on the left, for example
- Certificate Internet Explorer (Windows Vista)

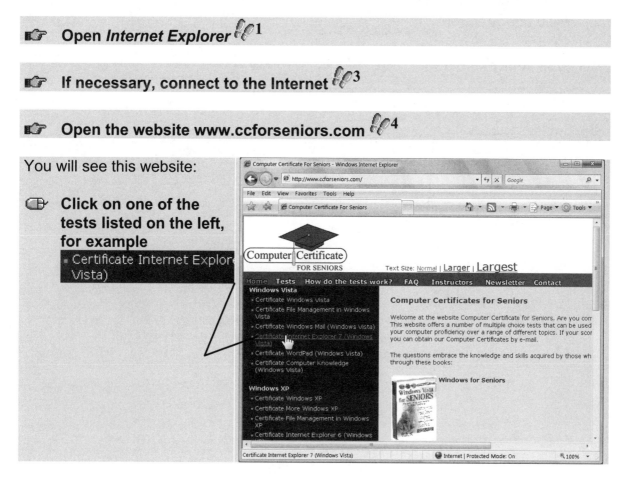

☞ **Using the scroll bar, scroll down to see the first question**

☞ **Read the question and click the right answer**

☞ **Continue reading and answering the remaining questions in this manner**

☞ **Scroll down further to see each question**

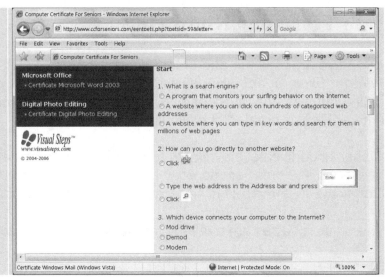

⌨ **Type your name and e-mail address**

☞ **Click** Score test

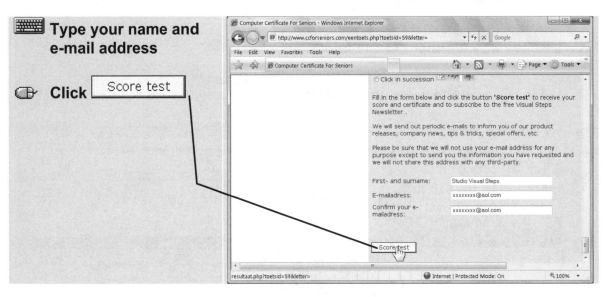

Your test result will appear:

If it is sufficient, you can request your Computer Certificate by e-mail.

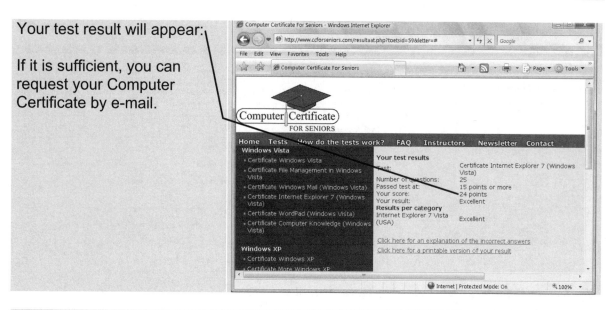

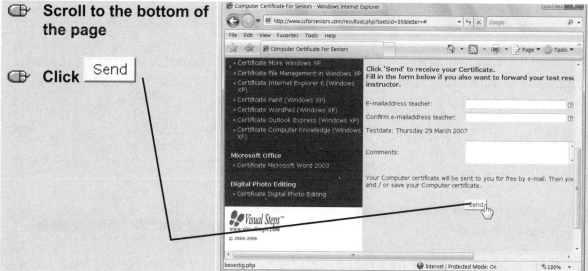

Scroll to the bottom of the page

Click `Send`

The Computer Certificate will now be sent to the e-mail address you entered earlier. You will see a confirmation:

The computercertificate has been sent to your emailaddress!

Open *Windows Mail* 35 and click Send/Receive

Open the e-mail message that you have received from ccforseniors.com 42

You did not receive it yet? Wait a few minutes and try again.

The Certificate is attached to this e-mail:

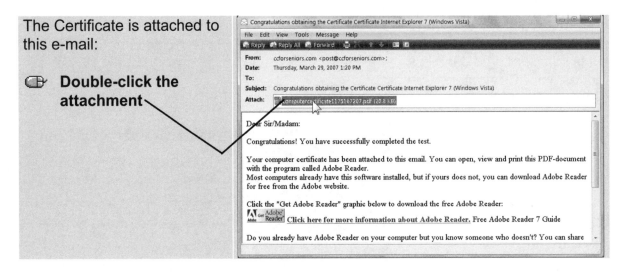

☞ **Double-click the attachment**

Windows Mail asks if you want to open the file:

☞ **Click** Open

The Certificate is a PDF file. It will be opened in the program *Adobe Reader*. On most computers this free program is already installed. If it is not on your computer, read the information in the e-mail about this subject.

You see your own Certificate:

Now you can print it:

☞ **Make sure the printer is switched on**

☞ **Click** 🖨

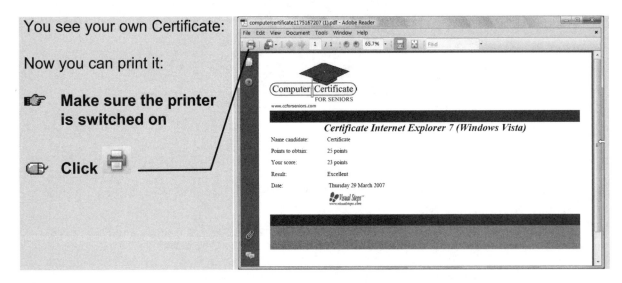

Your Certificate will be printed.

☞ **Close all windows** 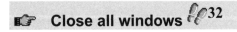32

9.27 More about Windows Vista

The book **Internet and E-mail for Seniors with Windows Vista** has taken you through the ins and outs of Internet and e-mail. Not only have you learned how to use Internet and e-mail to the fullest, you have also learned to take several measures to ensure your security and privacy.

Interested in gaining more skills? If you would like to know more about other books in the Windows Vista for Seniors series, please visit our website www.visualsteps.com.

 Tip

The Visual Steps Newsletter
Do you want to be informed about the release date of our new books? You can subscribe to our free Visual Steps Newsletter. We will send out periodic e-mails to inform you of our product releases, tips & tricks, special offers, free guides, etc.

☞ **Open *Internet Explorer*** 🦶¹

☞ **Open the website www.visualsteps.com** 🦶⁴

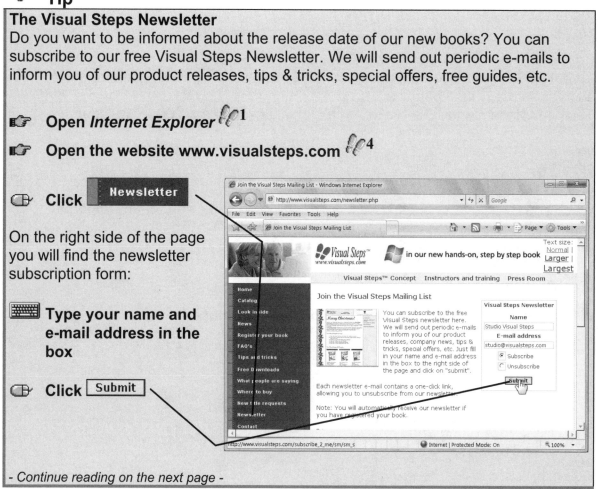

🖰 **Click** Newsletter

On the right side of the page you will find the newsletter subscription form:

⌨ **Type your name and e-mail address in the box**

🖰 **Click** Submit

- Continue reading on the next page -

This is an example of the Visual Steps Newsletter:

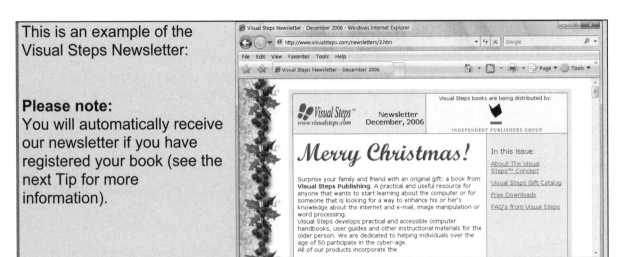

Please note:
You will automatically receive our newsletter if you have registered your book (see the next Tip for more information).

Privacy: Please be sure that we will not use your e-mail address for any purpose except to send you the information you have requested. We will not share this address with any third party.
Each newsletter contains a clickable link to unsubscribe from our newsletter.

 Tip

How to register your book
When you register your book, Visual Steps will keep you aware of any important changes that are necessary to you as a user of the book. Also, you will automatically be subscribed to the Visual Steps Newsletter.

☞ **Open *Internet Explorer*** 𝒞𝒞¹

☞ **Open the website www.visualsteps.com/internetvista** 𝒞𝒞⁴

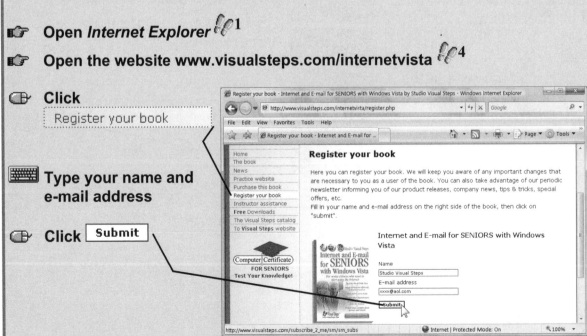

🖑 **Click**
    Register your book

⌨ **Type your name and e-mail address**

🖑 **Click** Submit

9.28 Background Information

Glossary	
Add-on	A program that adds extra functionality to a web browser like *Internet Explorer*.
Browsing history	The traces you leave on your computer when you browse the Internet. In *Internet Explorer*, the complete browsing history consists of the temporary Internet files, cookies, history, form data and passwords.
Cookies	Small text files that are placed on your hard drive while you surf the Internet.
Custom Scan	Option in antivirus or antispyware program to scan only the folders you specify yourself.
Firewall	Software or hardware that checks information coming from the Internet or a network, and then either blocks it or allows it to pass through to your computer, depending on your firewall settings.
First-party cookies	Cookies that come from the website you are viewing.
Form data	Information that you have entered into forms on websites or typed in the address bar.
Full Scan	Option in antivirus or antispyware program to scan all files and folders on your computer.
Https://	This prefix denotes a secure Internet connection.
Junk e-mail	Unsolicited commercial e-mail. Also known as spam.
Junk Mail Filter	In *Windows Mail*, the *Junk Mail Filter* prevents phishing e-mails and other junk mail from entering your *Inbox*. These messages are moved to the folder *Junk E-mail*.
Malware	Short for "malicious software"; software that is designed to deliberately harm your computer.
Microsoft Spynet Community	When you are subscribed to this community, *Windows Defender* automatically sends information to *Microsoft* about spyware, and potentially unwanted software.
- Continue reading on the next page -	

Parental Controls	Can be used to help manage how your (grand)children use the computer. For example, you can set limits on your (grand)children's access to the Internet, the hours that they can log on to the computer, and which games they can play and programs they can run.
Permanent cookies	Cookies that are stored on you hard drive, to be read by the website that created it when you visit that site again.
Phishing	Online phishing is a way to trick computer users into revealing personal or financial information through a fraudulent e-mail message or an innocent looking website.
Phishing Filter	In *Internet Explorer*, the *Phishing Filter* helps detect phishing websites. If the site you are visiting is on the list of reported phishing websites, *Internet Explorer* will display a warning webpage and a notification on the address bar.
Pop-up	A pop-up is a small web browser window that appears on top of the website you are viewing. Pop-up windows often open as soon as you visit a website and are usually created by advertisers.
Pop-up Blocker	A feature in *Internet Explorer* that lets you limit or block most pop-ups.
Quick Scan	Option in antivirus or antispyware program. Using this scan, only the locations where malware of often found are scanned.
Session cookies	Cookies that are removed when *Internet Explorer* is closed. Also known as temporary cookies.
Spam	Unsolicited commercial e-mail. Also known as junk e-mail.
Spyware	Malicious software that can display advertisements (such as pop-up ads), collect information about you, or change settings on your computer, generally without appropriately obtaining your consent.
Temporary cookies	Cookies that are removed when *Internet Explorer* is closed. Also known as session cookies.
Third-party cookie	Cookies that come from pop-up windows or banner ads.
Temporary Internet Files	When you view a webpage, *Internet Explorer* saves a temporary copy of that page so that the page can be displayed more quickly if you open it again later.

- Continue reading on the next page -

Trojan horse	Program that contains or installs a malicious program. The program may appear to be harmless useful or interesting programs, but are actually harmful when executed.
Tune-up	Part of *Windows Live OneCare* that performs maintenance tasks to keep your computer running smoothly. Among other tasks, tune-up defragments your hard disk, manages updates, removes unnecessary files and checks for viruses.
Virus	A program that attempts to spread from computer to computer and either cause damage (by erasing or corrupting data) or annoy users.
Windows Defender	Antispyware program that is packaged with *Windows Vista*.
Windows Live OneCare	Complete solution for your Internet safety. The program not only protects your computer against viruses, but also provides a firewall and antispyware protection.
Windows Security Center	System that checks your computer's security settings and keeps tracks of updates to *Windows Vista*.
Windows Update	System that checks if you are using the most recent version of *Windows Vista*.
Worm	Malware in the form of a self-replicating program. A typical worm sends out copies of itself to everyone in your *Contacts* folder, then does the same thing on the recipients' computers. This creates a domino effect of busy network traffic that slows down corporate networks and could possibly bring down the whole Internet.
Source: Windows Help and Support	

Safe surfing
In this chapter you have taken a look at various security settings in *Windows Vista*. But remember, your own actions play a very large role in your security. No matter how well you protect everything, there is always a risk that a virus or other malware sneaks onto your computer. New threats are developed every day. If you stop paying attention for even a moment, you can accidentally download something unpleasant onto your computer.

Here is a summary of things you can do to avoid mishaps:

- Always make sure you have a good, up-to-date antivirus program.

- Always make sure you have a good firewall.

- Always make sure that *Windows* is up-to-date.

- Use *Windows Defender* or another antispyware program to remove spyware from your computer.

- Have your antivirus and antispyware programs scan your computer regularly.

- If something strange happens while you are surfing, break the connection immediately.

- If you do not need access to the Internet for a longer period of time, break your connection. This reduces the chance that others can break into your computer.

- Protect yourself from pop-ups, junk mail and phishing attempts by using the measures discussed in this chapter.

- Download files and programs from trustworthy websites only.

- Enter as little personal data as possible on websites. Do not enter credit card or bank information, PIN codes or passwords unless you are absolutely sure you are on a secure website.

- Be careful when entering your e-mail address on websites. Some websites try to gather e-mail addresses to be able to flood them with spam later. It is a good idea to create an extra e-mail account with a free provider like *Hotmail, Windows Live Mail* or *Gmail* for use on the Internet. Use that e-mail address to register on websites for example. This way you can keep the spam out of your regular *Inbox*.

- Pay attention to the address and safety features of the website when you are doing your online banking or when you are buying something. The address (URL) should be <u>exactly</u> the name you expect and start with **https://**.

Paying on the Internet

As with any other type of financial transaction, buyers and sellers on the Internet demand a secure, reliable and fraud-free transaction. The customer wants to be sure he gets what he has paid for and in turn the merchant wants to make sure he gets paid. The merchant will request information from the customer. He needs to know where the order should be sent and where he can recover his losses if anything goes wrong.

To help consumers, a company called *ShopSafe* has developed online directories that list companies worldwide that practice "safe shopping". ShopSafe independently reviews the companies and lists only those that meet its criteria for safe shopping.

How can I pay online?

- **Credit Card or Bank Debit Card**
You provide the online merchant with your credit or debit card data.

- **Check or Money Order**
You place your order online, then send your paper check or money order by regular mail to the address listed on the merchant's website.

- **Electronic Funds Transfer or Electronic Check**
You provide the online merchant with your bank account number and routing number, and authorize him to deduct the funds directly from your account.

- **PayPal**
This is an increasingly popular alternative for individuals and small businesses accepting payments over the Internet.

- **C.O.D.**
You place your order online and pay the delivery person at the door when you receive it. Many merchants no longer accept this kind of payment.

Safe e-mail behavior

A regular e-mail message containing only text is not a big risk. Attachments to e-mail messages can be dangerous. Fortunately, different types of potentially dangerous attachments are already blocked by the security settings in *Windows Mail*. But it is still very important that you carefully examine every message before you open it.

Pay attention to these points:

- Always make sure you have a good and up-to-date antivirus program.

- Curiosity killed the cat! Never open unfamiliar messages or messages from unknown senders. Delete them immediately.

- Does the subject of the message seem familiar? Viruses sometimes use old messages and send them to random addresses in the address book on the infected computer. If you think it is an old message, or a message that is not meant for you, delete it immediately. You can also contact the sender by phone first.

- Does the message contain an attachment with a strange name or of a strange type? Do not be curious: delete it right away.

- Before you double-click on a message to open it, always view the message in the preview window first.

- Does the message offer you spectacular offers, prizes or wonder drugs? Do not respond to the message or click on an *unsuscribe* link. By doing that, you confirm to the sender that your e-mail address is real. This will result in even more spam.

- Not every phishing message is caught by the phishing filter. Never respond to messages from banks, credit card companies or online shops that ask you for confidential financial information. Remember, these e-mail messages and the websites they link to can resemble the real website very closely.

- Be careful with your e-mail address. Do not give it to anyone or enter it on every website. Before you know it, you will be drowning in spam or other unwanted messages.

- Consider getting an extra e-mail address. The first address is your primary e-mail address for friends, family, work and so on. The second address (such as a *Hotmail, Windows Live Mail* or *Gmail* address is the one you use when you are surfing and you are asked for information. If you start receiving too many unwanted messages at the second address, you can even get a third address.

- Remember that deleted e-mail messages are stored in the *Deleted items* folder. This folder should be emptied from time to time.

Hoaxes and Chain Letters
Hoaxes and *chain letters* are e-mail messages written with one purpose; to be sent to everyone you know. The messages they contain are usually untrue.

Hoaxes are usually e-mails that warn of virus threats. Sometimes these e-mails give detailed descriptions of how you can detect and remove a particular virus file from your hard drive. Often these are *Windows* system files. If you were to follow these instructions, *Windows* would no longer function properly. Other e-mails warn about e-mails with attachments that are sent out. **Never carry out the instructions and never forward these virus hoax e-mails to others.**

This is an example of such a hoax:

Subject: IMPORTANT-VIRUS ALERT!!!
Hi everybody, I just wanted to let you know you should check your computers by following the procedure that's next... I don't remember getting an e-mail with that file attachment, but I found it in my system. Since I found the dumb little bear in my computer, I'm sending you the info. The virus is called jdbgmgr.exe and it transfers automatically through Messenger and also through your address book and since I have all of you in my address book I have to send everyone this info. I'm sorry if this causes any problems. It certainly wasn't intentional. The virus isn't detected by McAfee or Norton and it remains in the folder for 14 days before activating and harming the system. It can be erased before it eliminates the files in your computer. To do so, follow these steps: (...) If you find this virus in your computer, please send this message to all the people in your address book before it causes any damage.

Other hoax messages contain stories about someone who is sick or needs your help. By sending the message to other people, money is supposedly raised to help this person. These messages are always untrue.

Chain letters have the same purpose as hoaxes. These messages generally offer money or good luck to anyone who passes the message on. And ofcourse, bad luck if you refuse to do that. Chain letters are often used to collect e-mail addresses and sell them to commercial organizations.

You usually receive a hoax or a chain letter from a friend or an acquaintance. That will make you more inclined to believe the story. You should always do some research to find out whether the information in the e-mail is correct. A good source of information is **hoaxbusters.ciac.org**. On this website you find an index of known hoaxes. Tou can search the database with a few keywords from the suspected hoax message you have received.

Always let the person who sent you the hoax know that it is a fake virus warning or a fake story and point him or her to this website!

Autodialers

An *autodialer* is a piece of software that breaks up your dial-up connection to your *Internet Service Provider* and creates a new connection. The new connection is made to an expensive number like a 900 number or an overseas number. You will have to pay significantly more when you get your next telephone bill.

Autodialers can be used legally and honestly. They are often used as payment for ringtones, games, music, and so on. But unfortunately they are often abused. Autodialers can even make a connection if you use DSL or a cable modem and your telephone modem is still connected!

Autodialer abuse occurs when:
- you have not been informed of the connection and the associated costs prior to the connection being made, or
- you have not given permission for the connection to be made.

The request for permission can be well-hidden; if you click OK too quickly you might just have given permission for the call to be made. You are most likely to encounter an illegal autodialer when you search for popular, hard to find or illegal content. Examples are illegal software or MP3 music files, pornography, questionable ringtones, online games or subscriptions to dating sites.

How do you now if there is an autodialer on your computer?

These may be signs that you have been infected with an autodialer:
- You receive a very high phone bill containing unfamiliar 900 numbers or international numbers.
- Your telephone company warns you that your bill has shot up in a short time.
- You discover an unfamiliar dial-up connection in your network connections.
- A strange icon is suddenly located in the *System Tray* of the *Windows* taskbar.
- You find new, unfamiliar shortcuts on your desktop or *Favorites Center*.
- The home page for your browser has been changed to an unfamiliar site.
- You hear your modem break the connection and start dialing again.
- You have a DSL or cable Internet connection but you hear a modem dialing.
- Your speed when surfing the Internet is slower than usual.
- New, unfamiliar software is listed in the *All Programs* list.
- You are online and you can receive e-mails, but you are unable to send e-mails through your own ISP.

- Continue reading on the next page -

What can I do to prevent autodialers from being installed on my computer?

- Never just click "OK" and never download something you have not asked for.

- Unplug your old telephone modem or ISDN adapter if you rarely use it.

- Turn off your computer and modem when you are not using it.

- It is possible to block 900 numbers and international numbers from being dialed from your telephone number. Keep in mind though, that 900 numbers can also provide useful information.

- Regularly check your Internet settings and dial-up connections.

- Keep *Windows, Windows Defender* and *Internet Explorer* up-to-date by downloading and installing security updates. Check regularly for new updates, or have these checks done automatically.

- Use a good antivirus program and keep it up-to-date.

- Use *Windows Defender* to scan your computer. Other programs that check for spyware and autodialers are *Ad-Aware, Hitman Pro, Spybot Search & Destroy* and *DialerDetect.*

- You can activate the *Task Manager* window in *Windows* by typing "control+alt+delete" once. This window shows a list of all programs and processes currently running on your computer. You can end autodialer programs in the *Task Manager,* after which you can delete them.

- You can file a complaint with your telephone company for the portion of your telephone bill caused by an autodialer. If you can not come to an agreement with your telephone company, you can contact the Federal Communications Commission (FCC).

- If software has been installed on your computer without your permission (as is often the case with an autodialer), you can file a complaint with the Federal Trade Commission (FTC).

For more information on autodialers and other Internet hazards, you can visit:

- *Federal Trade Commission (FTC)* - visit **www.ftc.gov** and select "For Consumers." Then select "E-Commerce and the Internet". You can also file a complaint here.

- *Federal Communications Commission (FCC)* - visit **www.fcc.gov/cgb/internet.html** for information or to file a complaint related to 900 numbers or overseas numbers dialed without your permission.

- *Internet Crime Complaint Center (IC3)* - visit **www.ic3.gov** if you think you have been the victim of Internet fraud.

9.29 Tips

 Tip

Antivirus software
There are a lot of good antivirus programs available on the market.

The most widely known programs are *Norton* and *McAfee.* But lesser known programs such as *Norman* or *Panda* also perform very well. Just like *Windows Live OneCare*, these programs offer free downloads for a 15, 30 or 60-day trial.

For more information check these websites:
- *McAfee*: us.mcafee.com
- *Norton*: shop.symantecstore.com
- *Norman*: www.norman.com
- *Panda*: www.pandasoftware.com

 Tip

Useful antivirus websites

us.mcafee.com/virusinfo	Virus alerts and information from *McAfee.*
securityresponse.symantec.com	Virus alerts and information from *Norton.*
www.lavasoft.com	Download the *Ad-Aware* antispyware program.
www.tucows.com	Widely respected dowload center for freeware and shareware, including the *Spybot* program.
www.misec.net/trojanhunter	Download the anti-Trojan horse program *TrojanHunter.*
hoaxbusters.ciac.org	Information on hoaxes, chain letters and phishing scams.
www.antiphishing.org	Information on phishing, with extensive archive and the possibility to report phishing scams.

Tip

Recognizing a secure website
When you buy something on the Internet, you should always check if you are on a secure website before you enter your credit card details.

The most important difference between a secured and unsecured website is that on a secured website information is transferred using encryption technology. The user enters his or her data, such as a credit card number. This information is encrypted using special software and then transferred to the seller, who decrypts the information. Only specially authorized parties are capable of doing so. This way you can prevent hackers from stealing and using the information when it is sent over the Internet.

The easiest and fastest way of recognizing a secure website is by means of the website address. Where this starts with "https://" rather than simply "http://", then you are on a secure website. The extra "s" stands for "secure".

Here you see an example:

https://www.bankofamerica.com/index.jsp

Another sign is the small padlock icon which will be shown in the address bar as soon as you enter the website. If this icon is missing, then the chances are good that the website is probably unsecured.

Please note:
Many websites have both secured and unsecured areas. For example, when you are looking for a book on www.amazon.com, the pages are unsecured. As soon as you log in to order and pay the book, you are directed to a secure area.

Only enter your personal data and credit card information when you are sure that you are on a secure website which ensures secure communication.

Tip

Breaking the connection
When something strange happens while you are surfing, you might want to break the connection immediately. This is the fastest way to do that for different types of connections:

Disconnecting your dial-up connection through *Windows*:

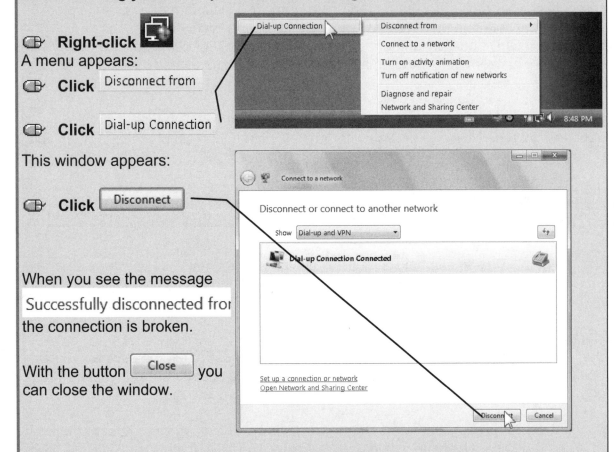

☞ **Right-click**

A menu appears:

☞ **Click** Disconnect from

☞ **Click** Dial-up Connection

This window appears:

☞ **Click** Disconnect

When you see the message

Successfully disconnected fro

the connection is broken.

With the button Close you can close the window.

Manually disconnecting your dial-up connection:

If the connection cannot be broken, you can also unplug the telephone cord that is used by your modem from the telephone jack:

The telephone plug   *The telephone jack*

- Continue reading on the next page -

Disabling your broadband or high speed Internet connection (DSL or cable) through *Windows*:

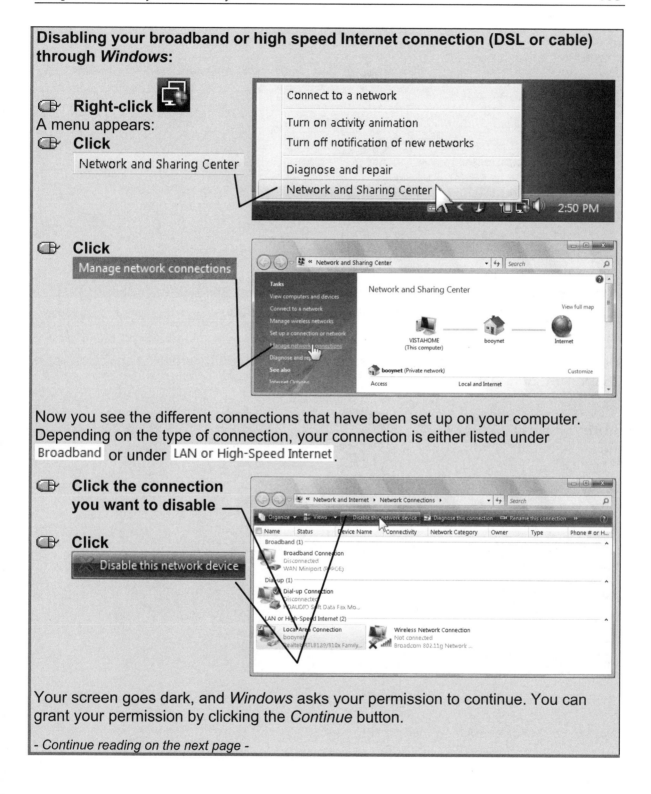

- Right-click

A menu appears:
- Click

  Network and Sharing Center

- Click

  Manage network connections

Now you see the different connections that have been set up on your computer. Depending on the type of connection, your connection is either listed under Broadband or under LAN or High-Speed Internet .

- **Click the connection you want to disable**

- Click

  Disable this network device

Your screen goes dark, and *Windows* asks your permission to continue. You can grant your permission by clicking the *Continue* button.

- Continue reading on the next page -

Now that the connection has been disabled, it looks like this:

✓ **Local Area Connection**
Disabled
Realtek RTL8139/810x Family...

To enable the connection again:

👉 **Click**

```
➡ Enable this network device
```

Your screen goes dark again, and *Windows* asks your permission to continue. You can grant your permission by clicking the *Continue* button.

Manually disconnecting your broadband or high speed Internet connection (ISDN, DSL or cable):

If the connection cannot be broken, you can also unplug the cable that runs from your ISDN, DSL or cable modem to your computer:

Cable modem   *DSL modem*   *ISDN modem*

Appendix A.
Setting up a Dial-up Connection

If your dial-up connection has not yet been set up, you can use this appendix to configure the necessary settings. First, check if your modem is ready.

☞ **Make sure your modem is connected to the telephone line**

Do you have an external modem?
☞ **Turn the modem on**

Do you have an internal modem?
☞ **You do not have to do anything**

⇨ **Please note:**

If you have an Internet access subscription, your *Internet Service Provider* (ISP) has given you a **user name** and a **password**. Also, you should have received a **phone number** that can be used to contact your ISP's computer.
Make sure to have these details ready.

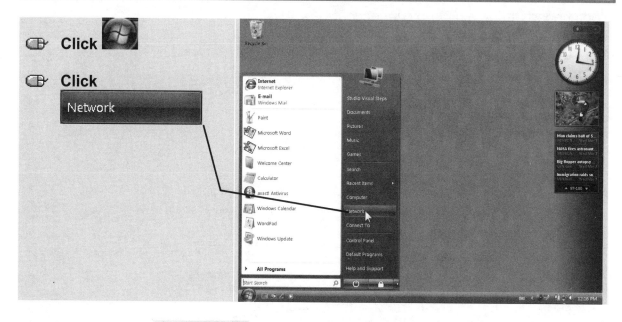

👆 **Click**

👆 **Click**

Network

The folder window ▶ Network is opened. From here you go to the window where you can add a new network.

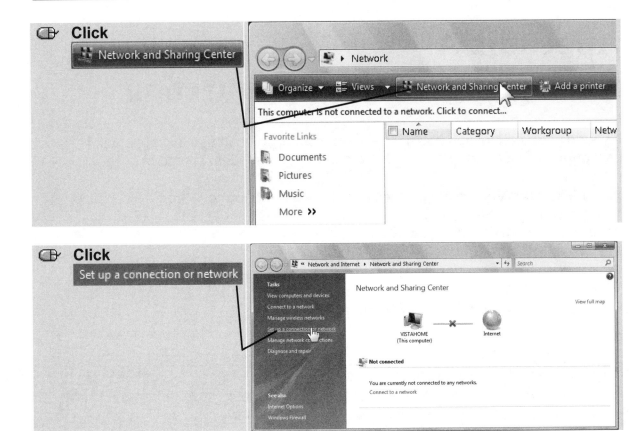

You choose *Set up a dial-up connection*:

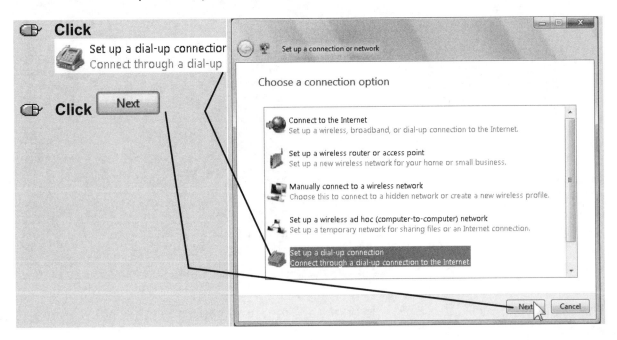

Now you can enter the details for your dial-up connection:

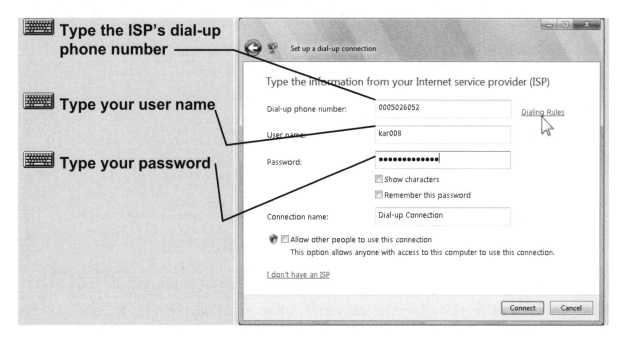

Type the ISP's dial-up phone number ——

Type your user name

Type your password

 Please note:

Whether you want *Windows* to remember your password or not depends a great deal on how accessible your computer is to others. If you are the only user and no one else has access to your computer, the situation is very different than when the same computer can be used by others.

Do Not Remember
If you choose not to let *Windows* remember your password, you will have to type it in yourself every time. This is recommended when you want to be certain that no one else can use your Internet connection.

Do Remember
If you are the only person who uses your computer and you are reasonably certain no one else can use it, you can choose the convenience of letting the computer remember your password.

Do you want your password
to be remembered?

☞ **Check the box**
   ☑ Remember this password

If you do **not** want your
password to be remembered:

☞ **Make sure this box is
   not checked**

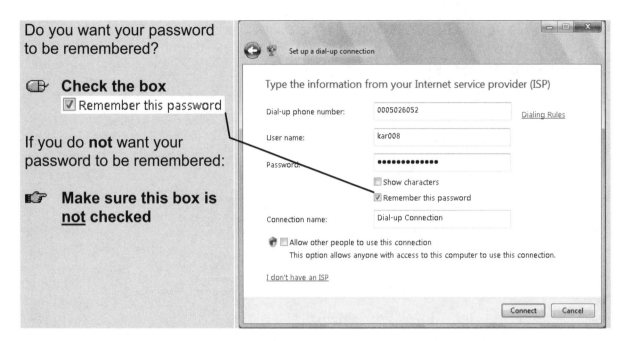

Windows Vista also offers the possibility to let other users with access to your
computer use this same dial-up connection. This means that other people with a
different account can see and use the connection you are setting up.

Do you want other users to
be able use this dial-up
connection?

☞ **Check the box**
   🛡 ☑ Allow other people to use th

If you do **not** want your
password to be saved:

☞ **Make sure this box is
   not checked**

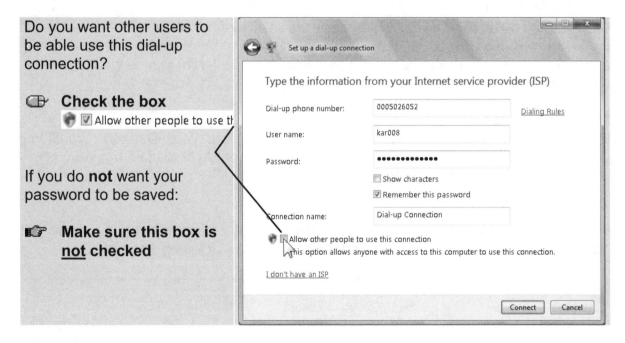

⇨ **Please note:**

As soon as you check the box , your screen
goes dark and *Windows* asks your permission to continue. Click the *Continue* button
if you want to apply this setting.

Now you can try the connection:

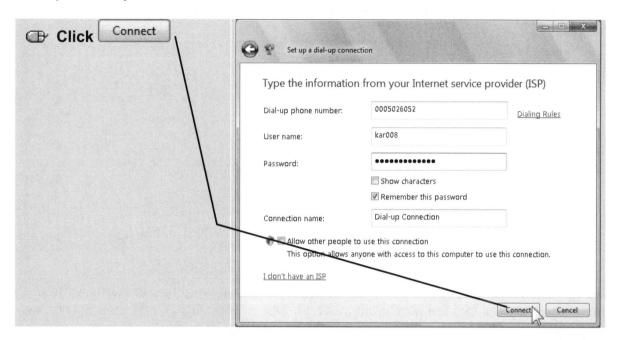

Click Connect

The connection is being made:

After that your password is verified and the connection is tested.

When the connection is
made, you see this window:

☞ **Click** [Close]

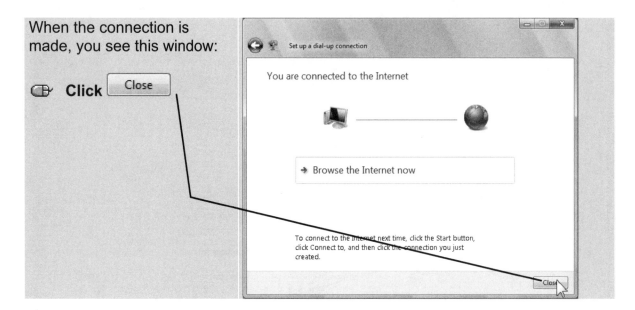

Now you see the window *Set Network Location*. The first time that you connect to a
network, you must choose a network location. This automatically sets the appropriate
firewall settings for the type of network that you connect to.

If you connect to networks in different locations (for example, a network at your
home, at a local coffee shop, or at work), choosing a network location can help
ensure that your computer is always set to an appropriate security level.

There are three network locations: *Home*, *Work*, and *Public location*.

Depending on where you are,
click the location that
describes your situation best.

For example:

☞ **Click**

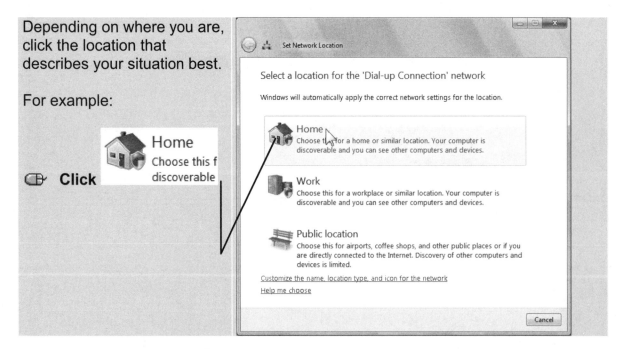

Please note:

As soon as you choose one of the locations, your screen goes dark and *Windows* asks your permission to continue. Click the *Continue* button if you want to grant your permission and apply this setting.

The settings have been configured.

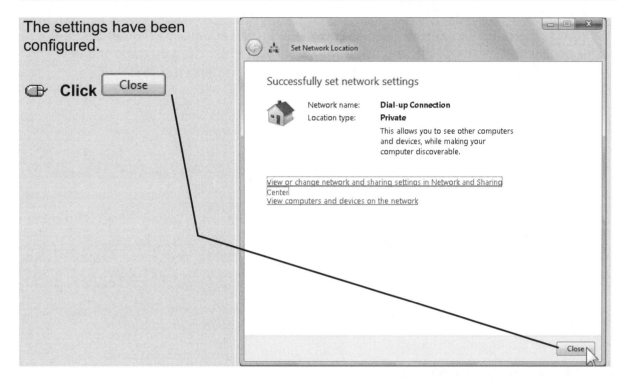

Click [Close]

Successfully set network settings

Network name: **Dial-up Connection**
Location type: **Private**
This allows you to see other computers and devices, while making your computer discoverable.

View or change network and sharing settings in Network and Sharing Center
View computers and devices on the network

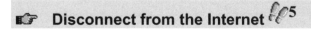 **Close the folder windows *Network* and *Network and Sharing Center*** $\ell\ell$32

Now that your dial-up connection has been set up, you can begin surfing the web. If you want to save that for another time, simply click disconnect:

Disconnect from the Internet $\ell\ell$5

Appendix B.
Setting up an Extra E-mail Account

Windows Mail is not limited for use with only one e-mail account. You can add an extra account, for example your work e-mail address. This way you can receive e-mail from two or more accounts at the same time. You need the following information:

- your second e-mail address
- the corresponding username and password
- the name of the POP3-server, for example mail.aol.com
- the name of the SMTP-server; for example smtp.aol.com

⇒ **Please note:**

Webmail accounts from providers such as *Hotmail*, *Windows Live Mail*, *Yahoo! Mail* and *Gmail* cannot be added as an extra e-mail account in *Windows Mail*.

☞ **Open *Windows Mail*** 𝓁𝓁 35

☞ **If necessary, connect to the Internet** 𝓁𝓁 3

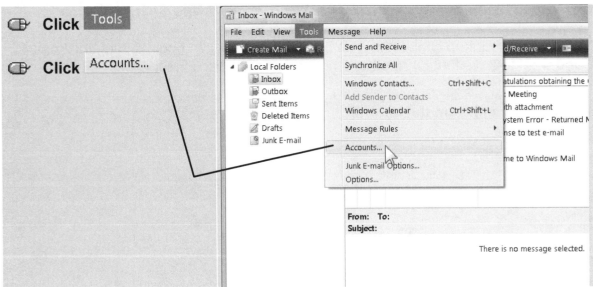

In this window you see the name of the account that is already active:

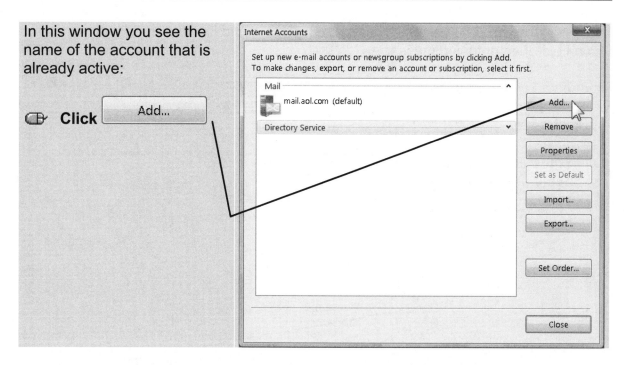

You are going to add an e-mail account:

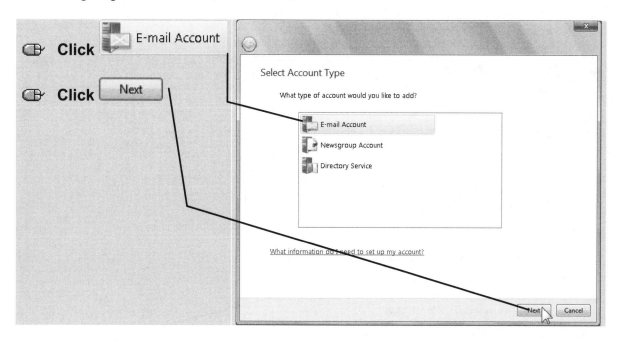

In the next window you can add your name as you would like it to appear in the *From*-field of an outgoing message.

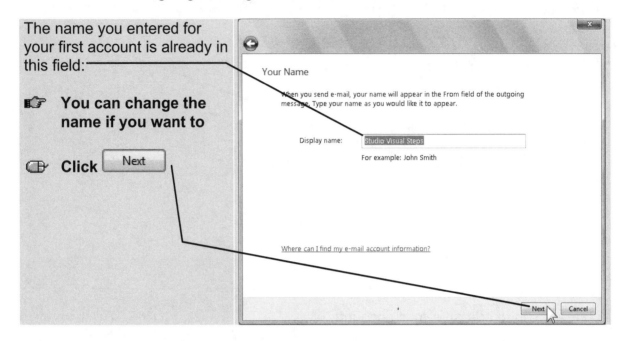

The name you entered for your first account is already in this field:

☞ **You can change the name if you want to**

🖱 **Click** `Next`

Now you can add the new e-mail address.

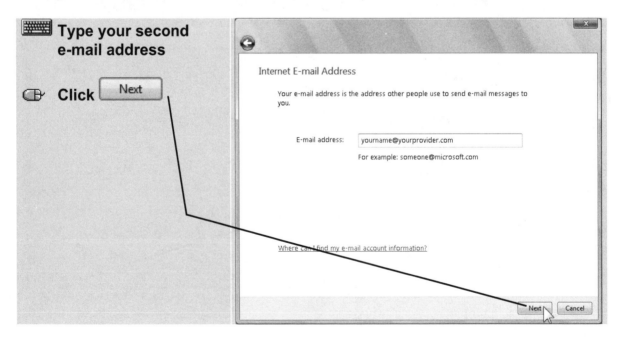

⌨ **Type your second e-mail address**

🖱 **Click** `Next`

Before you add the details of the servers for incoming and outgoing mail, please read the information below in the **Please note** box.

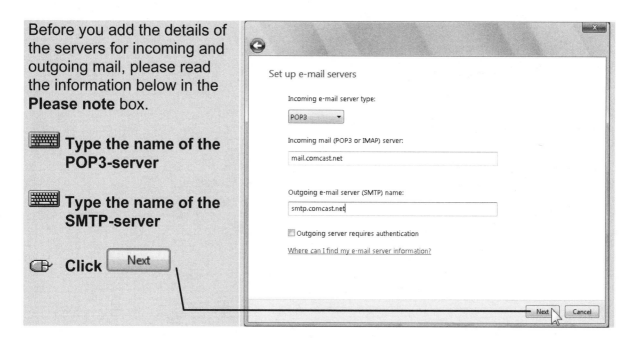

⌨ **Type the name of the POP3-server**

⌨ **Type the name of the SMTP-server**

☞ **Click** Next

⇨ **Please note:**

Settings when using a DSL-connection
When you use a DSL connection, the SMTP-server (outgoing mail) associated with your original e-mail account takes preference. Even if your second e-mail account is with a completely different provider. For outgoing e-mail from the other account(s), you use the following setting:

⌨ **Type the name of the SMTP-server associated with the DSL-account**

Outgoing e-mail server (SMTP) name:

smtp.xxxxxx.xxx

The other settings can be entered according to the specifications of the *Internet Service Provider* that provides the second e-mail address.

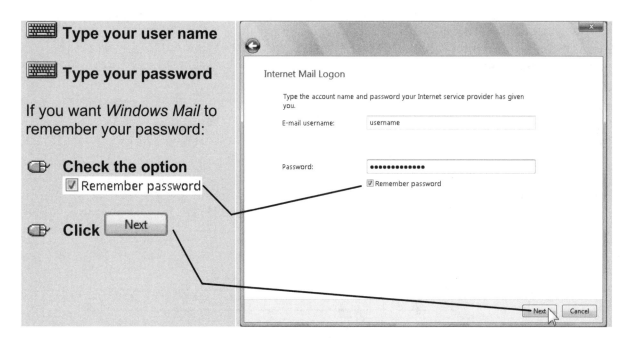

⌨ **Type your user name**

⌨ **Type your password**

If you want *Windows Mail* to
remember your password:

🖱 **Check the option**
   ☑ Remember password

🖱 **Click** [Next]

You have entered all the necessary information.

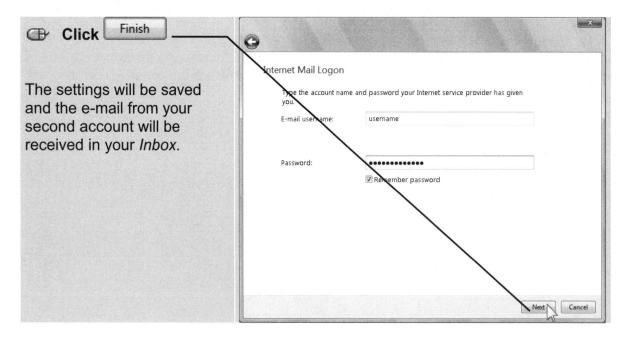

🖱 **Click** [Finish]

The settings will be saved
and the e-mail from your
second account will be
received in your *Inbox*.

You see that the second
e-mail account is now
included in the list:

The first e-mail account is the
default account. If you want
another account to be the
default account, select that
account, click

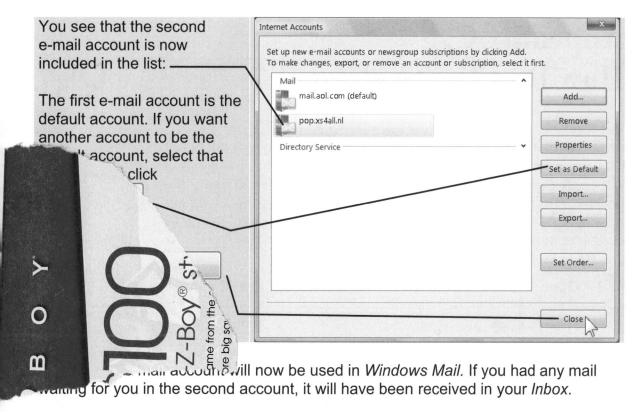

This mail account will now be used in *Windows Mail.* If you had any mail
waiting for you in the second account, it will have been received in your *Inbox.*

☞ **Close** *Windows Mail* ✍43

💡 **Tip**

Default e-mail account
When you create a new e-mail message, the default e-mail address will be listed as
the sender. If you would like to send an e-mail from the second e-mail account:

🖰 **Click the field next to**
From:

You see a list of the e-mail
accounts available in
Windows Mail:

🖰 **Click another e-mail
address**

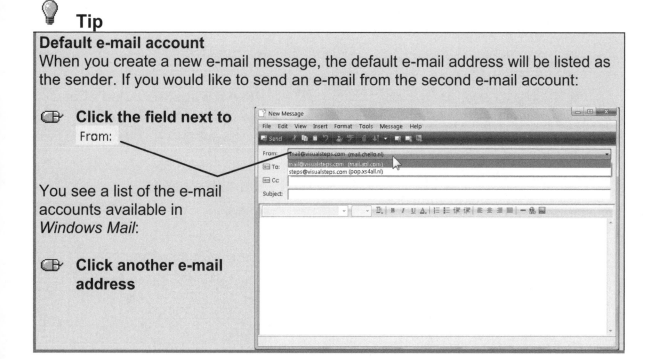

Appendix C.
How Do I Do That Again?

As you work through this book you may have noticed these footsteps: with a number beside them. This number indicates that there is a listing in the *Appendix C. How Do I Do That Again?*. Here you will find many short descriptions of how to perform specific tasks. Use the number to find the listing here in this appendix. This may come in handy when you have forgotten what is meant by a certain computer term.

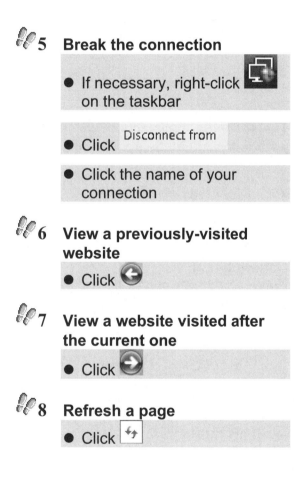

9 View the bottom of a page
- Click ⌄ on the scroll bar

Or:
- Drag the scroll box on the scroll bar downwards

Or:
- Use the scroll wheel on the mouse

10 View the top of a page
- Click ⌃ on the scroll bar

Or:
- Drag the slide box on the scroll bar upwards

Or:
- Use the scroll wheel on the mouse

11 Minimize a window
- Click in that window on ▭

12 Open a window from the taskbar
- Click the button on the taskbar

13 Close a window and stop the program
- Click in that window on ✕

14 Open a website from *History*
- Click ☆
- Click History
- Click the folder of the website
- Click the desired webpage

15 Make a website a *Favorite*
- Click ✦
- Click Add to Favorites...
- Click Add

16 Temporarily break the connection
- Right-click on the taskbar
- Click Disconnect from
- Click the name of your connection

17 Open a *Favorite* website
- Click ☆
- If necessary, click ☆ Favorites
- Click the website

18 Make a web address a *Favorite* and save it in a folder
- Click ✦
- Click Add to Favorites...
- Click ⌄ in ☆ Favorites
- Click the folder

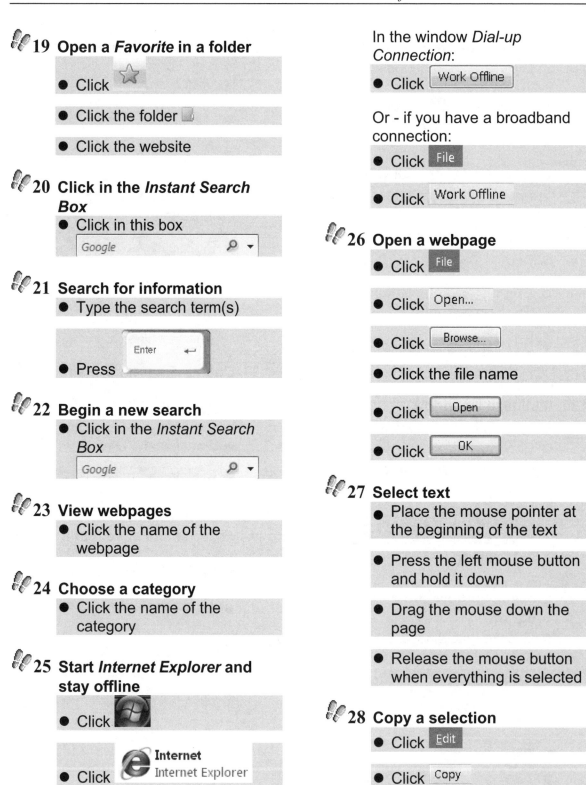

👣 **19 Open a *Favorite* in a folder**

- Click ☆

- Click the folder

- Click the website

👣 **20 Click in the *Instant Search Box***

- Click in this box

  Google 🔍 ▾

👣 **21 Search for information**

- Type the search term(s)

- Press Enter ↵

👣 **22 Begin a new search**

- Click in the *Instant Search Box*

  Google 🔍 ▾

👣 **23 View webpages**

- Click the name of the webpage

👣 **24 Choose a category**

- Click the name of the category

👣 **25 Start *Internet Explorer* and stay offline**

- Click

- Click **Internet** Internet Explorer

In the window *Dial-up Connection*:

- Click Work Offline

Or - if you have a broadband connection:

- Click File

- Click Work Offline

👣 **26 Open a webpage**

- Click File

- Click Open...

- Click Browse...

- Click the file name

- Click Open

- Click OK

👣 **27 Select text**

- Place the mouse pointer at the beginning of the text

- Press the left mouse button and hold it down

- Drag the mouse down the page

- Release the mouse button when everything is selected

👣 **28 Copy a selection**

- Click Edit

- Click Copy

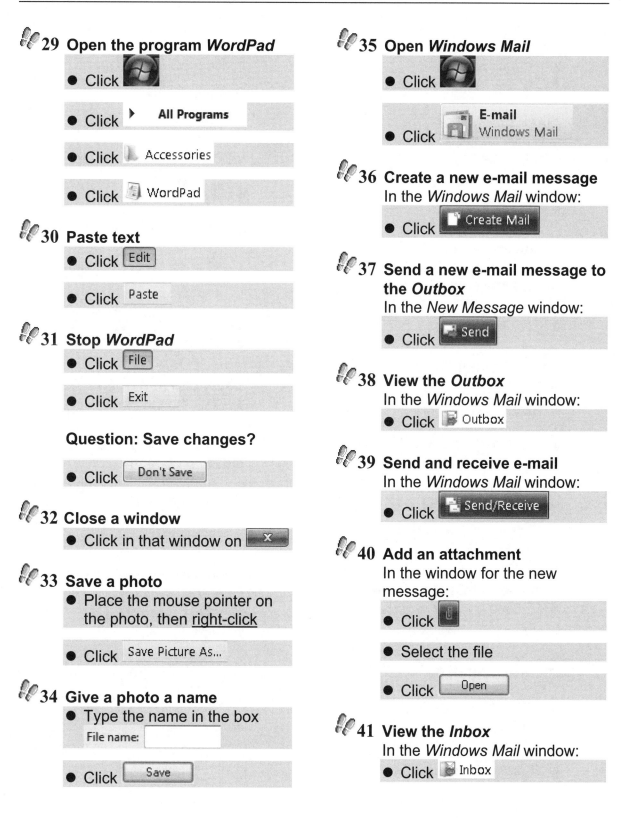

29 Open the program *WordPad*

- Click
- Click ▶ **All Programs**
- Click Accessories
- Click WordPad

30 Paste text

- Click Edit
- Click Paste

31 Stop *WordPad*

- Click File
- Click Exit

Question: Save changes?

- Click Don't Save

32 Close a window

- Click in that window on ✖

33 Save a photo

- Place the mouse pointer on the photo, then right-click
- Click Save Picture As...

34 Give a photo a name

- Type the name in the box
  File name:
- Click Save

35 Open *Windows Mail*

- Click
- Click **E-mail** Windows Mail

36 Create a new e-mail message

In the *Windows Mail* window:

- Click Create Mail

37 Send a new e-mail message to the *Outbox*

In the *New Message* window:

- Click Send

38 View the *Outbox*

In the *Windows Mail* window:

- Click Outbox

39 Send and receive e-mail

In the *Windows Mail* window:

- Click Send/Receive

40 Add an attachment

In the window for the new message:

- Click
- Select the file
- Click Open

41 View the *Inbox*

In the *Windows Mail* window:

- Click Inbox

42 Open an e-mail
In the *Inbox* window:
- Double-click the message

43 Close *Windows Mail*
In the *Windows Mail* window:
- Click File

- Click Exit

44 Delete an e-mail
In the *Windows Mail* window:
- Click the e-mail to be deleted

- Click ▣

45 Save an e-mail
In the message window:
- Click File

- Click Save

46 View the *Drafts* folder
In the *Windows Mail* window:
- Click ✎ Drafts

47 Choose a larger font
In the new message window:
- Choose a larger size using
  10 ▾

48 Choose stationery
- Click Format

- Click Apply Stationery

- Choose the stationery

49 Open *Windows Calendar*
If *Windows Mail* is open:
- Click Tools

- Click Windows Calendar

If *Windows Mail* is not open:
- Click 🪟

- Click ▶ **All Programs**

- Click ▥ Windows Calendar

50 Create a new appointment
- Click ▦ New Appointment

51 Download and open a file
- Click the file name

52 Open the *Internet for Seniors* practice website
If you saved this website as your home page:
- Click 🏠

If you saved this website as a *Favorite*:
- Click ☆

- If necessary, click ☆ Favorites

- Click 📖 Internet Book

- Click
  🅔 Internet and E-mail for SENIORS wi

- Click Practice website

Otherwise:
- Click in the address bar at the top left of the window

- Type:
  www.visualsteps.com/internet vista/practice

53 Save a webpage
- Click `File`

- Click `Save As...`

- Type a name in the box
  File name: [ ]

- Click `Save`

54 Choose a contact from the *Contacts* folder
- Click `To:`

- Click the name

- Click `To: ->`

- Click `OK`

55 Save changes to this message?
- Click `No`

56 Maximize a window
- Click in that window on

57 View an attachment
- Double-click the attachment

- Click `Open`

58 Display the whole page
- Click

59 Display the page at actual size
- Click

60 Open the window *Internet Options*
- Click `Tools`

- Click `Internet Options`

61 Open the folder *Downloads*
- Click

- Click your *Personal* folder

- Double-click
  Downloads
  File Folder

62 Open a new tab
- Click

63 Open a link in a new tab
- Press and hold `Ctrl`

- Click the link

- Release `Ctrl`

64 Switch to another tab
- Click the tab, for example
  `Visual Steps, com...`

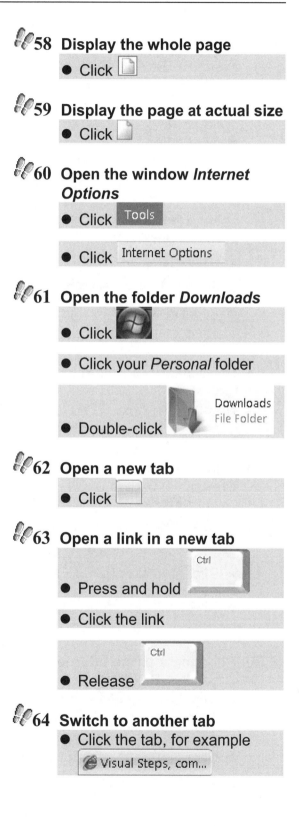

65 Close a tab
- Click ✕ on the tab

66 Display the menu bar
- Click 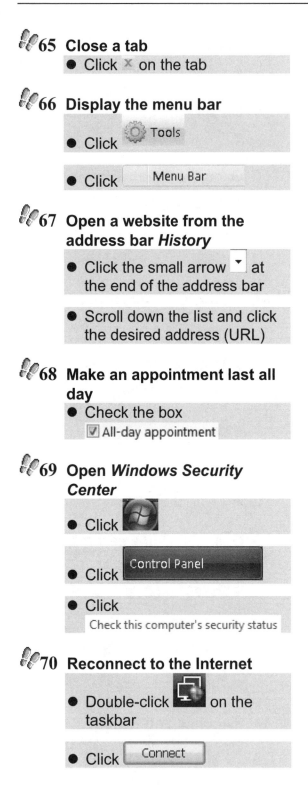 Tools

- Click │ Menu Bar

67 Open a website from the address bar *History*
- Click the small arrow ▾ at the end of the address bar

- Scroll down the list and click the desired address (URL)

68 Make an appointment last all day
- Check the box
  ☑ All-day appointment

69 Open *Windows Security Center*
- Click

- Click Control Panel

- Click
  Check this computer's security status

70 Reconnect to the Internet
- Double-click on the taskbar

- Click Connect

Appendix D. Index